WISHES COME TRUE

The smile Jake flashed across the table could easily melt hardened lava. "If I didn't know better, Red, I'd swear you made up that entire story just to come over and have breakfast with us guys."

"If that's what I wanted, Jake, I wouldn't have come over half-naked and dripping wet."

"Maybe there were other motives behind that little gesture."

Laurie shot him an angry frown. "Have you forgotten there are children present?"

"Okay, Red." He winked. "Next time you want to get half-naked and dripping wet, we'll do it in private."

Laurie groaned.

Jake's mustache twitched.

And her heart did a back flip.

WISHES COME TRUE

Patti Berg

AVON BOOKS  NEW YORK

WISHES COME TRUE is an original publication of Avon Books. This work has never before appeared in book form. This work is a novel. Any similarity to actual persons or events is purely coincidental.

AVON BOOKS
A division of
The Hearst Corporation
1350 Avenue of the Americas
New York, New York 10019

Copyright © 1996 by Patti Berg
Published by arrangement with the author
Library of Congress Catalog Card Number: 95-96049
ISBN: 0-380-78338-X

First Avon Books Printing: June 1996

AVON TRADEMARK REG. U.S. PAT. OFF. AND IN OTHER COUNTRIES, MARCA REGISTRADA, HECHO EN U.S.A.

Printed in the U.S.A.

RA 10 9 8 7 6 5 4 3 2 1

For Daddy, whose light still shines in my heart, and for my mother, whose patience, understanding, and love have helped make so many of my wishes come true

Prologue

"Look Grandma. Look." Annie Flynn burst into the dark and dingy kitchen, her emerald eyes alight with childish delight. "See what Mommy sent me?"

The Widow Flynn took a long drag on her cigarette and coughed out the smoke, never once turning toward the wide-eyed child, scowling instead at the cashier's check setting amidst the clutter on the gray Formica table.

Annie stood behind her grandmother's chair, her gift clutched to her chest, wishing the old lady would turn around and share just an ounce of her joy. "It's magic, Grandma," she whispered, her happiness somewhat overshadowed by her fear. "Mommy says so."

Mrs. Flynn spun around in her chair, dark, angry eyes narrowed to slits in her lined and crinkled face. "What did she buy this time?" she snapped. She grabbed the cashier's check and confronted the tiny redhead, waving the piece of paper before the child's eyes. "How does she expect me to support you on this? God knows it's never enough." Mrs. Flynn slapped the check back on the table and stared with cold, cynical eyes at the gift clutched in Annie's arms. "What's wrong, girl? You afraid to show that to me?"

Lips quivering, Annie slowly turned the picture frame around to give her grandmother a better look, wishing she'd kept it a secret, stuffed through a crack in the wall behind her bed where she kept her few precious and prized possessions. "It's a picture frame, Grandma."

"I should have known it would be something useless. Let me see." Mrs. Flynn wrenched it from her granddaughter's hands, examining the tarnished silver of the intricately carved eight-by-ten frame, mentally calculating its worth. "Nothing but trash."

"No, Grandma." Annie shook her head, her curls bobbing out of control. "Mommy said it's magic." She dug tiny fingers into the pocket of her hand-me-down dress and pulled out a wrinkled red, white, and blue air-mail envelope, slowly removing the letter from inside, pointing to the words on the paper. "See, Grandma. She wrote me all about it."

"You know I can't read without my glasses," Mrs. Flynn spat out, inhaling once again on the butt of a cigarette she held between nicotine-stained, arthritic fingers. "You'll have to read it."

Annie sniffed back a tear, holding the stationery in front of her face so her grandmother wouldn't see her cry. "*Happy birthday, my darling. I wish with all my heart I could be with you on your special day. It seems only yesterday you were born, not eight long years. Someday soon I hope to hold you again.*"

"Just like your mother to act like she cares," Mrs. Flynn interrupted, grinding out the butt in a dusty blue glass ashtray filled near to overflowing with the remains of long-ago-smoked cigarettes.

Annie lowered the paper and watched as her grandmother tapped a pack of Camels on the table and withdrew a new cigarette, flicking off a loose piece of tobacco, and sticking it between her lips. "Go on, girl. Let's see what other lies she's written."

"Maybe I shouldn't read any more, Grandma. It's upsetting you."

"You'll upset me if you don't read."

Annie stared down at her mother's flowing script, bold and beautiful and artistic, and daydreamed herself away from her grandmother's house, away from bare feet and tattered dresses, to her mother's dressing room on Broadway, where the pretty lady of her memories sat in front of a mirror, writing words of love before going out on stage.

"What are you waiting for?"

Annie's green eyes widened as her grandmother frightened her out of her dream, forcing her back to reality, to face a woman she could never manage to please.

"Do you think she's happy in New York?" Annie asked, forgetting the letter for a moment, thinking only of her mother.

"Fill somebody full of enough booze and drugs and they can be happy anywhere."

Annie lowered her head, looking again at the letter, praying she wouldn't cry, wishing her grandmother would just once say something nice, especially about the mother she loved. "Do you want to hear the rest?" she asked, looking up through long, pale lashes.

Mrs. Flynn tapped a thickened and chipped nail

on the tabletop, frustration evident in every move, every word. "I'm waiting."

"*I hope you'll love my birthday gift to you. It's magic.*" Annie raised her eyes once again to see if her grandmother was paying any attention, wishing the old woman would fall asleep just as she did most other times when Annie needed or wanted to talk. But Mrs. Flynn sat there in her faded yellow housecoat, puffing away, eyes trained on her granddaughter, while her fingers tapped a tattoo on the Formica.

"*The man I bought it from said miracles happen to those who own it. All they have to do is believe.*" Annie continued to read, her eyes trained on the letter so she wouldn't see any other signs of disgust on her grandmother's face. "*I didn't believe at first, but then it happened. I know it may sound crazy, but the woman in the picture winked at me, and I knew the magic must be real. I don't need more miracles in my life, Annie— I have you, and that's enough. But I'd like you to have a little magic in yours, so believe darling, always believe, and one day the woman in the picture frame will wink at you, and all the things you wish for will come true.*"

"Nonsense. Nothing but nonsense." Mrs. Flynn snatched the letter and envelope from Annie's hands, smirking at her daughter's frivolous and misguided ideas. She held the picture frame far enough away that she could see the rosy-cheeked woman with spectacles and fluffy white hair. "Doesn't look like much of a miracle worker to me."

"I believe it, Grandma."

"You're just a kid. What do you know?" Mrs. Flynn shoved the letter back in its envelope and wedged it between frame and glass, keeping a close watch on the woman in the photo, waiting for the wink she hoped would come. The magical story was too ridiculous to believe, yet, she thought, if anyone should be the recipient of miracles, it should be the poor old woman who'd been strapped with her daughter's bastard for the past six years.

"Can I have my gift back now, Grandma?"

Mrs. Flynn snorted. "She should have sent you new clothes or shoes instead of this ridiculous present. Go on out and play and forget all about it." She waved her granddaughter away while clutching her new possession to her chest. "I'll put it away till you're older."

"Couldn't I keep it in my room?" Annie begged, afraid she was losing her gift, and her mother's letter, the only rays of sunshine in her life.

"No! Go outside now. I have dinner to fix."

"Are we going to have birthday cake?" Annie asked, her voice full of hope and optimism. She'd never had one before, but every year she hoped her grandmother would relent, making the day bright and special.

"Birthday cake?" The dollar amount on the cashier's check glared up from the table at Mrs. Flynn, and she frowned in disgust. "Listen, girl. In my mind, today isn't much of a day for celebration."

Annie's shoulders and head sagged in familiar defeat. Why couldn't her grandmother love her? Why couldn't she have a home and family to love? And why had her grandmother once again robbed her, taking not only her happiness, but her mother's gift, grasping it—not her—securely in thin, frail arms?

Refusing to cry, Annie bit back her tears, letting

anger fill her eyes, and the emptiness in her heart. She started to turn, to run outside, to hide away in a treetop where she could watch happier scenes being played out in someone else's yard. But a twinkle of light glinting off the glass in the picture frame made her stop.

"What are you doing? I told you to go outside."

"I just wanted to look one more time, Grandma."

"Well, hurry up."

It might have been a daydream, it might have been shadows and light bouncing off the glass, but Annie thought the woman in the picture winked. The old lady looked sweet and kind, homey and cheerful and full of love, and Annie wished, with all her might, that someday, somehow, all of those mystical qualities would be part of her life. And maybe, just maybe, if she believed strongly enough, the old woman's magic would make all her wishes come true.

1

Laurie Langtry flashed a wholesome Miss America smile to the elderly ladies congregating outside the Presbyterian church, an old, familiar sentinel standing guard over the sleepy little town of Bunch Gulch, Montana.

The day couldn't have been more perfect for her return. Not a single cloud marred the wide, blue Montana sky, and the unusually warm June temperature screamed for bikinis and thongs. But not for Laurie. Spending wads on New York chic had long ago become a favorite pastime, and on this first tour through town in fourteen years, she wouldn't be caught in anything less than the crisp, white linen suit she'd had tailor-made to fit the curves of her less than five foot frame. The bright Picasso print silk scarf she'd swirled about her neck added just the perfect touch, she thought, and it waved gloriously over the back of her Corvette convertible, painted the same sparkling emerald of her eyes.

She adjusted her Ray-Bans to reflect the sun, and casually turned the corner onto Main, headed for the heart of town. Flicking the sound up on the CD, she raised her voice over Elton John's, enjoying the dazzling morning as her mood soared and the gentle valley breeze whistled through her short, curly mass of flaming red hair.

"God, it's great to be back," Laurie whispered to herself. "And it's great to be free."

Slowly, she cruised down Main, surveying her old haunts, noticing little had changed in Bunch Gulch, except the woman who'd just returned to town. The green neon *land and homes* sign still hung in the picture window of Nelson's Real Estate, but it didn't look nearly as good as it had when she'd ripped it off on Halloween and hung it in Mrs. Adams' barn. The Jolly Kone where she'd worked for three and one-half hours before getting fired for smoking in the kitchen, now sported white enamel patio furniture instead of splintered redwood. Even Tom Harrington, always so pious and pure, stood in front of his general store, broom in hand, sweeping nonexistent dirt into the street. She could swear he was still wearing the same faded and stained apron, but now he needed a new rug for his head, and liposuction could do wonders for the protrusion that hung way too far over his belt. She couldn't recall a more delightful scene—pure small-town Americana straight from a Norman Rockwell masterpiece.

Laurie waved at Tom, and even from the middle of the wide, dusty street she could see his old familiar frown, see his brain actively trying to place the stranger in the green Corvette. Finally, he raised his arm and hesitantly returned her wave. Funny, she thought, that he'd have so much difficulty remembering. She'd worked for him for an entire month to pay him back for the pack of Marlboros she'd been accused of swiping, and he hadn't taken his eyes off her for a moment while she swept and dusted and stocked shelves. He hadn't trusted her then; was it possible for him to trust her now?

Out of nowhere, a blur appeared through Laurie's windshield. She slammed her foot on the brake and skidded to a halt in the gravel that overflowed a rut in the road. "Damn!" She'd narrowly missed the tall, slim-hipped cowboy whose broad shoulders seemed to fill her entire line of vision. Where he'd come from she hadn't a clue, but now he stood just inches from her front license plate, his arms extended before him, anticipating impact, as if he were Superman and could stop the car if she couldn't. Her heart thudded from the shock and realization that she could have killed him. And before her calm had a chance to return, anger seized her. The stranger had startled her, and dammit, she hated surprise.

"What the hell are you doing?" she yelled through the windshield. "Don't you believe in watching where you're walking?"

Taking a deep breath, she pushed open the door and would have climbed out, but the cowboy and his tight, dusty Levi's blocked her exit, a decidedly worn and faded spot just south of the zipper jutting into her face. *Oh my*, she inwardly sighed, a crimson blush suddenly creeping up her neck to her cheeks, more than likely giving away her embarrassment, and maybe a trace of delight.

She looked up and grinned, only to meet the man's scowl. A sweat-stained Stetson tipped low on his forehead, shadowing his face, but she could still see the impenetrable squint of his eyes, and tightness in his jaw, even through the grunge of his scraggly beard.

"You're in my way," she growled, forcing herself not to flatten her hands against the man's ob-

viously rock-hard stomach, positioned just inches
from her nose, in an attempt to push him away.
But Superman—or Hercules, if she wanted to be
more descript—didn't budge, her words and tone
of voice apparently falling on stone-deaf ears, and
it looked as though he had no intention of moving
his slim hips from her direct line of vision.

The man's droopy Wyatt Earp mustache
twitched, whether in amusement or anger she
wasn't sure, until he spoke. "If you'd been watching where you were going, ma'am," he drawled in
an irresistible, laughter-filled tenor, "instead of
showing off like some highfalutin movie star, you
might have seen me." He knelt down, right there
in the middle of Main Street, his grizzled face only
inches away from hers. "Besides that, pedestrians
have the right of way."

"Look, I'm from New York," she fired back.
"We don't believe in right of way."

"Well, you're in Bunch Gulch now." He tipped
the Stetson up on his forehead and studied her
closer, his brow wrinkling in deep, intense concen-
tration. Did he recognize her, she wondered, or
was he just checking out the goods? His eyes
roamed from spiked jade heels to curly red hair,
as if she were a prime cut of beef and he the in-
spector. God, she hated being the target of
someone's attention.

"We don't stare at strangers in New York, either," she chastised.

"Well, ma'am, you could have fooled me." His
mustache twitched again, and she sensed an in-
sufferable-man type of grin under all that hair.
"You've been checkin' out my attire since you
nearly ran me down. Doesn't that qualify as staring?"

"Your attire, sir, is pretty hard to ignore when you've shoved your belt buckle into my face." She tilted her head, away from the zipper that intrigued her, to the grizzled face and sweat-stained hat that seemed so much easier to ignore. "Look"—as much as she hated apologizing, she knew she owed him something—"I was admiring your town, and the view. I wasn't expecting someone to appear out of nowhere."

"I was in plain sight the moment you turned onto Main. Why don't you just apologize and we'll forget it ever happened?"

Her eyebrows raised, along with her affronted voice. "Apologize?"

"Yeah, it's something we do around these parts when we're in the wrong." He stood, releasing his hold on the door and backed away. "Guess it's just not your style."

"I've got a lot more style than you might think. If it'll make you feel any better, you have my deepest and humblest apology."

Finally, she sensed a smile. "You know, you sound a helluva lot like a girl who used to live around here." Again, he neared the car, knelt down, and reached toward the unruly wind tousled curls she'd never been able to control. "She had springy red hair, too."

"Don't touch!" Her words and the sharp tone of her voice were more effective than a slap or grabbing his wrist.

His fingers stopped just an inch from a curl, then instantly retreated to rest on a dusty jeans-clad knee. "Annie? Annie Flynn?"

"Langtry," she bit out. "Laurie Langtry, formerly and never again to be Annie Flynn." She watched the obvious departure of his eyes from her face as they sought out her hand and, more than likely, her marital status. She wiggled the ring finger on her left hand, then answered his question. "Single. Never married, and if you really must know, Langtry was my mother's name."

He snorted out a laugh and his mustache twitched, not on one side, but two. "Well, I'll be. What are you doing back in town?"

"Visiting." He was awfully nosy for a stranger. But how could he be a stranger if he remembered Annie Flynn? She studied his face, searching for some clue to his identity, but the mustache, the scraggly hair on his face, and the Stetson hid all traces of anyone she might have known before. Of course, the shoulders and arms that looked like he weight-lifted cows for a living seemed awfully familiar.

With a perfectly manicured crimson fingernail, she stabbed the brim of his Stetson and tilted it back on his head. A lone, wavy lock of blond hair fell from under the hat and across his forehead. Remembrance brought an instant smile. "Jake?"

"Yeah. Bit older. Bit uglier."

She couldn't see much under the beard, but Jake McAllister was someone she'd never forgotten, and Jake McAllister, high school heartthrob, star athlete, and guy most likely to succeed, had been far, far from ugly. "I thought you'd left Bunch Gulch years ago."

"You been keeping tabs?"

"Not exactly. Just thought for sure you would have been in some big city by now. An attorney. A doctor."

"You've got me mixed up with someone else if you think that. Truth is, my folks sold their place a few years back, and I stuck around. They went to New Mexico when Dad got tired of trying to make a living at being a rancher."

"So, what *are* you doing?" she asked, although from the dust and sweat he seemed to have bathed in, she had the uncanny insight to rule out banker or accountant.

"Still ranching—sort of." He swept the hat from his head and plopped it in his lap, making an attempt to comb his fingers through unruly hair that refused to stay anywhere but flopped over his brow.

"What's it been, Annie?" He laughed and shook his head. "Sorry. Laurie might take some getting used to." He scratched the back of his head and Laurie fought the urge to cringe. "Must be at least ten, eleven years since you've been around."

"Fourteen."

"Damn! I remember now. The Fourth of July party at the Grange."

"I'm surprised you remember."

"Hell of a night, or so I've been told," he said, and she remembered the friendliness in his eyes, laugh lines and minuscule wrinkles at their corners now, where time was just beginning to wreak a little mischief on the face that could once have belonged to Adonis. "Guess I got a bit drunk."

Laurie's fingers tightened on the steering wheel as she remembered that Fourth of July. Jake was right. It had been a hell of a night, and the next morning she'd finally found the courage to run away from her grandmother, and from the town that had scorned her existence. But those were old memories, this was a new life. If it hadn't been for that disgusting incident, she might never have left, might never have become successful, might never have changed from a hate-filled child to a more understanding and patient adult. It seemed only right to make light of that humiliating moment that had become the turning point in her life. "As I recall, you retched all over my party dress."

The smile plummeted from his face. "Yeah, I heard about that. God, you must have hated me."

"Let's just say you put a damper on any feelings I might have had for you at the time." Talk of the past was uncomfortable, and she nervously twisted the diamond tennis bracelet, watching his eyes drop to the sparkling gems that glimmered in the rays of the sun.

"You don't look much like the old Annie." Again, he checked out her freckled legs camouflaged by silk stockings, the short length of her tailored skirt that barely covered her thighs, and the two-carat diamond studs glistening in each ear. "You've done well for yourself."

"I've done okay." She tossed off the nonchalant remark as if success didn't matter, but it did.

"Do you have time for some coffee? It's been awhile. Maybe we could catch up on old times."

As if she had somewhere to go, she glanced at the clock on the dash. "Wish I could. Maybe some other time," she said, remembering that years ago, when Jake McAllister had turned every head and melted every heart, she would have jumped at the chance. But she'd changed over the years, and so had her tastes. She liked hundred-dollar haircuts, Armani suits, and Gucci ties. She'd cultivated her life, and men like Jake McAllister just didn't fit in. But, in spite of that sweat-stained Stetson, and the gruff, unkempt exterior, there was something warm and comfortable about Jake McAllister.

"You staying in town?" he asked. "I know your

Grandma's place was torn down a few years back."

At my direction, she wanted to scream. She'd hated the place and couldn't destroy it fast enough after her grandmother passed away. But, again, she bit back her anger and swallowed the pain. "Actually, I'm staying at your folks' old place."

His Montana blue-sky eyes narrowed, obviously pondering her words. He was uncomfortable with her statement. She recognized the look, the way his eyes darkened to shadowed pools of cobalt. "You're renting it?"

"I own it."

He shook his head, his disbelief visibly overwhelming. "They never told me."

"I doubt that they knew. My attorney took care of everything, and the name Langtry wouldn't have meant any more to them than it did to you."

"Yeah, well, they were pretty anxious to sell." Bitterness raged in his voice. "I tried to buy it, but, hell, I couldn't compete with your offer. It wasn't worth what you paid, you know. What did you do when you left here, Laurie? Rob a bank?"

"Contrary to popular opinion, no."

"Well, you stole that house right out from under me. I wasn't happy when it happened, and according to popular opinion"—he threw the words back in her face—"I'm still not thrilled." He stood up, adjusted his Stetson, pulling it low over his eyes, but she could almost feel the heat and anguish radiating behind the brim.

He shoved the door closed on Laurie's Corvette and stepped back. "I live in an old cabin you can see from your place. Guess I should be thankful you didn't rip that off, too."

She gripped the steering wheel and willed herself to remain calm, although Jake McAllister was doing his best to ruin her mood and her perfect day. "I don't see any reason to get angry, Jake. The place was on the market. I wanted it, I bought it—and I don't regret it. If you want to know the truth, I didn't give the least bit of thought to anyone else. As far as I knew, the McAllisters no longer wanted the place and were moving out. So don't throw any of your *poor me* crap up in my face." She eased her foot off the brake and the car rolled slightly before she jerked it once again to a stop.

"Look, Jake. I hate to fight. It's not productive." She stuck out her hand. "So since we're going to be neighbors, maybe we should consider being friends."

Like a marble statue of a Greek god, he stood motionless in the middle of Main, the only movement the blond hair that had escaped from under his hat, and gently swayed in the breeze blowing across the deserted street. "My friends are few and far between, Laurie," he stated, his voice flat, void of any emotion, "and adding the new owner of my rightful home to that list just isn't gonna happen."

Laurie rolled her eyes at his stubbornness, and withdrew her outstretched hand, knowing, most definitely, he didn't intend to acknowledge her truce. "Okay, maybe we don't have to be friends. But we *are gonna* be neighbors, because I don't plan on giving up my new home."

"It's *my* home, Laurie. Not yours." His fingers tightened into a fist, and Laurie could see his jaw clenching in obvious anger. "I was born there, I grew up there, and dammit, no one else has the right to be living there."

"That's where you're wrong," she fired back. "I have every right, and it's all perfectly legal. Maybe my being there doesn't set well with you, but setting well with people has never been one of my better known attributes. And, you know what, Jake? I quit caring what other people think a long time ago. If you want to stew about the house, go right ahead. Won't bother me a bit. I'll sit on my front porch and smile at you every time you drive by. If I remember correctly, you've got to go through my property to get to yours, and I'm not too partial to strangers. So, I suggest, if you want me to make access to your place halfway easy, you knock that blasted chip off your shoulder and consider being neighborly."

Jake gripped the edge of the door, and leaned close to Laurie, his burning gaze meeting hers head on. "You through mouthing off?"

"I'm never through, Jake. That's just one more thing about me you might have to get used to."

"Don't think getting used to you is possible, Laurie. You've always been a breed of your own."

"You're right there. And I don't give up, either." She took a deep breath and forced herself to make amends with this man she was positive would make a better friend than enemy. "Tell you what. I've been known to make a halfway decent cup of coffee. Why don't you stop by on one of your treks across my property. Maybe we could laugh about the good old days."

He hitched his thumbs over the rims of his pants pockets. "I'll consider the offer, but I'm busy most of the time."

"Yeah, well, I don't waste much time socializing, either. But I'm a woman, Jake, and occasionally I change my mind. Maybe you'll wise up one of these days and consider changing yours."

With that, Laurie switched her foot from brake

to accelerator and gunned away from Jake McAllister, the tarnished remains of a fond old memory.

Jake watched the Corvette's trail of dust till the car and the redhead ran the easy-to-see stop sign at the edge of town, and turned left onto the highway. In spite of his anger at Laurie for ripping part of his inheritance out from under him, and his ongoing bitterness at not having the power or resources to do anything about it at the time, he managed to smile at her antics. It may have been fourteen years since she'd disappeared from Bunch Gulch, she may have robbed a bank or found a sugar daddy to change her from rag-tag poor to glitzy rich, but she still had that spitfire attitude that had long ago intrigued him.

Of course, that's not all that intrigued him now. She had the most damnably cute freckles and turned-up nose he'd ever seen on a grown-up woman. She looked like a pixie, a petite piece of perfection who should be flying around on fairy wings instead of driving a lethal weapon, and whispering sweet nothings instead of spouting venom. And, although he hadn't touched her, really touched her, he knew she was soft and curvy, and made to be . . .

Ah, hell! He didn't have time, the money, or the inclination to dwell on Little Annie—Laurie Langtry.

Langtry? He scratched the nape of his neck, concentrating on the name that nagged at him. It had a slightly familiar ring, but one he couldn't place. Shaking his head, he finally continued the trek to the post office he'd begun before the pretty redhead with flashing green eyes nearly ended his life.

"Afternoon, Tom," he said, stomping dust and

dirt off his scuffed and faded black leather boots as he stepped onto the boardwalk in front of Harrington Mercantile.

"Afternoon." Tom shoved his broom into the widening crack between two wooden planks and rested his hands on top of the handle. "You know that woman in the 'Vette?"

"Used to. Remember Annie Flynn?"

Tom's fleshy jowls slackened. "Can't be. What'd she do? Rob a bank?"

"Don't think so." Jake laughed. "Goes by the name Laurie Langtry now."

"Laurie Langtry?" Tom looked down at the handle of his broom until recognition dawned, and then his eyebrows raised. "You mean the writer?"

Jake shrugged. "Don't know much about writers."

"I've got some books inside," Tom said, leaning his broom against the building next to an oak barrel overflowing with profusely blooming red and white geraniums. "Come on. Let's see what I can find." He wiped his hands on his stained gray apron as he lumbered down an aisle. "The wife makes me keep books in stock. Don't pay too much attention to them myself, of course, except for stacking them on the shelf. But that name sure rings a bell."

Jake followed, grabbing a loaf of bread and a can of tuna as they walked through the store to the small, cluttered variety section that occupied a far corner of the room.

"Let's see." Tom stood before a revolving rack of books, turning it slowly, studying the names.

Jake grabbed the rack in mid-turn and pulled out a violet-covered paperback with the name Laurie Langtry blazing across the top. "Well, I'll be."

He traced the raised white letters of her name with the tips of his fingers, giving little thought to anything else on the cover, not even the title, flipped it over, and read the italicized quote that grabbed his attention. *"Mesmerizing! Hypnotic and sensual! Laurie Langtry has done it once again."*

"What is it?" Tom asked. "One of those romance novels?"

"Don't know," was all Jake said, finding himself much more interested in finding out if this Laurie Langtry and the Bunch Gulch hellion were one and the same. He opened the front and flipped through half a dozen pages of reviews from *Publishers Weekly* and the *Chicago Tribune*, even Rex Reed, and many more names that didn't register at all in his brain. There was a listing of other books by Laurie Langtry and he slid his finger down the page, counting twenty-seven, but nothing at all about the author. Finally, he turned to the inside back cover and there she was, Laurie Langtry, in living color—Betty Boop lips, pixie nose, and flaming red curls. "Damn!"

"What?"

"It *is* her. Listen to this." Jake began to read.

" 'Award-winning novelist Laurie Langtry has captivated readers since she burst on the scene in 1985, weaving her own special magic that transports readers into the past—from Norman conquests to Civil War battlefields, from Highland fortresses and castles of kings, to prairie shanties and palatial cattle baron estates.

" 'A New Yorker at heart, Ms. Langtry is host of a nationwide radio talk show, and appears weekly on "America Today," dishing out advice for the lovelorn, and romantic wisdom to an audience that knows no age or gender.' "

Jake shut the cover. "I knew I'd heard the name somewhere. Must have seen her on TV or something." He shrugged. "Pretty impressive, huh?"

"Yeah, if you buy all that trash. My wife's been reading that stuff for years and there's just no pleasing her anymore. Too much romantic nonsense filling her head these days."

"You ever read one?" Jake asked.

"You gotta be kidding."

Jake flipped the book over in his hand, checking out the price on the spine, wishing it was a few dollars cheaper. "Well, I'll give it a quick read and let you know if you're missing anything."

"Sure you wanna spend money on that?" Tom asked, frowning as he nodded at the book. "Can't eat it, you know."

"Have to splurge once in awhile," Jake tossed back, tucking the book under his arm, noting Tom's shrug and the roll of his eyes as he walked to the front of the store. Jake hated the fact that Tom, and too many other people in town, knew the state of his finances, or lack thereof. It wasn't something he was proud of, but something he'd learned to live with and ignore.

Again, Jake turned to Laurie's short biography and read the words, momentarily wondering how the poor troubled kid he'd grown up with had turned into a star, and wondered, too, why she'd come back to Bunch Gulch when, from all appearances, she belonged in New York.

Hell, maybe she wants to get back at me for throwing up all over her party dress, he thought. Maybe that's why she stole my house—to get revenge. He spun the creaking metal book rack and watched the name Laurie Langtry circle around and around, taunting him, just as he was sure she would do every time he drove down that blasted drive. He could picture that grin of hers quite clearly, that petite ball of fire sitting on the big front porch in his grandmother's old redwood bench swing, rubbing in the fact that he was too damn down on his luck to be living in his old home.

And then other fleeting memories sped through his thoughts: a little girl with bouncing red curls peeking around the corner of his house while he wrestled in the grass with his dad; a wild, unruly teenager crying when the drunken boy who'd tried to grope her budding breasts emptied the contents of his stomach on her crimson spaghetti strap dress. The visions weren't funny, and, until now, he'd almost forgotten them. But those days seemed vivid in his mind, and he wondered how life could pull such a switch, making him the outsider looking in, and Laurie the new queen of the castle that should rightfully have been his.

Damn! He gave the book rack one more spin and headed to the back corner of the store where a bank of ancient brass postal boxes lined the wall.

Pulling a ring of keys from his front pocket, he shoved one into his box and pulled out half a dozen envelopes. Thumbing through, he tossed the advertising into the black Rubbermaid trash can in the corner, and tensed when he found the envelope from Bishop Well Drilling. He ripped off the end of the white envelope, blew it open, and pulled out the final bill for the new well he'd had drilled last summer when his old one ran dry. He wished he could wad it up and throw it in the can right along with the rest of the junk mail, but, instead, stuck it into his pocket and made a mental note to call

Bob Bishop and ask for another extension. He hadn't had the money last month to make the payment, and this month didn't look much more promising.

When he found the lilac-scented lavender envelope, he leaned his shoulder against the wall of boxes and pried open the flap stuck together with a dab of gold sealing wax stamped with the letter M. Quickly he scanned the contents, his mustache twitching more than once as his lips turned up at the corners, then dropped the way they usually did when he read the last of his mother's words. When would she quit asking him to move to New Mexico? When would she quit telling him he should provide a better home for his family? When would she ever realize that he loved Montana, he loved what was left of his land, and being a rancher made him happy?

He shoved the flowery card back into the envelope and tossed it into the trash. He loved his parents, and he missed them, but all their attempts to get him to move had failed, and would continue to fail. They may have run away from Bunch Gulch because ranching, for them, had turned into a losing proposition. But for Jake, it was the life he knew, and loved, and he'd be damned if he'd run away, too.

2

Laurie curled up on the window seat in her second-story bedroom, clutching a ruffled white eyelet pillow to her stomach, and looked through sparkling glass at the valley beyond. Acres of tall, green grass waved in the wind, immense pines butted up against the rugged cliffs to the east, and thousands of feet of posts and barbed wire separated her small piece of property from what she now realized was Jake's. She loved every ounce of dirt, every rock and tree, and the house—especially the house.

"It's an obsession," her agent had chastised her. "Bunch Gulch? Why the hell would anyone want to live in a town called Bunch Gulch when you have all of New York?" her attorney had moaned. "You're out of your mind," her real estate agent had muttered when Laurie insisted the woman keep a close eye on property for sale in a town that wasn't much more than a wide spot on a highway in southwestern Montana. But the real estate agent had watched, and Laurie reacted, snapping up the house and the twenty acres surrounding it. She hadn't known and hadn't cared why the owners were selling. It didn't matter. All that mattered was that she'd wanted this house—her dream—

and when Laurie Langtry wanted something, she made a point of getting it.

Four years ago she'd bought the place. Four long years. And she'd waited for the perfect time to return—when her career was at its highest point; when she'd achieved all her goals; when she'd built up the courage to face the townspeople of Bunch Gulch and show them she was better than they thought, that she'd made something of her life, and she was just as good and decent and upstanding as any one of them. She'd wanted to prove that as a child, but she had too many strikes against her, and back then it was easier to play their game than to fight.

She'd long ago achieved her goals and risen to the top in her career, but none of that had made her return. It was the madman who'd haunted her, and terrified her, who'd forced her to run to a place where she hoped she'd find peace.

Now, though, she faced a new nightmare, and it came in the guise of Jake McAllister. He despised her, quite obviously, for buying what he felt rightfully belonged to him. She wasn't in the habit of explaining herself to people, she hadn't done it as a kid, she didn't do it now, but she had the strangest urge to make him realize she hadn't bought the place to hurt him; she'd only bought the place because she thought it would bring her a little joy, and hope, and love, to make up for a childhood that hadn't been fair.

Certainly life hadn't been fair when she was growing up. The townspeople of Bunch Gulch, along with her grandmother, had made her existence painful. She was a bastard, she was a troublemaker—she was downright no good, or so she'd been led to believe. But, in spite of the sneers and

snubs of the good citizens, in spite of her grandmother's bitterness and scorn, she had loved the
town. She could never pinpoint a reason why she
loved it—she just did, and that love had stayed
with her for thirty-two years. Perhaps it was the
beauty of the Bitterroot Valley, surrounded most
of the year by rugged snow-capped peaks, and
deep, dark canyons. Perhaps it was the territory's
rich history of gold and copper, of Indians and
crooked sheriffs and vigilantes. Maybe, just maybe,
it was the love she had witnessed between mother
and father and son when she'd hid behind the
trees near the old McAllister house, wishing, just
once, she could be part of their family.

In truth, that was the biggest reason she returned. She did love the valley. She did love the
mountains and rivers and streams. She did love
the lush green pastures in summer, and the win-
tertime snow. But, most of all, she loved that feeling that warmed her heart every time she got close
to the McAllister house. The family knew how to
love. Now, she only hoped a little of that love remained in the house, and that perhaps part of it
could rub off on her.

And, too, she hoped it would be the perfect
sanctuary, the perfect refuge and hiding place from
the horror she'd lived through in New York.

She ceased her musing, shoved the pillow between her knees, and pushed open the window,
letting the cool late-afternoon breeze into the room.
She sucked in the fresh summer scents of newly
mown lawn, the sweetness of roses winding in and
out of her picket fence, of a barbecue burning
somewhere in the distance. Children's laughter
carried on the wind, filling her room right along
with the thud of a hammer, the loud, irritating

squawk of something unknown, and in the background, the wind rustling through aspen leaves down by the stream.

Suddenly, she had a desire to be closer to those sounds, to add her voice to the laughter. She tossed the pillow to the floor, retied the shoestring on her right Nike, grabbed hold of the window frame, and pushed herself out to the two-foot-wide ledge. It seemed a crazy thing to do, but she'd never let convention or right or wrong stand in her way. She'd scaled trees, but never the side of a house. She didn't even know if she could, but she liked taking chances.

Adrenaline rushed through her veins as she inched her way toward the drain pipe. Cautiously, she wrapped her hands around the cold, sturdy metal, and shook it to test its strength. It didn't budge an inch. Holding on for dear life, she peered over the edge to the ground—a long, death-defying drop below.

She swallowed a deep breath, remembering all the times she'd climbed out the window of her bedroom as a child, sneaking away from her grandmother. But that was a long time ago, she lectured herself. She was thirty-two now, not twelve, this house was three stories, not just one, and she hadn't climbed in a helluva long time. But maybe, just maybe, she thought, she hadn't lost her touch.

"Well, here goes," she whispered to God and anyone else within earshot. Turning around backwards, she jabbed the toe of one tennis shoe into the side of the house, at least a foot below the ledge, and slowly, carefully began her descent. Her heart pumped hard and fast with each foothold. The palms of her hands burned from the icy cold of the pipe, from the tightness of her grip. Her head throbbed from the insanity of her daring feat, and, when the reality of what she was doing finally sank in, she wondered what on earth she was trying to prove. But it was far too late. She couldn't turn back now.

She kept on moving, one foot after the other. Finally, she heard the rustling of hedge as her right foot brushed against the leaves, and without stopping to think about the madness of her actions, applied both feet firmly to the side of the house, and pushed. Her body propelled away from the wood siding at the same time as she let loose of her grip on the pipe, and somehow, miraculously, she jumped safely to the ground.

Her joints slammed together, every muscle screamed, but within seconds, the vibrations died. With a self-satisfied smile, she rubbed her hands on the backs of her jeans, rose from her crouched position, and sauntered off toward the happy noises and the cabin she knew must be Jake's. Not bad, she laughed to herself, for a writer whose most strenuous exercise consisted of signing autographs and typing.

Long shadows had slipped across the land by the time she reached the fence that marked the boundary between her property and Jake's. She crouched low and slipped under the bottom strand of barbed wire, careful not to catch her t-shirt, or any part of her anatomy. Her right shoulder still bore the scar from an old run-in with a sharp, electrified barb. Absently, she rubbed the shoulder, remembering the pain of the cut, the shock of the jolt, and her grandmother's anger over the rip in her dress.

Tossing the memory aside, she walked through

the cow-patty-strewn pasture, strategically dodging land mines, and the ever-present stones that dotted the ground. She zigged and zagged, avoiding ground squirrel holes along with the piles of green, grassy goo, and somehow, without tripping or stepping in something she'd instantly regret, she found the sought-after noise.

"Throw it to me, Daddy."

"No, Daddy. It's my turn."

"Over here, Daddy."

Jake stood by a battered barbecue grill, out of the line of smoke, and tossed a miniature football to the tallest of three tow-headed boys. "Great catch, Jacob," he yelled, darting across the lawn toward the boy, tackling him to the grass, his arms encircling and protecting the child as they rolled.

Laurie's heart warmed as she watched the game being played, as she hid behind a tree and observed the interaction between father and sons, so much like the scenes she'd longed to be part of years and years before. The two littlest boys dove into Jake's outstretched arms, and all four laughed and hooted as they rolled over and over, their blond hair filling with freshly mown clippings, their bare knees and elbows staining with streaks of green. And somehow, Laurie found herself holding her breath, watching, waiting, for wife and mother to step from the rustic cabin to either join in the fun or scold.

But a woman never appeared, and finally, Jake pushed himself off the ground, a small, wiggling boy captured under each arm. "Hot dogs will be ready any second," he said, standing the boys on the ground and ruffling their mops of hair. "You guys go in and get cleaned up."

"Gee, Dad. Do we have to?" the tallest boy

whined. Even from a distance Laurie could see Jake's eyes narrow, his commanding look, his nod toward the house speaking louder than words, and in an instant the boy who'd whined and the other two ran up the stairs and slammed through the screen door.

Jake brushed grass from his hair, shaking the thick, wavy mane that curled behind his ears and over the neck band of his grass-stained t-shirt. Only on construction sites, and in her novels, had she seen such remarkably muscular arms. Did he wrestle bulls in addition to weight-lifting cows for a living? she wondered. The white cotton strained across to-die-for pecs, and that obviously granite stomach, and her fingers tingled, itching to stroke the rock-hard ripples she'd briefly considered touching as they'd stood nose-to-buckle earlier in the day.

Voyeurism wasn't her style, nor were sweat, grass stains, and scraggly beards, but she had the wickedest desire to stay hidden behind the tree and watch him for hours. But hiding was something she swore she'd never do again—she'd left that behind in New York. Instead, she stepped from behind the tree, loudly announcing her arrival as her tennis shoes crunched through a thick bed of gravel in the drive. "Good evening."

Jake spun around, a wiener stabbed in the tines of the long-handled fork, waving like Excalibur between himself and Laurie. "Didn't expect to see you here tonight," he stated quite flatly, and with very little interest.

Such a gentleman, she thought, wishing she could rip the beard off his face to see the tilt of his lips, to see if he bore even the slightest trace of a smile. "I got tired of unpacking boxes," she remarked, all perky and sweet. "Hope you don't mind my coming over."

He shrugged his shoulders, avoiding her eyes, and she watched him drag his gaze slowly over her body, taking in the shortness of her cropped turquoise t-shirt, and the tight, faded blue jeans that rested just above her hip bones and left her belly button clearly within view. She hadn't meant to shock him, she'd just opted for comfort, but she rather enjoyed his obvious unease. His Adam's apple rose and fell in his strong, corded neck, and the fabric stretched even tighter over his chest as he sucked in what appeared to be a life-saving breath.

Turning away, he shoved the blackened wiener between a bun and added it to the two others he'd already placed on a platter. "I'd invite you to stay, but I'm a little short on hot dogs," he stated, his clipped words nearly carried away in the breeze.

He wanted her to leave. She could sense it, but he wasn't going to get his way. "No problem." Laurie clasped her hands over her stomach, willing the sudden growl to remain quiet and unobtrusive. "I'm not hungry anyway."

As if he'd willed it, as if Mother Nature was on his side, the wind changed directions and surrounded her in a billowing cloud of white smoke. The smell of burning hickory assailed her sinuses and burned her lungs. She moved quickly, out of the line of fire, but the smoke followed until she slid behind the safety of Jake's broad and muscular back. "Mind if I hide back here? The smoke doesn't seem quite so attracted to you."

He shrugged again, but when he turned, the plate of hot dogs in hand, she looked up and finally saw a grin, the uncontrollable twitch of his mustache, and she hoped his mood had changed, that he wasn't just amused by her predicament. "They come eight to a pack," he informed her as if she didn't have a clue. "I usually eat five, but if you're hungry, I'm willing to share."

It was a pretty lousy offer, but she wasn't about to walk away. "Thanks, but I'm more interested in company than food at the moment."

"What? That old house too lonely for you?"

"No, just too quiet. It's not exactly New York around here."

The cabin door slammed against the rough-hewn log wall, and three childish voices reverberated through the evening's calm as the boys scrambled from the house, chasing each other until they caught sight of Laurie, and stopped dead in their tracks. They didn't speak or move, they just stood there and stared from their dad to Laurie and back again.

"You wanted noise?" Jake laughed. "Well, you're in for a treat."

The boys had lined up like tin soldiers, straight, tall, and silently at attention, and Laurie paced in front of their ranks, inspecting the imps who were miniature replicas of their dad, two of them clones of each other. "I'm Laurie Langtry," she said, kneeling slightly to address the tallest boy face to face. "And who are you?"

"I'm Jacob McAllister, Jr.," he stated, sticking a thumb into his chest. "I'm six. My brothers are four. That's Joshua." He pointed to the twin on the right. "And that's Joseph. He's got a scar. See. Right here." He stuck his finger on a jagged, half-inch scar at the bottom of Joseph's chin. "It's the only way strangers can tell them apart."

"I'm pleased to meet all three of you." She

stretched out her hand, gracefully acquainting herself with one little boy, then another, then another.

She looked up at Jake and smiled. "Working on your own football team?" she asked, remembering full well the way Jake had looked on the field. He'd been the only reason she'd ever gone to a game, and she could well imagine the way these little boys would send the girls' hearts sailing when they reached their teens.

"Stopped a few short of a team, I'm afraid." He ruffled the hair on the oldest boy's head, and set the plate of hot dogs on the redwood table next to squeeze bottles of catsup, mustard, relish, and a big plastic bowl full of barbecue chips.

"Have a seat, Laurie." He didn't practice the gentlemanly fashion of waiting for the lady, but swung one leg over a bench, then the other.

Following suit, she checked for splinters in the redwood then sat across from Jake and Jacob Jr. Joseph, the twin with the scar, squeezed against her right side, Joshua her left. Joseph instantly reached for a bun but Jake fixed him with a death-defying stare, and Joseph's hand sprung back into his lap, his gaze lowering to the bottom edge of his white paper plate. Laurie hadn't the slightest idea what the child had done to deserve his father's scorn, until Jake folded his hands and lowered his head.

He cleared his throat. "Dear Lord. The dogs are burned, as usual, my beer's probably warm, but I'm truly thankful for the bounty before us. Suppose I should thank you for the company, too. Trouble doesn't normally come in such a pretty package." Laurie looked up from her own folded hands to meet Jake's studying gaze. His mustache twitched and under the hair she could see the slow smile covering his face. He winked, and once again closed his eyes. "Amen."

"Okay, guys. Dig in," he said, and six little hands and arms reached and collided and grabbed. Laurie squeezed catsup on buns for each of the twins, drenched one in mustard for herself, and picked at the barbecue chips the boys had scattered on her plate. Over and over she was jabbed with elbows, a blob of catsup dripped from Joshua's bun onto her jeans, and she loved every moment.

"I haven't had a good hot dog in ages," she stated, and shoved the concoction into her mouth and took a bite. "Mmm. Delicious."

Laurie munched on the dog, entertaining the giggling boys as she smacked her lips in obvious, and possibly feigned, delight. It did taste good, she realized, in spite of the charred and crinkled skin, and the thought that she was indulging in half a million grams of valve-clogging fat. But she would do it ten times a day, maybe even eat whale blubber, if she could continue to share the camaraderie she was enjoying at the McAllister table.

"May we be excused, Dad?" Jacob mumbled, his mouth full of chips.

"Sure, but don't play so far away that you can't see me."

They scrambled across the lawn and through the nearest pasture, chasing circles around a slow-moving cow chewing peacefully in a stand of tall grass and clover.

"Would you like a beer?" Jake asked, pushing up from the table and crossing to the cabin door in a few long strides.

"Sounds good," Laurie said as he went into the house, but what sounded better was the thought of relaxing conversation with a man she'd wanted to know as a teen, who she thought she might like knowing now.

When he returned, she studied his walk, his form, as he ambled toward the table and straddled the bench. He had an Olympian swimmer's body and grace, and a vivid picture of Jake in the skimpiest fluorescent Speedo flitted through her mind, the vision almost strong enough to make her forget he looked as if he'd been living with cattle rather than the gods.

He pushed the cold bottle of Budweiser across the table. "You're staring again," he teased. "Hell if I know what you find so intriguing about me."

"I'm a writer, Jake. I study everything. And since I write romance, studying men comes natural. Hope you don't mind being the current target of my research."

"You could buy a copy of *Playgirl*."

"I prefer the total picture, someone who not only looks good, but talks, too."

He balanced his elbows on the table and took a swig from the amber bottle, his blue-eyed gaze passing beyond Laurie to the pasture where the boys were playing, and she knew he planned to ignore her comment.

"You happy to be back in town?" he asked.

"For the most part. The farmhouse is everything I ever expected, and more. I'm far from settled, but that's going to take time. Of course, the welcoming committee hasn't exactly been beating down my door." She aimed a steady, convicting gaze straight into his eyes. "Haven't been welcomed by anyone yet, including you, but guess I didn't really expect it."

"Too many strangers been buying up property

around here the last few years. Most folks, including me, haven't been happy about it."

"I'm not a stranger, Jake. I was born here, so that buying up property excuse only applies to you." She took a drink of beer, keeping her eyes leveled with his, waiting for some kind of response, an apology, a welcome, but it never came. She sighed deeply. "The rest of the people in this town don't need a new excuse, Jake. They've got one left over from fourteen years ago. They plain old don't want me around."

Most men would have looked away, Laurie thought, when confronted with that statement. But not Jake. He kept his gaze firmly on her eyes. His mustache twitched slightly, and his words, when they came, were slow, filled with regret. "I wish I could say that's not true. But I can't."

Laurie forced herself to sit there, to accept the truth that had hurt her so much as a child. Dammit, it hurt now, but she wasn't going to run away—not this time.

Jake downed another swallow of beer, and slowly, he shook his head, his eyes twinkling as his mustache twitched over an obvious grin. "What did you expect? You were a hellion, Laurie."

She swirled the beer around in her bottle, letting his laugh sink in and erase a bit of her hurt. "Hellion? You're too kind. As I recall, my reputation went far beyond hellion. True or false, labels stick."

"I heard others, but what the hell. You know," he said, scratching the infernal hair on his cheek, "I used to be jealous of you and your moniker."

"Jealous? You've got to be kidding."

"At least you didn't have somebody's grand

scheme to live up to. When you're dubbed 'most likely to succeed,' some people, especially parents, have a tendency to expect a helluva lot. It gets old, real old, and when it doesn't pan out, well, some people aren't too thrilled."

"Who? Your folks?"

He laughed. "They had college and a good career in mind. I had Bunch Gulch and a ranch. Guess that's pretty much the reason they sold the house and part of the property out from under me. I think they figured I'd go to New Mexico with them and get a real job."

"You don't regret it? Staying here, I mean."

He shook his head, and by the light she saw in his eyes when he looked past her toward the boys playing in the pasture, to the bright orange sun dipping below the purple mountains in the distance, and the pines, and aspen and willow, she knew it would take a whole lot more than parental persuasion to get him to leave. "My great-grandparents homesteaded this place over a hundred years ago. They built the cabin first, then the farmhouse. Half the fence posts around here were made from felled timber off this land, and most of the ditches were plowed by hand. It's a *legacy*, Laurie, not just a piece of property." He shoved his fingers through his hair, pushing an errant strand from his forehead. "No, I don't regret anything I've done. Those boys," he said, nodding toward the twins, toward Jacob Jr., "will inherit all of this someday. I doubt I'll ever be able to give them much more, and I sure as hell can't leave them that house you're living in, but at least they'll have this, and God, I sure hope they'll want to keep it and hand it down to their kids."

"And your wife?" She hadn't seen one, hadn't

met one, and for some reason hoped there wasn't one, but she had to ask. "Is she happy here?"

He took a long swig of his beer and when he set the bottle back on the table, the thick bottom where his fist wrapped around the amber glass hit a little too loud, a little too hard. "No wife, just three kids. And no, she hated it here."

Laurie refused to look down at her hands, at her own bottle of beer, and refused to be embarrassed for asking. Now, she wanted to know more. "Has she been gone long?"

"Drop it, Laurie. Subject's closed." He pushed up from the bench and strolled across the gravel drive, through the tall grass, not looking back even once to see if Laurie followed.

He stopped at a fence post where a coil of barbed wire lay on the ground, and grasped the top, looking off toward his old home.

Laurie walked up behind him, wanting to offer comfort, wanting to put her hands on his back, on his shoulders, wishing he would tell her more about his life, and his loss, but she knew now wasn't the time to ask. Instead, she steered the conversation away from his problems, to the subject that might keep them from becoming friends. "Want to know why I bought your place?"

"Not really."

His response didn't surprise her, but she wouldn't be brushed aside. There was nowhere to lean except against the barbed wire or Jake's back, and Laurie had the distinct feeling both would rip her apart. Instead, she chose to walk around him, sitting atop a moss-dotted boulder that seemed to have been placed there as a convenient resting spot, a place made just for her to face an angered, surly male. "Want to know why I left Bunch Gulch?"

"I can pretty much guess, but sure, tell me the story."

No one else knew the story, and she had no clue why she felt compelled to tell him now. But it was a day for new beginnings, for renewing old acquaintances, and for digging up long-buried secrets. "Did you know my grandmother very well?"

"Heard about her. Nothing good, though."

"She might have had a few good traits, but I don't remember many. Even towards the end, when I put her in a home and called her every day, she resented me. She didn't exactly like being saddled with her daughter's kid, and tried her hardest to make me regret ever being born."

"Wasn't your fault."

"No. That she blamed on my mom." Laurie smiled, fondly remembering the face she'd embedded in her memory as a child. "I don't remember much about my mother, only that she was pretty and she went off to New York to become an actress." The wistfulness slowly left her face. "My grandmother never forgave her for running away. Told me she was a drug addict—and a whore."

"Nice words to dish out to a kid," he said, his words laced with sarcasm and regret, and then he looked up, tenderness filling his eyes, as though he wanted to gather Laurie into his arms and make her forget the horror of her grandmother's words. "Did you leave Bunch Gulch to find your mom?"

"Not at first. All I wanted to do was run away, from my grandmother, from the people around here who were convinced I'd end up behind bars, and, I suppose," she hesitated, studying Jake's face, "from a bunch of guys who thought I'd be a great roll in the hay."

"Were we that obvious?" Jake asked, admitting his guilt with downturned eyes.

"Some more than others. One guy took me into the trees and promptly threw up on my graduation dress."

His shoulders sagged, and he shook his head in shock and disgust. "Look, Laurie. I'm sorry about all that. Really. I was drunk. I never would have—"

"It doesn't matter anymore, Jake," she interrupted. She'd forgiven him and the rest of the people in Bunch Gulch a long time ago. "I've put all that behind me, but I figured since I'm dishing out my life story, I might as well get that out in the open, too. I promise, it won't come up again."

"I did go to your place the next day to apologize."

"I know. I'd just sneaked out of the house headed for the bus stop when I saw you at the door. I heard you asking for me, and heard my grandmother telling you to go away. I'm glad I didn't run into you. I'm glad you didn't have the chance to apologize. If you had, I might have stayed, and, if I had, I might have ended up like everyone expected."

"Well . . ." He laughed, and took a swig of beer from the bottle he still held. "I never thought throwing up on a pretty lady would be the turning point in her life."

"Don't try to claim all the credit," she teased. "All you did was heave, I'm the one who got on that bus and didn't have a clue where to go. I'm the one who was afraid my grandmother would send the cops after me."

"Why? Did you think she'd want you back?"

Those words startled her, then she laughed. "Hell, no! The last thing she wanted was to have me around. But I ripped her off. Took all but a few dollars out of the coffee can she hid over the stove."

Once again, Jake smiled, and it warmed her soul. "Gutsy, weren't you?"

"Three hundred and seventy-four dollars worth of guts." She drew her knees up close to her chest and wrapped her arms around them. "You know how far you can go on that much money?"

"Not far."

"A bus ride to New York, a few nights sleeping in an alley, scared to death and hungry."

She watched Jake's Adam's apple rise and fall heavily in his throat as he swallowed, and for the first time she was reminded of the young boy who'd offered to give her his kitten, and the pre-teen she'd followed when he ran from the cemetery after his grandfather died, and sat by the river and cried for hours. She'd envied him that day, just as much as she had any other. He had a family to cry for—and she had no one. That was one of the things she remembered about him—his sensitivity when no one was looking, now it seemed as though he had much more trouble hiding his feelings, even when he tried to mask them behind anger and indifference.

He balanced the empty bottle on top the fence post, and he settled beside her on the boulder, his long legs stretched out, his mud-crusted boots digging into dirt and grass to keep him from sliding to the ground. "You didn't have to sell your . . ." His words trailed off, but she knew where his thoughts were headed.

"Never. I figured if some guy wanted this body of mine, tiny though it is, he'd have to pay a damn sight more than ten or fifteen bucks or whatever the going rate was back then."

Absently, she picked at a nub of thread on the knee of her Levi's, remembering the tattered and torn ones she'd been wearing when she'd arrived in New York. At least, she laughed inside, she'd picked an alley in Manhattan. "Actually, I dodged security guards and sneaked into an office building on Madison Avenue, cleaned up as best I could, and started going from office to office asking for work."

"You're kidding?"

"Guts, remember? I had about five dollars left of it, and I knew it wasn't going to last much longer. You get pretty desperate sleeping behind a Dumpster, even on Madison Avenue."

Jake leaned over and snapped up a long, thick blade of grass, drawing it over and over between his fingers. "So, you got a job, and got rich and famous."

"I scrubbed toilets." Laurie laughed. "Then I opened mail at a publishing company."

"And," he said, tilting his head toward Laurie, his mustache twitching once again, "I suppose you moved sleeping quarters from alley to mail room?"

"Not quite. Two bachelors took me in. They were looking for a maid, and probably a little something extra on the side." She wiggled her copper brows, remembering so vividly the beginning of the best years of her life. "I cleaned more toilets, firmly planted my knee in two overactive crotches, and got a room of my own with a lock to keep them out."

"Ever write a book about your adventures?"

"Too tame. Besides, I prefer history—mine not included."

Suddenly realizing she'd talked about herself till only a thread of sun peeked over the mountains, she hopped down from the boulder and headed for the well-worn path that connected her home to Jake's. "I can't believe I've gone on and on about myself. I'm not usually so open about my life."

Jake also left the boulder, standing beside her now, more than a head taller, a lifetime of differences separating them. "I'm glad you told me. It's a whole lot different than life in Bunch Gulch." He reached out and captured a ringlet of red, coiling it around his finger, keeping her from going any further.

And then, as if that strand of hair had caught on fire, he dropped it, backing away, distancing himself physically. "What happened next?" he asked, hooking his thumbs over the back pockets of his Levi's. "After the mail room?"

"I read a romance and fell in love. And then I wrote one, and another, and another, and finally convinced someone to look at my work. Thirteen rejections later—and the rest is history. Took awhile before I made any money, but book number five, *My Captain*, took off." Laurie followed his lead and shoved her hands in her pockets, afraid if she kept them out she'd latch on to a strand of Jake's long hair or his t-shirt and pull him close, and she wasn't sure how he'd react to that just now. She wasn't even sure why the thought entered her mind, or how she'd react if she came in contact with his body, so, slowly, she backed away. "Look, it's getting late. I need to go."

"Don't." He blurted out the word and, as if by

sheer instinct, he seized her arm and held her back. "Not yet anyway."

Laurie glared at the hand that held her, uncomfortable with his quick, forceful gesture, but when she looked into his eyes and saw his smile, the way his mustache curved up at its sides, she was reminded once again she had nothing to fear in Bunch Gulch, or from Jake.

"I didn't hurt you, did I?" he asked, his fingers gently massaging the tender, sensitive skin of her arm.

"No. I startle easily, that's all. I really do have to go, Jake. Books don't write themselves, and I've left my heroine in one hell of a predicament."

"Then let me walk you home."

"What about the boys?" Laurie looked toward the pasture and saw them playing atop and beside a fallen tree, old and bare of bark, the wood polished smooth from years of climbing and pretending.

"They'll be fine, besides, I can see them all the way to—your place." He pushed open the gate that severed the path at the borderline of their properties, and walked at her side along the hardened dirt trail.

"You never told me about your mom," he stated, his pace slow, methodical, his long legs knowing just how to move so her short legs could keep in step. "Did you find her?"

Laurie's throat constricted and she bit at her lower lip to hold back tears, the same thing that happened every time that question was asked. After fourteen years, she still wondered when she'd be able to forget, or hurt a little less. "Yeah, I found her not too long after I got to the city. She'd been a dancer on Broadway once, or at least that's what

I remembered from a letter I'd seen when I was young. I asked around at the theaters but no one had ever heard of her—not Connie Flynn, and not Laurie Langtry." Laurie looked at Jake through tear-filled eyes and stuck a fist under her nose, trying to hide the trembling of her lips. "It was her stage name. My grandmother told me over and over how crazy my mom was, thinking she could be a star, thinking someday her name would be known around the world. She never became a star, never became famous, and I never found anyone who knew her, not even the person who buried her."

Slowly, Jake wrapped his arm around her shoulders as they walked, attempting to offer comfort.

"I've never told anyone, Jake. I don't know why I'm telling you now."

"Maybe no one's ever had the time to listen. I've got nothing but time, Laurie. Tell me the rest."

She breathed deeply, sucking in the sweet scents of pine and the roses that grew in profusion around her house, and for the first time in fourteen years, she had a pleasant memory to associate with her mother's death. "I went to the *Times* and looked up obituaries," she said, thoughts of the microfiche flipping through her mind, "and that's how I found her. Someone paid for a plot, and someone put a marble marker on her grave. I don't know who, I don't know why, but at least I was sure she'd had a friend when she died."

"She had you."

"I was only eight, and she left me when I was two. I never knew her, only her memory. I remember her holding me one night in bed, telling me she loved me, telling me she might not always be around, and the next day she was gone. At first I cried, but that made my grandmother just that much angrier. When I finally realized she wasn't coming back, I got mad, and I hated her for a long time, just as my grandmother did. But every once in a while a letter would come, a small gift, and I knew she loved me, just as she had said. She never said why she left. She never blamed anyone, but for a long time I thought it was because of me. God knows my grandmother wanted me out of the house, and I imagine she made my mother's life pure hell when I was born. In her letters she told me about her dream of wanting to be a star, of being famous. I couldn't blame her for wanting her dream. I had dreams, too, and I knew someday I'd run away to find them, just as she had done. Didn't seem fair for either of us. Doesn't seem fair for any kid to grow up without a mother."

"Hell, Laurie, you might have been separated, but at least she told you she loved you."

"She did. In every letter she sent, in every dream I ever had of her. My mother's love is something I never doubted."

"Not every kid's that lucky," he said, and she knew he was thinking of his own three boys. He wiped a tear from her cheek with the pad of a callused thumb. "Why did you take her name?"

Laurie closed her eyes, remembering the moment she first saw the headstone, *Laurie Langtry* carved at its center, a smattering of stars surrounding the name. She'd laid down on the grave and sobbed, her tears hitting the marble stone. She'd cried until there were no more tears to shed, till she knew in her heart and her mind what she had to do. "I wanted her to have her dream," Laurie said. "I wanted the world to know her name. It didn't happen in her lifetime, not like she wanted, but I swore it would happen in mine."

They stopped at the gate of the white picket fence that surrounded the farmhouse and a grassy lawn and garden, an oasis in the middle of thousands of acres of cattle land. Jake easily drew her into his embrace, and it felt good to rest her cheek on his chest while her tears dried and her heart calmed. His fingers lightly caressed her back, his soothing touch lightening her mood.

She forced herself out of his arms, turning away so he wouldn't see her vulnerability. She'd been tough once, hardened by years of pain and hurt. She'd long been able to hide her insecurities, but she couldn't with Jake. Even if she put up a shield, she had the feeling he'd see through it.

She wiped her eyes with the back of her hand. "You'd better get back to the boys."

"You'll be all right?"

She took a deep breath and released it in a short, quick rush. "Positive." She pushed against the swinging gate and let it close on its own as she stepped into the confines of her yard. "Thanks for dinner."

"You're welcome." He smiled, and his mustache twitched as the smile turned to a grin. "You plan on reciprocating soon?"

"I make lousy hot dogs."

"What can you cook?"

"Not much. Actually, I'm pretty useless around the house. Except for toilets."

"But you do make a great cup of coffee? You told me that."

"I lied." She grinned, holding up her hands in supplication. "I'm a storyteller by trade, remember?"

Jake laughed, and somewhere in the distance a

cow bawled, she heard the heavy flutter of birds' wings as a dozen or so jays flew from a nearby pine, and all the noises blended together with the rapid thud of her heart.

"Hey, Dad!" one of the children cried out, the voice echoing across the meadow. "Come play with us."

"Seems I've got to go, too," he said, and Laurie noted a tinge of reluctance in his voice.

She shrugged, half-glad, half-sad, to finally have an escape. "Go on. Next time I brew a good pot, I'll give you a holler."

He backed away, slowly, his gaze never leaving hers until he stumbled, the heel of his boot catching in a ground squirrel hole. "Gotta be careful around here," he called out, finally turning away to run across the field to his kids, and Laurie wondered why she'd waited so long to come home.

3

Laurie crept up the steps leading to the attic, studying each footfall, each creak in the hundred-year-old wood, learning where to place her feet so she wouldn't make a sound on the next trip. It was a crazy thing to do and not the least bit necessary, but it came with years of practice, once a necessity, now a habit.

She clutched the ancient key in her trembling fingers, and in the dim light of a yellowed, low-wattage bulb, she found the keyhole, listened for the click, took a deep breath, and slowly, cautiously opened the door.

A sliver of morning light shone through the slats in a circular window at the peak of the ceiling, shedding a glimmer of light on the silken webs strewn from wall to wall, box to box, and hidden item to hidden item. The room smelled of must and mildew, not at all what she'd expected after paying so generously to have the place cleaned.

Feeling her way around dusty boxes, she caught a glimpse of the pull string attached to a single bulb in the center of the ceiling, reached on tiptoe, and brought shadows to life in the room, and old memories of her grandmother.

Dented and ripped cardboard containers rested

in the center of the wood plank floor, only partially sealed with tape, now peeling and cracked, leaving space for years of dust and dirt and probably insects to slip inside and disturb the contents. They were her grandmother's belongings, locked away for years in the basement of that old, decaying home, hidden and forgotten, and never allowed to be touched when Laurie was young. They should have been discarded when the old house was torn down. They should have been hauled to the dump like the stained and faded sheets and towels, like cracked glasses and chipped dishes, but Laurie had given specific orders that the boxes be kept in storage, until she had time, until she was ready to satisfy her old curiosity, and find out what treasures her grandmother had secreted away. Two years ago she'd had the boxes moved to the attic of her new home, where they'd remained unopened and untouched, unlike the rest of the house which she'd had refurbished and decorated. There were no old memories in the rest of the house—only here, and now she longed to look inside for any remembrances of her mother, for a picture of a pretty lady with red curls, smiling and happy and full of life. It was the way Laurie remembered her, but it was only a child's memory, faded and distorted through the years.

A pile of what appeared to be old rags was heaped in a box in a corner, and when she pulled one out to use as a dust cloth, she found a child's dress, ragged and discolored, its fibers filled with years of dust that came close to choking her when she shook it out. But she remembered the dress, remembered wearing it to church on Easter Sunday, her hand clutched in her grandmother's as she was ushered into the sanctuary of that holy place, where her grandmother had told her, many times before, and after, she didn't really belong. She was a bastard, after all, and bastards deserved very little. The billowy, ruffled sleeves of that calico dress had hung past her elbows, the waistline hugged her hips, and instead of standing perky and stiff with layers of ruffled petticoats underneath, it draped limply below her scuffed knees. She'd been such a sorry sight walking into that sanctuary when all others were in their new Easter bonnets, their flowery pastel dresses, and their shiny pink or white patent leather Mary Janes. Laurie wore scuffed and dirty tennis shoes, their laces dragging on the floor, and stuck her tongue out at everyone who stared. She proved to the congregation that she didn't care, but deep inside she was crying.

With a jerk, she ripped the dress in half, and feverishly used the scraps to wipe years of dirt and dust from the tops of boxes. She coughed as the particles flew through the air, then settled lightly on the wood plank floor. At the window, she tore down the old sheet that had been thumbtacked at the top to block out the light. She struggled with the latch, stuck in a mire of dried and thickened white paint, but finally it twisted and she pushed open the window, letting in a gush of fresh air and light. She sucked in a healthy dose of pine, and exhaled most of the stale memories.

One box was indistinguishable from another. No markings. No hint about what rested inside, so she grabbed hold of a piece of old masking tape on the nearest box and easily ripped it away, opened its flaps, and jerked in surprise and shock when the grinning face of a clown popped out.

Her hand flew to her chest, waiting for her

nerves to calm and her heart to slow. And then she
laughed. It was only an old jack-in-the-box. Carefully she tucked its head into its red, yellow, and
orange polka dot container, closed the lid, and
turned the handle, the clanking, distorted music of
"Pop Goes the Weasel" filling the attic with childhood noise.

She delved further into the box and found a naked rubber babydoll, one arm rotten and eaten
away with age. It cried when she pressed its belly,
and Laurie hugged it to her chest, stroking its head
and the hole in the rubber curl of hair where a bow
should have been. She remembered her mother's
bosom and how she had once held Laurie, playing
with her curls, then kissing her goodbye. After
that, all Laurie remembered was being as lonely
and forlorn, and as tattered and torn, as the doll.

In box after box she found more toys, old
clothes, and faded black and white photos with
crimped edges that looked as though they had
been taken in the forties. A man in a sailor suit
clutching the hand of a little girl in pigtails, dangling what appeared to be a necklace in front of
her eyes. Her grandfather? Her mother? A birthday or Christmas gift?

She turned it over in her palm, looking for
names, or even a date, but, sadly, no one had taken
the time, or felt the necessity, to jot down the now
desired and important information.

Laurie slipped the photo into the pocket of her
t-shirt, anxious to put it in a silver filigree frame
to place next to her bed, to cherish and love, and
to say goodnight to when she went to sleep.

She found no further photos. No school pictures
with funny hair, and twisted and toothless smiles,
no Christmas pictures of a family sitting next to a

tree surrounded by toys, no babies, or graduations, or weddings. She sighed deeply, wishing she had dozens of memories to scatter around the house in frames.

"Someday," she whispered.

She almost left the last box closed, knowing it would be relegated to the discard pile with everything but the doll and the photo, but as she started to toss it aside, a faint twinkle of light, shimmering through a crack in the lid, caught her eye. A trace of a memory flickered through her heart and her brain, and she remembered, just faintly, another picture frame.

It's magic, Grandma!

Memories of a child's joy-filled voice reverberated through the dusty old attic.

Again, she ripped off tape and flipped open the lid. Resting on top of shredded paper was her tarnished silver picture frame, a gift from her mother, and her mother's last letter in an old red, white, and blue air-mail envelope wedged between glass and silver.

Gently, she removed it from the box and set it in her lap. Taking out the envelope, her throat tightened at the thought of seeing her mother's words once again. The picture frame didn't matter right now, only the words.

Carefully, afraid the paper might crumble in her hands, she removed the letter and read each word, lovingly touching the script, her mother's broad, artistic stroke. Laurie closed her eyes and saw her mother again, sitting before a mirror, surrounded by other dancers and singers, laughing and talking and having a great time, while she wrote a letter to her darling daughter before she had to go on stage.

Laurie wiped tears from her eyes and swallowed a sob. She'd cried too many times over the past for the mother she'd never really known, now all she could do was go forward.

Again, she read the letter. *"Believe darling, always believe, and one day the woman in the picture frame will wink at you, and all the things you wish for will come true."*

Laurie had believed. And she'd wished, again and again and again. She'd believed her mother would return, but her wishes had never come true.

Laurie folded the letter and put it back into its envelope, adding it to the old cherished picture she'd already tucked in her pocket.

The frame was dusty, and tarnished till only a trace of silver could be seen through the blackened metal. It needed hours of gentle scrubbing with a soft cloth and silver polish, a chore for a quiet evening. A thin film coated the glass, and with the end of the old tattered dress, Laurie tried to wipe it away, but it needed a long soak in soapy water. Later. Right now, Laurie wanted to see the woman in the photo, the one her mother claimed to be magic, the one who had winked at her—but didn't grant wishes.

When the old dress didn't work, Laurie tossed it into the discard pile and used the bottom of her cotton t-shirt to buff the glass. And there she was, the remnants of an old woman, faded beyond recognition.

"Dammit!" Laurie swore to the picture and to God. "She thought you were magic. She believed. She truly believed. So why couldn't you grant her wishes?"

A tear fell from her eye and splattered on the glass, sliding across the woman's face. The glass

sparkled, and Laurie looked to the window to see
if sunlight was shining through, to see if it had hit
the glass to make it shine. But the sun was now
too high in the sky, and all she saw was blue.
Again she looked at the photo, and through her
tears she saw the woman wink.

"This is crazy. Absolutely crazy."

But she looked at the frame again, at the woman's eye, and willed herself to believe.

"If you are magic," she said, absently rubbing
the edge of the silver with the pad of her thumb,
"couldn't you bring a little joy into my life."

Tap, tap, tap.

Laurie jumped at the faint sound of the knock
on the door downstairs. She didn't expect her
housekeeper until tomorrow, she didn't expect
Jake at all, and the fear of a stranger intruding on
her solitude frightened her.

Tap, tap, tap.

Laurie ran the back of her hand across her eyes
and nose, and brushed the remnants of tears on
her Levi's. With the frame grasped tightly in one
hand, she once again closed and locked the attic
door, slowly walking down the stairs, missing the
spots that had creaked on her way up, hoping the
person at the door would be gone by the time she
arrived.

Tap, tap, tap.

Persistent bugger, she thought, as she opened
the door.

"Hello. I'm Meghan O'Reilly, the unofficial welcoming committee."

Laurie barely heard the woman's words, barely
saw the woman's face. Instead, she stared at the
long-stemmed yellow rose the stranger held in her
hand. The fear returned, and nausea. She fought

for control, taking a long, deep breath.

"Are you okay?" the woman asked.

Laurie's gaze remained fixed on the rose. "I'm fine." But she wasn't. She hated yellow roses—they reminded her of the man who'd made her leave New York, the man who'd forced her to live in hell for well over a year.

Slowly, she extended her hand. "I'm Laurie Langtry." She forced a smile and took the rose, discarding it without another thought on the lace-draped table next to the door. "Won't you come in."

"Thank you." Meghan frowned slightly at the discarded rose as she stepped over the threshold into the farmhouse.

Meghan wasn't a bit like a welcoming-committee woman, Laurie decided, at least not the stiff, starched, gray-haired creatures she'd always envisioned. No, Meghan stood tall and slender, with an abundance of board-straight hair, the color of fine old mahogany, hanging past her waist. She wore a scoop-necked gingham shift that draped softly to her calves, and acorn-colored Birkenstocks that showed off pearly pink polished toenails that wiggled with an ounce of impatience or nerves.

"I'm afraid I don't have any coffee to offer you," Laurie apologized, ushering Meghan around boxes that hadn't yet been unpacked.

"No, please. Don't apologize. I should have brought coffee for you, or cake, it's the least I could do to welcome you. But, I didn't want to take much of your time, and, really, I can't stay very long anyway."

Laurie liked Meghan. She knew it the moment she welcomed her to town. She'd never had a girl-friend, someone to share confidences with. Maybe, just maybe, Meghan would be a first, and another change in her life.

"It's a mess in here," Laurie admitted as she wound her way between boxes and paper she'd tossed aside when unpacking her crystal.

She offered Meghan a tall, wing-backed, floral print chair, scattered with round and square ruffled pillows in matching shades of forest green and rose and Dresden blue. She herself sat in its twin, separated by a glass-topped, brass-legged table with an immense Waterford vase setting in the middle, overflowing with roses of every hue—but yellow—that she'd picked just that morning from her garden.

"I'm not used to barging in on people's privacy," Meghan stated, "but Jake told me you'd moved into the house and, well . . ." Her words trailed off, her gaze turning to her hands, which twisted in her lap. "I'm sorry, Ms. Langtry, but I'm a big fan of yours, and I'm a little nervous. I've never met a celebrity before."

"I've never claimed to be a celebrity, just a writer," Laurie cheerfully consoled her, a smile overtaking her face, "and I can't think of anyone I'd rather know than an honest to goodness fan."

Meghan smiled at Laurie through the longest, thickest, blackest lashes Laurie had ever seen. The girl was much too gorgeous, the perfect heroine for one of her novels. "There's really no welcoming committee in town," Meghan admitted. "Jake told me you had bought his old house. Well, actually, he told me he finally met the person who stole his home. I was so surprised when he told me it was you, and I wanted to meet you. I didn't think Jake would introduce us, or anyone else. Strangers usually aren't welcome additions to town."

"I'm hardly a stranger." Laurie laughed. "Born and raised right here in little old Bunch Gulch."

"Yes, I heard that yesterday from Mr. Harrington and the ladies at church." Meghan gave up the twisting of her hands and captured a hunk of hair, casually weaving and unweaving a braid. "You're the latest topic of gossip, I'm afraid."

"Gossip doesn't worry me much anymore." Laurie leaned back in the chair, drawing her legs and bare feet beneath her, relaxed in Meghan's company. "I have the feeling you didn't believe what you heard."

"I've heard a lot of gossip from the ladies. I listen like everyone else, but I'd rather draw my own conclusions."

Laurie's admiration for this woman was increasing with every passing second. "I appreciate that." She smiled, and wished Meghan would relax, wishing people wouldn't always be so intimidated in her presence. She was a writer, after all. Not a god.

"You seem to know a lot about me." Laurie set the tarnished frame she'd been clutching on the glass tabletop, studying that strange winking eye one more time, wondering if the sweet lady sitting across from her was a portion of the joy she'd wished for. Meghan O'Reilly, she decided, was an absolute delight. "So, Meghan, why don't you tell me about yourself."

"Me?" Meghan's dark eyes widened, obviously surprised that Laurie would ask. "Well, I'm from San Diego originally. I moved here when I got married."

"And your husband?"

"Steve talked about moving here for ages. Thought it would be a great place to raise a family.

So we came here about five years ago." Meghan twisted the gold band on her finger, around and around and around.

"And has it proved a great place for a family?"

Meghan shook her head. "Steve died just a month after we got here."

Laurie wished she hadn't asked. "I'm so sorry."

"It's okay. Really." Meghan's shoulders drew up as she released a deep sigh. "I didn't come here to talk about me. I really did come to welcome you, and I would have done that even if you weren't a celebrity. Jake said you seemed rather lonely, and thought you might need a friend."

"He did, did he?"

Meghan nodded. "He's not big on talking about himself or anybody else, and he's not crazy about having lots of friends around, so it surprised me when he suggested I stop by. He's been rather bitter since his wife left, and since his folks sold the house. Honestly, I'm surprised he's given you the time of day."

Laurie laughed. "He's all bluster. I've got the feeling he's in as much need for friends as I am. But then," Laurie studied Meghan's face, understanding how a man could care deeply for her, "he has you, and why would he want to give anyone else any of his time?" She kept a smile plastered on her face as she asked the question, hoping her mouth wouldn't turn into an instant frown when she heard the answer.

"Oh, no. There's nothing between us. Well, we're close, and he helps me out a lot, and I take care of the boys once in a while. But I'm not the least bit interested in him if that's what you mean. He's just not my type."

"Thank God." The words slipped between Laurie's lips before she could control her tongue.

Meghan's eyes brightened. "You're interested? In Jake?"

She hadn't thought so, until now. "You find him that odd?"

"It's not that. It's just that he's not interested in women. He's not, well, you know, but he doesn't date, or socialize, or go to church, and he's told me hundreds of times that he'll never get married again. I think his wife must have really hurt him."

Quiet Meghan had suddenly become a fountain of knowledge, and Laurie put on her interviewer's cap, hoping to learn more. "Do you know what happened?"

"No, and he won't talk about it. I've asked, but he always changes the subject."

"What does he tell the boys?"

"Nothing bad, I'm sure. That's just not his style. He's one of the kindest men I've ever met, but too much of a loner, except where his boys are concerned." Meghan's face lit with a blissful smile. "Steve would have liked him if they'd ever met."

So much for dragging out information, Laurie thought. Meghan simply wasn't a gossip.

Meghan looked at the slim, black leather-banded watch on her left wrist. "I really have to run." She stood and smoothed the crinkles at the front of her cotton dress. "I've got choir practice this afternoon, but maybe you could stop by sometime."

"I'd like that." Laurie unfolded from the chair and followed Meghan to the door.

"We're having the Fourth of July party planning meeting at my house in a few days. Mrs. Adams will be there. I don't know if you remember her, but she normally does all the planning, and"—

Meghan laughed—"in the last few years, I've done the work."

"Don't tell me. Bert Ramsey will play his old seventy-eights, and the teens will disappear somewhere and get drunk."

"Exactly. I want to make some changes but she won't listen to me. I thought maybe you might have some influence with her."

Laurie laughed. She'd gotten caught TPing Mrs. Adams' elm tree and the old lady had made her live to regret it. A face-off now, Laurie thought, might be rather lively, and fun. "Just let me know when and where, and I'll be there."

Meghan started through the door, then stopped. "Laurie?"

"Yes."

"I've seen you on TV before, giving advice on . . ." She hesitated, looking down at her hands, at the wedding ring she was twisting and slipping on and off her finger. "Well, on love."

Laurie couldn't help but smile. "Guess I'm sort of a fairy godmother. Make a wish, and Laurie Langtry makes it happen—at least when it comes to getting people together. Haven't been quite so successful with my own love life I'm afraid." But, in spite of her own affairs, Laurie sensed Meghan needed help, and advice, and had no one else to turn to. Heaven knows, she'd been in that boat her entire life. "Why do you ask, Meg? Is there someone . . ."

"Kurt Elliott," Meghan blurted out. "He's tall and handsome and the sweetest man I've ever known, but he's not the least bit interested in me."

"You're sure?"

"Positive. He's my pastor, and, well . . ."

"Ministers need love, too," Laurie tossed in

quickly, before Meghan had a chance to change her mind about wanting help. "Give me some time to think about this. I can't just snap my fingers and make things fall into place."

"No, of course not." Meghan seemed a touch dismayed. Had she really thought it would be easy? "Will you come over for lunch? Day after tomorrow? I'm a great cook, and we could talk, and maybe—maybe you'd autograph my books."

Laurie smiled at Meghan's fresh exuberance. "I'd love to. You can tell me all about Kurt, and who knows, if we put our heads together, we might dream up some kind of miracle."

With the old photo she guessed to be of her mother and grandfather propped up in front of her computer, Laurie stuck in a disk and brought Chapter Eight to life on the monitor, wishing she could bring the characters so easily to life.

Stranger in the Night was due in two months, but for the past six she'd done little more than stare at a blank screen, visions of the stranger who'd haunted her days and nights appearing before her, making her afraid to go out, making her afraid to stay in alone. She'd run to Bunch Gulch to escape. Only her editor, agent, attorney, and the movers knew where she'd gone, and it felt good to finally be away, and free.

The words, she felt, could now pour from her fingers, her characters snappy and sassy, bold and daring and adventurous. "Look out, Chapter Eight," she challenged, "I'm going to have you complete within the hour."

Tap, tap, tap.

"Oh, hell!" Who could it be this time? she wondered. Another member of the so-called Bunch Gulch welcoming committee?

She clicked the mouse on "save" so she wouldn't lose the one and only word she'd typed, and bounded out of the picture-perfect office lined with built-in oak bookshelves that she'd filled, neatly, and in alphabetical order, with her favorite authors. And right there at eye level, *Langtry* jumped out at her. The name graced the covers of books around the world, and Laurie Langtry was famous. She'd set herself a tremendous goal, but like so many other things in life—if she wanted it, she figured out how to get it.

Down the stairs she ran, skipping the creaks, giving half a thought to sliding down the banister from second floor to first. Maybe later, she thought, when someone wasn't incessantly knocking on her door.

Tap, tap, tap.

Maybe it was Meghan again, and that thought delighted her. She needed a friend and wanted a friend, and the girl who couldn't be much older than twenty-five, with her freshly scrubbed, makeup-free face, seemed the perfect candidate.

She could see just the faintest shadow of a rather short figure through the leaded glass swagged in creamy Venetian lace. Definitely not Meghan; definitely not Jake. Cautiously, she turned the knob and opened the door just the slightest crack. And a great gust of icy air blew it from her hand. Wind whipped around the room, stirring the Dresden-blue chintz draperies and the lace that hung underneath, knocking petals from the roses on the coffee table, scattering them about the glass.

Laurie shivered at the sudden drop in temperature, rubbing her arms, as a little old lady bustled into the room, dropped two candy-cane-striped carpetbags on the floor at her sides, and shoved her folded arms under her more than ample bosom. "Good afternoon, Miss Langtry. I'm Merry Nicholas, your new housekeeper."

Laurie stared, open-mouthed, at the unfamiliar rosy-cheeked woman who stood before her.

"Close your mouth, child, or heaven only knows what will fly in." Merry tilted her head and surveyed Laurie, and the room, over the rectangular wire-rimmed spectacles perched on the tip of her nose.

"My, my, my," the woman muttered, bustling around the unpacked boxes, and clutter of paper and dishes and all manner of things that needed to be put away. "I see we have much to do around here."

Laurie pinched the bridge of her nose, feeling a sudden, unexplained headache. "I'm sorry, Ms. Nicholas . . ."

"*Mrs.* Nicholas," the woman interrupted. "Merry, spelled M-E-R-R-Y, if you please. My, my, my, I just don't hold with all that Ms. stuff. Either you're a miss or a missus, there's just no in-between."

"All right, Merry then. But I hired a Mrs. Nolan."

"No, no, no." The words clicked off Merry's tongue. "Mrs. Nolan had a sudden inclination to retire. Dear me. Left town in such a hurry you would have thought someone had set a fire under her Hush Puppies."

"I take it you're her replacement."

"Replacement? No, no, no. I'm the one you should have hired in the first place."

Laurie closed the door, took one long look at

Merry, and began her inspection from head to toe.

"Excuse me, dear. What is it that you're doing?" Merry asked, as Laurie began to circle.

Laurie stopped, cocking her head to one side as she placed a crooked finger to her lips. "Checking you out, Merry. I don't allow just anyone into my home."

"This is unheard of," Merry spouted. "None of my employers has ever checked me out before."

"Well, Merry, I'm not just any employer. I'm Laurie Langtry, and you're not who I hired. If you want to stay, I have to know everything about you."

"No, no, no. That won't do at all."

"Is it your intention to stay here, Merry, or do you have another employer in mind?" Laurie grinned as she continued her perusal of the little lady whose fluffy white hairdo would have made a Gibson girl proud. Her cheeks were red and round like fresh cranberries, and her billowing crimson dress and white eyelet apron did nothing at all to slim down the plumpness of her figure.

Merry shoved her fists into her hips, and tapped one toe of her black, laced-up, ankle-high boots that looked like she'd ordered them from the 1898 Sears and Roebuck catalog. "Are we almost finished?" Merry asked, her patience rapidly ebbing.

"Almost." Laurie stopped directly in front of Merry and, standing eye to eye, came close to chuckling at the way the woman's wire-rimmed spectacles sat precariously close to the tip of her nose. Mrs. Claus, Laurie laughed to herself, had just come to life.

"So, Merry, do you have references?"

Merry lowered her head, increasing her double chins from one to two, and shot a disgruntled stare over the rims of her glasses. "No one has ever questioned my work, and no one has ever asked for references."

"Well, I'm not everyone, Merry, and I don't just let strangers into my house without a clue who they are."

"I'm not a stranger, young lady. I'm your new housekeeper. Now, if you'll excuse me, I have work to do." Merry bent over one of her carpetbags and pulled out a large feather duster, instantly going to work at the table where the petals had fallen. "Oh, dear." She swept the petals into her palm, crushed them in her pudgy little fist, opened her hand, and blew, scattering their fragrance, but none of the petals, around the room.

Laurie fought to keep her mouth from falling open once again. "I've never seen that done before."

"Of course not, child. I told you I'm good, but for some odd reason you just don't want to listen."

"Okay, I'll listen. How did you do that?"

Merry touched her finger to her nose, her eyes twinkling in impish delight as she winked at Laurie. "Magic. Just a little bit of magic." She swatted Laurie away with the feathers of her duster. "Now, you have work to do. My, my, my, you're never going to make the deadline on that book of yours if you intend to supervise everything I do around your home."

Laurie gripped the edge of the banister. "How do you know about my deadline?"

"Oh, it's just a knack I've picked up over the years," Merry muttered, brushing off Laurie's question as easily as she dusted furniture. "Now, run along, child."

"But, Merry—"

"No, no, no. I don't allow any buts in my house. Upstairs with you, child. I'll call you when it's time for dinner. Let's see," she tilted her head from left to right, from right to left, obviously giving Laurie the once-over. "A home-cooked meal is definitely what you need. Mashed potatoes and roast beef dripping in thick mushroom gravy, and a nice thick slab of my very favorite pumpkin pie."

Laurie felt her stomach rumble, and her mouth watered at the thought of something so delectable, but she wasn't about to give in so easily. She just didn't eat big meals, and Merry had better get used to that fact right now, or they'd butt heads day in and day out. "That's way too much."

"Nonsense. I'll hear none of that, young lady. I have everything in control, including your life, and things are going to be *so* much better. Just you wait and see."

Laurie hadn't been dismissed quite so quickly or easily since she'd been a child, only Merry's way of doing it was easier to take than her grandmother's. In fact, Laurie realized, Merry embodied every good and wonderful aspect of a make-believe grandmother.

The little old woman smelled as if she'd just stepped out of a holiday kitchen covered in bits and pieces of absolutely delightful treats. Hints of cinnamon and cloves, sugar and peppermint, spiced apples and red hots, seemed to waft through the air around her. Laurie halfway expected to walk downstairs at any moment and find a dish of dark chocolate fudge, pumpkin pie, and maybe a punch bowl full of eggnog spiced with a bit of brandy, all laid out on the dining room table, just waiting for guests to arrive.

Yet, as delightful as the woman seemed to be, Laurie couldn't reconcile Merry's knowledge of her impending deadline, the way she knew her name, or the way she knew that Laurie had dreamed as a child of, just once, having roast beef and mashed potatoes and gravy for Sunday dinner.

Could Merry, as she said, be magical?

Laurie smiled, shaking her head at her creative thoughts. Magic only happened in books and movies and in her mother's letters—it didn't happen in the Langtry home.

Shivering, Laurie gathered her sweater close to her neck, thinking about the way the temperature dropped in the house the moment Merry stepped inside, the way she scooped up the rose petals and made them disappear in thin air. Of course, there were logical explanations to all those things. The house was old—very old, over one hundred years, and it was perfectly natural for a fuse to blow, or for something to go wrong with the air conditioning. It had been rather warm for June, and she had cranked the temperature down to keep the house comfortable. Maybe the automatic thermostat wasn't working correctly. As for the rose petals— any magician could do sleight-of-hand tricks. Apparently, Merry had learned that art just as well as she'd mastered the ability to pluck a feather duster out of a carpetbag and make dust disappear with the twinkle of an eye.

Of course, there was always the explanation that she was Mrs. Claus come to life. Laurie preferred that thought, although she knew the insanity of even thinking such a thing.

She pushed up the sleeves on her sweater, rubbed her hands together for warmth, and once

again sat before her computer, checking her out-
line, and finally, for the first time in months, got
carried off to another time as she created her story
of two hearts desperately trying to become one.

Hours later, when she heard the buzz of a saw,
the laughter of children, and Merry's incessant, but
delightfully pleasant, hum of Christmas carols, she
leaned back in her chair and stared into the blue
Montana sky—remembering Jake's laughing eyes,
his Olympian-god body, and the night he'd
thrown up on her dress, when what she'd wanted
was a kiss from the boy she knew she'd never be
worthy of.

"My, my, my, young lady."

Laurie jumped at the sound of Merry's voice,
surprised that the woman had been able to sneak
into her office without being heard. "I sent you up
here to work, not to stare off into the clouds."

"I write my best books that way."

"I can't dispute that—and you do write very
good books, dear. But there's so much more to life
than daydreaming. You've shut yourself off from
the world far, far too long, and I have every intention of changing all that."

"Excuse me, Merry," Laurie said, spinning
around in her chair, "but how is it you seem to
know so much about me when I know so little
about you?"

"Why it's written all over your face. You're too
pale. Definitely need more time in the sun. You
need to go on a picnic, or soar sky high in a swing,
or, oh dear me—" Merry's breathy words trailed
off as she crisscrossed her chubby hands over her
ample bosom. Her cranberry cheeks turned crimson. "Perhaps you should romp in the grass with

a hero who has a little more substance than the ones in your books."

"What's wrong with my heroes?" Laurie fumed.

"Nothing whatsoever, child. But they're paper and ink, not flesh and blood, and, my, my, my, flesh and blood is ever so much nicer. You take my Nicky now . . ."

"Nicky?"

"Oh, my. Have I somehow forgotten to tell you about Nicky. Why, he's my husband, child. We've been married for nigh on an eternity. Jolliest old soul you'd ever want to meet, and believe you me, he's no fantasy." Merry's eyes grew wistful, and her bosom rose and fell with her deep, passionate sigh. "That, Laurie dear, is the kind of man you need."

"A real-life hero, huh?"

Merry nodded, her rectangular glasses slipping further down her nose until she pushed them back into place with the tip of a pudgy finger. "Now, in case you haven't smelled it, I've a nice hot roast beef dinner downstairs waiting for you."

"I've never eaten big meals, Merry." Laurie saw the scold in Merry's eyes long before she could utter any words of admonishment. "So, I hope you'll join me."

"Why, of course, Laurie dear. We have ever so much to talk about."

Merry turned and shuffled across the room with Laurie right on the heels of her black lace-up boots. "So, Merry, what do you think of my home?" Laurie asked as she trailed her housekeeper down the steps.

"Home? No, no, no. This isn't a home child, it's a nicely decorated house. A home," Merry corrected, "is a house filled with love. That's one of the things I'm here to teach you."

"I know what a home is, Merry. It's a place filled with warmth and laughter and sharing and caring, it's ..." Laurie's shoulders dropped. "Okay, so this isn't a home. There's not too much I can do to change it."

"But of course there is. First, you need pictures. Lots of pictures. Family. Friends. Children."

"And where do you propose I get them? I have no family, no children, and my friends are business acquaintances. I'm not about to spread their pictures around my house."

"You have one picture. I saw it propped up next to your computer. Lovely photo. Lovely girl, your mother. And, I dare say, your grandfather was a right nice fellow, too."

"You're doing it again, Merry."

"Doing what?"

"Acting like you knew my mother and grandfather."

"Like I said, child. I have a knack for knowing things. But sometimes you just have to look in a person's eyes, or study a picture, to understand their personality. The man was holding the little girl's hand, giving her a necklace. She was looking up at him and smiling. Yes, dear. There was a lot of love in that picture, and those who truly love are good people. Now, that one picture might be a start, but you need ever so many more. So, I've decided to share mine until you get some of your own."

Laurie stepped on the bottom stair and stopped, her mind soaking up all the homey touches Merry had spread about the room. It had been beautiful before, decorated just as she'd instructed the interior designer, in country charm, but now it seemed more cozy and snug, intimate with picture frames of every size and style scattered over mantle and tables. Crocheted doilies had been tossed over the backs and arms of chairs, giving the room the feel of yesteryear instead of country modern. And Laurie loved it.

Going to the mantel, Laurie picked up one of the frames and admired the family photo. An auburn-haired beauty, a giant of a man whose steel-blue eyes beamed down at her with love, a black-haired girl of maybe five or six, and an infant, cuddled in the big man's arms.

"That," Merry said, standing at Laurie's side and pointing to the distinguished gentleman with strawberry-blond hair, "is a very dear friend of mine. McKenna O'Brien. Ah, how I miss that man. My, my, my, but did he ever need my help when I showed up at his door. And that's his wife Kathleen, and their daughter Julie. Of course, you can't tell much about the youngster in the photo. He was just barely a few weeks old when it was taken. McKenna Jr. Oh, my, such an enchanted family. I just wish I could gather them all into my arms and hug them to pieces."

"And all the others?" Laurie questioned, looking around the room at the smattering of photos.

"All dear friends. Nicky and I never had any children of our own, y'know."

"I'm sorry, Merry." Laurie smiled, watching the way Merry moved from photo to photo, lightly floating her duster over silver and gilt and ceramic. "You would have made a wonderful mother."

"Yes, that's true. But we've managed to compensate. My word, Nicky spends just about the entire summer making toys to give out to good little boys and girls. That's why I take on housekeeping jobs this time of the year. That husband of mine gets so absorbed in his work he hardly knows I'm around. And, of course, he has so many helpers I just always seem to be underfoot."

Toys? Helpers? Good little boys and girls? Laurie's thoughts that Merry might be Mrs. Claus were becoming more firmly embedded in her mind, but she didn't care. She'd realized for many, many years that she needed a little touch of magic in her life, and if Merry was the one to bring it, all the better. "You're not underfoot here, Merry," Laurie admitted without a trace of doubt. "I can't tell you how happy I am to have you around. It's like having a family for the very first time."

"It's just the beginning, child." Merry nodded, her double chins shimmying. "Just the beginning," she mumbled as she bustled off toward the dining room.

Laurie followed Merry but stopped short when she saw the vase of yellow roses on the table. Again, the horror returned, a chill ran through her body, making the fair hair on her arms stand up. "What are those doing in here?" she demanded to know.

"Why, they're making the room smell sweet, of course."

"I don't like yellow roses, Merry. Take them out. Please." A lump stuck in her throat and she fought back tears and fright. "And do me a favor. Hire someone tomorrow to get rid of all the yellow roses around this place."

Merry moved close to Laurie and took hold of her trembling hands. "Oh, child. It isn't the roses you want to get rid of, it's what they represent—

someone mean and evil. The roses cannot harm you."

Laurie jerked away. "How do you know?"

"I've told you Laurie. I have a knack for knowing things. It helps me take care of those I love."

"You're my housekeeper, Merry, not my mother, not my grandmother. You don't have to love me, you don't have to know things about me, all you have to do is get rid of those roses."

Merry shrugged. "Very well."

Laurie watched Merry lift the heavy crystal vase from the table and shuffle out of the room. Damn! How could she have yelled at the poor old soul like that? She was just trying to make Laurie feel better, to ease her fears.

"Merry!" Laurie pushed through the swinging door into the large country kitchen and found Merry at the counter already arranging a new bouquet. Laurie rubbed her eyes, wondering if she was seeing things. But the roses were definitely red, not yellow, and the old ones were no longer in sight. Was this some kind of trick Merry was playing? Had she waved her crazy feather duster and turned the yellow roses into red with just a quick flick of her wrist?

Merry looked over her shoulder and smiled at Laurie, her eyes twinkling, bringing a touch of merriment to the room. "What do you think of the red ones, child? Do you like the smell?"

The tension eased in Laurie's shoulders, and in spite of the chilly temperature in the room, her body warmed, and so did her heart. "They're lovely, Merry. And—I'm sorry. I shouldn't have yelled."

"Nonsense, dear. I had hoped you'd left all your fears behind in New York, but you haven't. That's just one more thing we have to take care of."

"Do you really think you can help?" Laurie asked, giving in, at last, to the unbelievable fact that Merry was psychic—or magical.

"Why, of course. Now, aren't you just the least bit hungry?"

"Starved." Laurie lifted the white ceramic lid covering the platter on the table, and took a long, deep sniff, looking up at Merry and smiling. "I've been smelling this roast all afternoon."

"And what about my pumpkin pie? Have you smelled that, too?"

"Couldn't miss it."

Laurie took the vase from Merry's hands and stuck her nose into the petals of a wide-open rose, inhaling its sweetness. "They're lovely, Merry. I wish you could turn all my yellow roses into red ones just like this."

Merry stopped abruptly, shook her head, and looked heavenward. "Oh, Nicky, Nicky, Nicky. It's going to be a very busy summer."

4

"You've got to get married, Dad."

"I what?"

"Get married. All the guys at school have moms. We want one, too."

Jake rubbed the bridge of his nose, and rolled his eyes. It wasn't the first time Jacob had thrown the having-a-mom-thing at him and he was positive it wouldn't be the last.

Weaving his fingers together behind his head, he leaned against the headboard of the twin bed, crossing his legs at the ankles, his booted feet butting against the footboard. Jacob Jr. straddled his stomach, while Joshua and Joseph bounced on their knees at either side of his chest. All three boys had been on his case about one thing or another since they'd had hot dogs with Laurie Langtry. Now this.

"I thought you guys liked things the way they are—just the four of us."

"We've been talking about it, Dad." Jacob Jr. put his hands on his nonexistent hips and twitched his lips from side to side, obviously deep in thought.

I'm in for it now, Jake sighed to himself.

Joseph pulled one end of Jake's shaggy, downturned mustache. "You never bake cookies, Daddy."

Hmm. Cookies? he thought. So that's what this is all about? "Let me get this straight. You want me to get married so someone will bake you cookies?"

"You like cookies, don't you, Daddy?" Joshua pulled the other side of the mustache.

"Yeah. But if all you want are cookies, I can get them at the store."

"Baked cookies, Dad," Jacob Jr. said in youthful exasperation. "Not Oreos. And we want real food. Tommy's mom makes pot roast on Sundays."

"You trying to tell me you're tired of peanut butter and jelly?"

All three boys nodded, and Jake had to admit they were right. "I guess I am too."

Damn! If he had money he could hire a housekeeper to take care of the things the boys wanted. Cookies. Pot roast. He didn't need a wife for those things.

Actually, he could only think of one reason he'd want a wife, and if he got desperate, he could get that from someone other than a spouse. From experience, he knew a marriage had to be based on a hell of a lot more than sex to make it work.

Jake sat up, lifting Jacob Jr. off his stomach, then wrestled all three boys until they lay side by side, giggling on the bed. He leaned over them. "You know, guys, there's a lot more to getting married than having someone around to cook and clean."

"Yeah. I know that, Dad." Jacob Jr. put his hands behind his head, and crossed his ankles, mimicking his dad. "Tommy told me all about it. Gee, Dad, don't you think a wife should at least make decent food if she's going to lay in bed at night and scream and moan?"

Jake choked on a gulp of air and began to cough. He felt like he was wearing a dress shirt and tie and wished he could loosen the stranglehold it had on his throat. Hell, if he didn't have that beard and if he looked in the mirror, he knew for sure he'd see a face as crimson as Laurie's had been when he'd first seen her blush.

He took another deep, careful breath, and scratched his cheek. "Well, I suppose you've got a point there, Jacob. But, you know, if I do get married again—remember, I said *if*—I've got to love the woman. A lot."

"More than us?" Joseph asked, his lips turning to a pout.

Jake smoothed the blond hair away from his four-year-old's brow and planted a kiss on his nose. He couldn't imagine loving anyone more than he loved his sons. "Not more. But just as much."

Jacob's forehead wrinkled as he blinked away tears. "Did you love our mom as much as us?"

How could he answer his son? What could he say about the woman who had deserted them? He refused to say anything bad about Amy, no matter how he felt. But he'd always been truthful with his kids. "No. I didn't love her as much as you," he finally admitted. "If I'd loved her that much, she wouldn't have gone away, and I wouldn't have let her go. When you love someone, I mean really, really love someone, like I love you, you make things work out, you don't run away."

Jake suddenly sprang forward and tickled the three boys, lightening the mood. They giggled and laughed, tossing pillows about the room till it looked like a herd of buffalo had stampeded through, and then, when the merriment subsided, and the boys had relaxed, he continued, a hint of laughter still in his eyes. "And you know what else?"

The boys shook their heads.

"When you love someone like I love you, it doesn't matter if they can bake cookies or make pot roast."

"But it helps?" Jacob asked.

Jake smiled and shook his head. "No. It doesn't matter if they can cook, or clean, or ride horses, or look pretty. Sometimes you just see someone, and fall head over heels in love."

The boys giggled again.

Jake ruffled their hair. "When you guys get older you'll understand. When you fall in love, you won't care about cookies or pot roast."

"So," Jacob added when his dad ended his dissertation on love, "when *will* you get married?"

Jake sighed and rolled his eyes. So much for his heart-to-heart attempt at explanation.

An hour later, boys tucked into bed and sound asleep, he paced the front porch, one of his grandfather's ancient, intricately carved Meerschaum pipes clenched tight between his teeth, the smell of cherry tobacco wafting through the air along with white circles of smoke.

Marriage. It wasn't a subject he wanted to discuss, or to consider. Amy's desertion had put a bitter taste in his mouth that nothing, no matter how sweet, could wash away.

In the past four years he'd had little time to think of anything but his boys, his failing ranch, the close to zero balance in his bank account. Marriage had never crossed his mind, and women had been nice to look at, but that's about all.

Now, though, as he paced in the cool night air, he thought about the redheaded pixie who'd stolen his house, and could easily steal his heart if given half the chance—a chance he didn't want to take. Laurie Langtry had a history of running away, and he wouldn't subject himself or his boys to that ever again.

Laurie paced.

She couldn't sleep, so she prowled, and finally, when she tired of listening to the quiet patter of her bare feet on the hardwood floor, she climbed onto the seat at the open window, and looked across the valley. Moonlight shone on the tall silvery grass, waving calm and serene in the light breeze of night. An owl hooted unseen in a neighboring tree. Brush stirred and she thought she saw a pair of luminous yellow eyes peering out through the thicket. And off in the distance, she saw Jake's cabin, golden light shining through one of the windows, and the darkened shape of a man pacing back and forth outside. What thoughts tormented him enough to keep him awake? she wondered.

Soon her eyes turned to the star-filled sky, to a bright, twinkling light directly above the top of the tallest tree. A wishing star. "Star light. Star bright." She leaned against the windowsill, wistful and dreamy. "I have so much," she whispered to the star. "It doesn't seem fair to ask for anything more." And then she smiled, remembering her earlier talk with Merry. "But, if you're in the mood for granting wishes, I wouldn't mind someone new in my life, a hero to love, to make this house a home."

Stealing one last look at the apparition that paced before the lighted window off in the distance, Laurie, with eyelids grown heavy, climbed into the folds of crisp, sweet-smelling floral sheets, closed her eyes, and drifted off to dreams.

Thump!
Laurie bolted upright in bed, opening one hesitant eye, then another.
Thump!
The dull thud came from downstairs.
Thump!
She swallowed her fear, swung her feet over the edge of her bed, slipped into the fuzzy bunny slippers she had received from an admiring fan, and shoved her arms into the pink chenille robe that had slipped from the bed to the floor.

Cautiously, she headed for the stairs.
Thump!
It sounded as if the movers had returned and were tossing boxes of books from the truck to the hardwood floor. That couldn't be, of course. *Merry*? No. She'd left late and said she'd be back around noon. Maybe—Oh, Lord!—maybe *he* had found her.
Thump!
She snatched up the three-pound dumbbell she used as a doorstop—never for exercise—and quietly opened her door, avoiding memorized squeaks in the floor as she headed to the stairs. She stopped to listen, and heard the unmistakable sound of giggling.

"Thank you, Lord," she whispered.

Certain she had nothing to fear, that the thumping noises weren't her worst nightmare come to haunt her in Bunch Gulch, she set the dumbbell next to the banister, placed a confident foot on the first step, the second, the third, remembering too late the distinct, loud creak of a loose board on the fourth. The room below her grew still, quiet. Then, when it had been quiet far too long, she heard a muffled laugh.

"Shhh," someone whispered.

Laurie took another step and heard the snapping crack of wood, rolled her eyes and inwardly groaned as she added the steps to a rapidly growing list of repairs the contractor had neglected.

As she stood on the landing, just three steps above the floor, she watched a shaggy blond head peak around the corner of one of the packing boxes, then once again pop out of sight. "She's coming. Keep quiet."

More giggles.

Laurie put a hand over her mouth to stifle a laugh.

"Shhh!" The voice was no longer a whisper but an irritated roar of air. "Quiet! She'll hear us."

Without making a sound, Laurie crept toward the carefully arranged grouping of boxes, two high in places, three in others, and rested her elbows on one marked *crystal*. She peered over the edge. Three shaggy blond heads huddled together, Jacob Jr. with his index finger to his lips, the twins with hands tightly clasped over their mouths to hold back their laughter.

She waited till all was quiet, then cleared her throat.

Six wide blue eyes looked upward, they looked at each other, then back again at Laurie. She didn't see one ounce of guilt written on any of their little faces, only disappointment that their game had come to an end. Obviously, getting caught was nothing new.

"Excuse me, gentlemen." Laurie beckoned them toward her with a wiggle of her index finger. "Would you mind stepping out of there so we can talk." They looked like angels caught in the midst of something devilish.

The boys climbed on top of the cardboard containers, then one after the other jumped to the floor.

Thump!
Thump!
Thump!

They lined up like tin soldiers—a well-practiced routine, Laurie was sure—spines and scrawny necks straight, bony shoulders thrown back, their chins turned up to Laurie for inspection.

She scrutinized their faces. Traces of mud circled Joseph's and Joshua's mouths, and without any thought she pulled a lacy white handkerchief from the pocket of her robe and wiped away the crustier parts. "I used to eat dirt pies, too," she said, tucking the soiled piece of cotton and lace back into her pocket, never once taking her eyes from the boys.

The twins fidgeted, and Jacob stepped forward. "Are we in trouble?"

"Should you be?"

"Well, my dad might not be too happy if he knew we were here."

"Hmm." Laurie, looking thoughtful, and contemplating his comment, sat down on the bottom step, wrapping her robe around her knees. "Why don't you tell me what you were doing."

"Building a castle," Jacob announced.

"I see. And I suppose you're knights in shining armor?"

Jacob drew his scrawny shoulders back and puffed out his little boy's chest. "Heroes," he pronounced, a smile touching his face, his eyes glistening. "We're saving the castle from a big, ugly dragon."

"Heroes, huh?"

"Yep."

Laurie laughed to herself. She'd wished for a hero but somewhere along the line the wish got garbled in the transmission. She'd wanted a grown-up hero, not three little ones. Perhaps she'd better give up wishing.

Joseph sat next to Laurie on the step, and pulled the sleeve of her robe for attention. "Do you have any cookies?"

Joshua sat on Laurie's other side and, like his brother, pulled on her sleeve. "We like cookies."

Laurie had the strangest feeling her face would permanently freeze in a smile if she spent much time with Jake's little boys. "But it's much too early for cookies. You'll spoil your breakfast."

"Nah. We've been up for hours. Dad fed us peanut butter and jelly on toast this morning." Jacob sighed with exasperation as his shoulders drew up toward his ears then heavily dropped back into place. "Dad's got this thing for peanut butter and jelly."

"There *are* worse things than peanut butter and jelly," Laurie admitted.

"Not if you eat it at least once a day." Jacob stared at Laurie's bunny slippers, squinting his eyes and cocking his head slightly to the right as he looked back into her face, obviously sizing her up, and Laurie wondered what could possibly be going on in his mind. "You aren't married, are you?"

She smiled and shook her head.

"Got a boyfriend?"

"No."

Jacob looked at his brothers, his grin stretching from one ear to the other. "So—do you have any cookies?"

From peanut butter, to husbands, to cookies. How had the topic changed so many times? she wondered. Was it always this way with children? "How about Oreos?" she finally answered.

It wasn't difficult to miss the shrug of their shoulders, their outright disappointment. Jacob shrugged too.

"Well, it's pretty obvious you don't like Oreos," Laurie said.

"They're okay." Jacob sighed. "S'pose they're better than nothing."

"Cookie baking isn't one of my specialties," Laurie admitted.

"How 'bout pot roast?" Joseph asked, his eyes narrowed as if he were analyzing her again.

Laurie shook her head.

"Can you do *anything?*" Joshua softly wailed.

Laurie thought long and hard, then she smiled. "I tell stories."

Finally, the boys grinned. She'd at least come up one notch in their estimation.

"Our Daddy tells us lots of stories."

"Like King Arthur."

"And Merlin."

"And cowboys and Indians."

"What kind of stories do you tell?" Jacob asked.

"Happily ever after stories." She'd never spun a tale for a child, but the thought delighted her.

"Will you tell us one?" Joseph asked, playing with the ears on one of Laurie's slippers.

"Maybe later. Right now, I think you'd better head for home before your dad starts to miss you."

Joseph tugged on Laurie's robe. "We get Oreos first."

How could she have forgotten something as important as cookies? "Tell you what. I'll get out the cookie jar and while you're eating, I'll get dressed."

"Can we have more than one?" Joshua asked, eyes wide and hopeful.

"Afraid not." The boys' smiles turned to pouting lips. "Maybe later." Laurie winked. "I'll walk you home and see if it's okay with your dad."

"He won't mind," Jacob stated.

"We'll ask anyway." Laurie stood up and smoothed out her robe, and with the boys following close behind, she pushed through the kitchen door and stopped in mid step, her eyes focusing on the plate full of cookies resting on top of the kitchen table.

"Those don't look like Oreos to me," Jacob stated.

"No." Laurie shook her head. "No, they don't." She'd heard Merry humming in the kitchen late last night, and wondered what had kept her so occupied. Now she knew. "Look pretty good, don't they? Why don't you try them out."

The boys charged to the table, carefully inspecting the platter and the iced cookies it held, then looked at each other and grinned, rather secretive smiles, and Laurie wished she could step inside their minds to get a taste of what her charming neighbors were thinking. From their faces she knew their thought processes were working on something more than how many cookies they could devour.

She dragged a chair out from the table, slumped in the cushioned oak seat, and gazed at the room and the homey touches Merry had added. A poinsettia in a white porcelain planter sat at the end of the sparkling Wedgwood-blue tiled countertop, a tall crystal vase Laurie recognized as one of her own sat at the other end, filled with red roses.

Suddenly her eyes darted back to the poinsettia. *Poinsettia*? She'd only seen them at Christmas, never in June. Where on earth, Laurie wondered, could Merry have gotten a poinsettia?

"Gosh, Laurie," Jacob exclaimed. "You sure fixed this place up nice."

"Thank you very much, young man."

It did look nice. Her decorator had hung lacy white priscillas at the windows and painted the plain wood cabinets a glistening white. Wedgwood-blue flowers dotted the creamy background of the paper decorating the walls above the bleached oak wainscoting, and matching flowers had been stenciled on the buffed and polished hardwood floors. It had been beautiful, and Laurie had loved it, but until this morning, until the boys filled it with their magical laughter and fidgets, it had seemed a room as flat and lifeless as a layout in *Architectural Digest*. And magazines, Laurie knew, didn't smell, not like this. Not like cinnamon and sugar, hot apple cider, and that scent of pine that always reminded her of what she thought Christmas morning should be like.

Lost in wistful thoughts, Laurie nearly missed little hands picking through the assortment of cookies looking for the perfect one. She spied hers immediately—an angel with glittering gold wings, silver sprinkles scattered around feathered edges. Of course Merry would bake Christmas cookies, Laurie surmised. Why not? They went perfectly with Christmas carols and her Mrs. Claus image. It would be a great advertising gimmick, Laurie thought, if Merry ever advertised.

She might be wacky and eccentric, but Laurie liked Merry's optimistic, cheerful spirit, her almost cherubic qualities. She couldn't help but wonder why or how she knew so much about Laurie's personal life, and her thoughts, but she'd pushed her initial worries about that aside and considered Merry's psychic talent to be an asset she'd hate to live without. She brought a special magic into the house, as did the boys sitting at her table, cookie crumbs dusting their lips and chins. All of those touches made the old farmhouse a home.

Laurie excused herself from the table, and, nibbling on the wings of her angel, went to her room to change. T-shirt, jeans, and boots were the call of the day. No more linen suits and silk blouses. Not out here. She quickly washed her face, brushed her teeth, stroking a coating of sable mascara on her almost translucent eyelashes, and picked out the curls in her hair. She was going to see Jake, and that strange feeling came over her again—she wanted to look somewhat close to her best.

Running down the stairs, she pushed through the kitchen door and once again stopped in her tracks. The cookie tray was empty. The boys' pockets bulged and so did their cheeks. She shoved her fists into her hips, tilted her head down, and attempted to look annoyed and disappointed that they hadn't obeyed. "Apparently you didn't hear me. I said one cookie each," she chastised with a wicked grin.

"That's all we ate. Honest," Jacob declared.

She pointed to his left pocket. "And what's this?"

"For later. You didn't say anything about taking a few extras."

He was right, of course. And perhaps they had only eaten one each, but she doubted it.

"Well, young men, why don't we go see your dad."

"He's fixin' the fence Sue Ellen knocked down," Jacob stated, marching out the kitchen door, his brothers and Laurie right behind.

"Who's Sue Ellen?" Laurie asked.

"The cow. Gertrude's the goose."

"Ah, the goose. That must be the horrid noise I hear at night."

"Yep." Joseph nodded. "She likes to squawk something awful."

Jacob led the way across the well-worn path that meandered in a winding fashion through trees and shrubs and over a bridge that consisted of three loose two-by-fours stretching from one side of a minuscule stream to the other. Laurie already knew the path by heart, but hopping and skipping and jumping gave new life to the plain dirt trail she'd traversed several times before.

"We all have to take care of Sue Ellen," Jacob informed Laurie, "but Gertrude belongs to Joshua."

"She's better than a watchdog," Joshua added.

"Yeah, and she won't let anybody but Josh play with her." Joseph made an abrupt about-face, stopped, and Laurie nearly collided with the youngster. He stuck out his chin. "She's the one who gave me the scar. I needed a feather 'cause we were playing cowboys and Indians. Boy, she sure didn't like me pulling on her tail."

"So she bit you?" Laurie asked, absently rubbing a smudge of dirt from Joseph's scar.

"Nah! Gertrude doesn't bite. She chased me, squawking like crazy. Made me trip in a ground squirrel hole."

"And you hit your chin?"

"Yeah, on a big"—Joseph emphasized each word as he threw out his arms, wide, then wider—"humongous rock."

Joshua hopped in front of Joseph to gain Laurie's full attention. "And he got blood all over everything."

"Well," Laurie said, "I'll stay away from Gertrude. Are there any other animals I need to worry about?"

"Nah," Jacob informed her with a shake of his head. "Dad had to sell all the other animals, except Sue Ellen and Reb. That's the mule. Nobody wanted a lazy old thing like him."

So, Jake had to sell his animals. Was he having a tough time financially? she wondered. Of course, she had noticed the rips and tears in the jeans the boys were wearing, the scuffs on their boots that seemed one or two sizes too big and wobbled on their skinny legs. She'd also noticed that, like their dad, they were long overdue for a haircut. But was there anything unusual about any of that? They were boys—all four of them, or so it appeared—and they didn't have a woman around to take care of their needs. She'd noticed nothing unusual about the cabin. The yard immediately around the old log home was well manicured. The wood appeared to be recently stained, the railing around the porch was sturdy. Jake did have an ancient Jeep parked in the yard that appeared to be on its last leg. But was he monetarily strapped, or did he like things that way? Of course, if he did have money problems, perhaps she could help.

They continued across the pasture, skipping along the path, strategically maneuvering around cow patties and the infamous ground squirrel holes. The boys pointed out the trail leading to the best fishing hole west of the Rockies, kicked up dirt and rocks with their boots, and stopped every now and then to pick up a stone to toss.

Jake looked up as they neared the fence, his rough bearded face hiding the smile she sensed lurked behind all that hair. He dropped the post hole digger and grabbed up a running twin into each outstretched arm, captivating her soul. And when the twins planted kisses on his bristly cheeks, she nearly melted.

"Mornin'," he drawled, walking toward Laurie in that long, ambling gait, his bare, Olympian god–like chest glistening with perspiration in the warmth of the early morning sun.

"You're staring again, Red."

Red? When, she wondered, had she acquired that nickname? She knew it was fitting, especially now when she felt an uncontrollable blush rise from her breasts to her cheeks. Not one of her heroes had ever looked so good in sweat and dirt, so it was only natural to stare. Lord, she wondered what was happening to her senses.

Somehow, she took control of her breathing and donned a grin. "I like the view," she finally admitted, openly and honestly, with a slight grin and wiggle of her brows. No need to try to hide the fact—her blush would always be a dead giveaway.

"Guess there's just no accounting for taste," Jake laughed, setting the twins on the ground. He lightly patted their bottoms, then ran his big hand over Jacob's hair and cupped the back of his head. "Why don't you and your brothers play up by the house. I'll be there in a minute."

"Can't we stay here with you and Laurie?"

Jake said nothing, just lowered his head and raised his brows.

And they understood completely.

"Okay, Dad," Jacob said with a theatrical touch of dejection, then shot off ahead of his brothers toward the house. "Last one to the swing is a rotten egg," he taunted, never once looking back, as Joseph and Joshua scrambled after him.

Laurie shaded her eyes with her hand and watched until Jacob grabbed hold of a tire suspended by rope from a rickety-looking jungle gym, and swung out of his brothers' reach. "Nice boys."

"I'm rather partial to them."

She looked back at Jake, who was holding the post hole digger once again, his work-gloved hands crossed at the top, his chin resting on his knuckles. His Montana blue-sky eyes shone out from under his hat, radiating with love when he spoke of his sons. "Hope they weren't bothering you. They've always fancied that house up there. Guess we all figured we'd live there someday."

Laurie'd already heard enough of Jake's belly-aching about *her* house, so she made a point of ignoring his last comment. "They were building a castle out of my packing boxes."

Jake's eyebrows raised again. "They break anything?"

"No, they were just having fun."

Jake took off that despicable sweat-stained hat Laurie was growing to like, and wiped his forehead with the back of a gloved hand. He didn't take his gaze from Laurie, and now she saw the sparkle, the mischief, another resemblance between father and sons. "Most kids build forts, mine have a penchant for castles. Three Robin Hoods and not a Wyatt Earp or Doc Holliday in the bunch."

"Much better choice. Helping the poor and downtrodden's more rewarding than shootouts at the OK."

Jake adjusted the hat back on his head, tilting the brim low over his eyes. "Yeah, I hear helping the poor and downtrodden's one of your specialties. Meg said you plan on helping her with Kurt. You think it's smart to interfere?"

"She asked, and what could it hurt?"

"Maybe Kurt doesn't want someone intruding. Maybe he'd rather be left alone."

"Like you, I suppose."

He shrugged. "Not everyone wants to be helped out, or wants to bare their soul."

"Like I did?"

"You wanted to talk, I didn't mind listening. But I don't make it my business to offer solutions."

Laurie frowned, shoved her hands in the back pockets of her jeans, and circled Jake, studying him just as she'd done Merry. "You got a bee up your butt or something this morning?"

"No, just got the feeling you plan on interfering in my life, too, so I'm stating my case before you get any silly-assed ideas about trying to fix what isn't wrong." He lifted the post hole digger, pulled the handles apart, and walked back to the place where he was working before Laurie and the boys showed up.

"Unless you need anything else," he said, his dismissal more than obvious. "I've got a helluva lot of work to do." He raised the digger, slammed it down into the ground, his eyes on the dirt instead of the redhead who watched his every move.

Laurie threw up her hands and headed for the path, then changed her mind, tramping back to the spot where Jake pounded the digger up and down in a hole that would end up in China if he didn't ease up. She planted her petite but full of hellfire body smack in front of his chest, tilted her head, and glared into his way too scraggly looking face. "What the hell have I done?"

"Nothing, yet. Do whatever you want for Meg. Do whatever the hell it is you plan on doing to Kurt. But let me make it perfectly clear, before you try redeeming me, that I don't like people butting into my personal life. Haven't you done enough already, buying up my family home?"

"I've got a damn sight more important things to do than butt into your life, Jake McAllister. But let me point one thing out. I don't butt. Far be it from me to interfere in your miserable life. Far be it from me to try to offer to help you out when I know you're hurting financially . . ."

Jake stopped digging his way through the center of the earth. "Who told you that?"

"It's obvious. Look at this place. There's only one cow in sight. You've got one lousy mule, a goose that ought to be shot, and the boys told me you had to sell everything else. I've got money, Jake. You could help me out, I could pay you."

Fire blazed in his eyes. "I don't need your money, and I don't want it. Did you ever think maybe I don't want a lot of animals to tend or extra work to do? Did you ever consider the fact that I might like things just the way they are?"

"Don't feed me that line of bull. You told me all you want is to be is a rancher."

"My first mistake. I should have kept my mouth shut."

Laurie drew in a deep breath and let it out slow and easy. "You know, Jake, there's nothing wrong with having problems or letting people help you when you need it. That's all part of friendship, or being neighbors."

"Don't analyze me."

"Okay, I won't. I've never liked being analyzed either. I've had too much of that over the years."

"Isn't that all part of the celebrity thing? You want to make big money, you want to have your name in the limelight, so you get analyzed?" He pulled the digger out of the ground and dumped the dirt into a pile next to the hole.

"I've tired of that life, Jake. That's part of the reason I came home."

"Then go home, Laurie. Go back to that house you think is yours and bake cookies or chocolate cream torte, or, better yet, write your blasted books. Analyze all the heroes and heroines you want. Write all the happy endings you want but, please, leave my life alone. It's not broken, it doesn't need to be fixed. And, while we're at it, I'm not very neighborly, either, so don't try to change that along with everything else."

"I have no desire to change you. Personally, in spite of being rude, crude, and in need of a barber, I like you just the way you are, although I'd prefer you without the bee up your butt.

"Now, I could lie and tell you I make a halfway decent chocolate cream torte, but I don't. I can't even bake cookies. I write quite well, I make buckets of money, and I'm in the habit of saying what

I mean." She halted her speech and took a deep breath. "I hide very little, Jake, and I won't hide the fact that I want to be friends, good friends, and, dammit, you feel exactly the same. You can push me away if you want, run me off with your stubborn sense of pride, but I've run away one too many times in my life, and I'm not going to do it again."

Jake dropped the post hole digger, ripped off his gloves, threw them on the ground, and clutched Laurie's shoulders. She had the distinct, uncomfortable feeling he had every intention of giving up on the digger and pounding her into the hole.

His gleaming chest heaved from exertion and probably anger. "You finished yet?"

"Maybe," she stated, forcing her eyes away from his glossy pecs, looking off in the distance with an apathetic stare. "Maybe not."

"Can't you ever give me a straight answer?"

She looked again at his chest, calm now, his breathing light and even. She tilted her head and looked into eyes that patiently waited for an answer. "Okay. I'm finished."

"Good, then shut up."

Laurie's eyes narrowed. Her shoulders drew up. "Excuse me?"

"Shut up, Laurie, and give me your hand."

"Why?"

There it was again, the tilt of his head, the sedate lift of his brows, that same do-as-I-say-look he gave the boys. She wasn't the least bit thrilled that he was using it on her, but she'd be darned if she wouldn't give him her hand. She stuck it out and he grabbed hold as if he wanted to shake.

"Truce?" he pleaded, his mustache uncontrollably twitching on both sides.

Somewhere under the hat and under the hair, she saw a trace of a smile, a hint of a sparkle in his eyes. And somewhere in her brain, maybe in her heart, she realized she'd never been touched by anything so warm and tender as the rough, sandpaperlike calluses on his fingers and palms.

"Truce," she answered back, looking up into his Montana blue-sky eyes, wondering just how long it would last.

5

Jake slammed the post hole digger into the dirt, twisted it, turned it, then crossed his hands over the top and forgot about the blasted hole and focused all his attention on the sweet derriere of the woman walking away.

He sure liked Laurie's fiery temper. It matched her hair, short and flaming, and tightly sprung. He wondered if she'd be as deadly a shot with a pistol as she was with the words that spewed from her mouth. And *oh* what a mouth. He'd never seen one quite like it, except maybe in the cartoons. Betty Boop lips, almost a perfect heart, dainty and pink and puckered. If he was given to fantasies, he could just imagine what those lips could do to a man.

But, no. He wasn't fanciful. He didn't want to know just how sweet those lips tasted, he didn't want to know how they'd feel against his mouth or any other part of his body, and he didn't want to know what her soft, delectable curves would feel like pressed against him. Well, maybe he did. But getting that close meant she'd want to get even closer, and he sure as hell didn't want another woman around on a permanent basis. One bad marriage in a lifetime was more than enough.

And then he remembered the boys, remembered their words last night. *We want a mom.*

But Laurie Langtry? She couldn't cook, couldn't bake, couldn't even make a decent cup of coffee. He'd told the boys those things didn't matter, but when he thought of Laurie Langtry, he had to think of a few extra excuses for wanting her to stay away.

He continued to watch Laurie from afar. She was a sight to behold with that bare span of skin showing between hip-hugging jeans and one of those infernal crop tops she liked to wear, clothes that showcased her belly button and made him squirm. No, Laurie Langtry wasn't mother material.

If he was looking for someone with those particular instincts, Meg O'Reilly would have to be the one. And Meg was definitely beautiful—no doubt about it.

Hell! What was he thinking about? Meg O'Reilly was the perfect candidate for the preacher. She sang in the choir and did endless hours of charity work. And she'd probably try to convert him given half the chance.

Just like Laurie Langtry.

Damn! A woman couldn't be happy unless she was trying to make a man over to suit her whims. And he wasn't about to get involved with another woman who wasn't happy with him just the way he was.

Hell! He pulled the digger out of the hole then thrust it once again into the earth. The way Laurie Langtry maddened and frustrated him, he figured he could fence the circumference of the globe in less than a week.

* * *

Laurie stomped along the well-worn path, wondering what had possessed her to convince that insufferable man to be friends. It couldn't be his looks. Jake McAllister looked worse today than he had yesterday, that grungy beard hiding all traces of cheek and chin, and that sweaty hat covering his eyes. Well, she did have to admit his eyes were rather inviting, rather intriguing and bright and blue when he removed that hat. They smiled, too, over something as simple as a child's hug. My word, she liked that in him.

She kicked a stone, swagged around a cow patty, and skirted the edge of the white picket fence surrounding her house, walking into a heavily wooded area she hadn't yet explored. Where the pines cleared and gave way to a view of the clear, sunny western sky, someone had long ago planted roses, now grown wild and rambling, with deep blood-red buds and full-bloom flowers scattered profusely about. She picked a delicate, just-opening flower, held it to her nose, and relished the scent. The entire area was filled with their sweet, heavenly smell. Later, she'd come back to this spot and pick a vase full to set next to her computer for inspiration. For now, though, she tucked the bud behind her ear and continued her tour.

An old wooden plank swing hung suspended from a thick lower bough of a tall, spreading pine, the rope ancient and frayed from too many years in the sun and the wind and the rain. It didn't look the least bit sturdy, but it looked like a challenge, and she was in the mood for something fun. She sat on the weathered wood, noticing below her the deep grooves in the hardened ground where other feet had slid across the dirt when the swing was in use. The grooves were covered now with long green grass, trampled, it appeared, by an animal, or maybe a human, in the night.

A sudden chill ran through her at the thought. Had a human being been roaming around? Lurking? No, that wasn't possible, she convinced herself. He was in New York, she was in Bunch Gulch. There was no way he could know where to find her. She was safe here, she had no need to worry any longer.

She forced the old nightmare from her mind, and wrapped her fingers around the ropes, tugging gently to test their strength and safety. Cautiously, she sat on the plank, pushed her feet against the ground, beginning a slow back and forth movement, building momentum as she began to swing. She started gradually, then pumped her forelegs back and forth as the swing settled into a rhythm. Higher and higher she soared. Cool air whispered through her hair, across her cheeks, and she felt like the child she'd always wanted to be. One with no worries. No cares.

Up. Up.

Higher and higher.

Snap!

She heard it before she felt the rotted rope break away from the branch of the tree. Suspended in midair, the seat collapsed from under her, her left hand falling with the broken rope, her right hand sliding painfully down the raffia on the one still in tack, holding on for dear life, long before she even thought about jumping.

And then she did it. She released both hands and sailed through the air toward a pine. She closed her eyes and prayed. There wasn't time to put out her hands, wasn't time to brace herself

against the collision. Wasn't time to think of anything but hitting the tree.

Thud!

It didn't feel like a pine.

"I see you've added flying to your list of head-
line-making feats."

It didn't sound like a pine.

She cracked open one eye, then the other. It
didn't look like a pine, or smell like one, either.

Instead of bark and sap, her nose was smashed
into Jake McAllister's chest, and at the moment she
didn't know which she would have preferred—
brawn and sinew, or unyielding pine. She doubted
she would have knocked over the pine, doubted it
would have wrapped its boughs around her to
hold her close, like Jake McAllister was doing now,
his cow-lifting, bull-wrestling, Olympian god arms
strapped tightly around her waist as she lay atop
him, his body stretched out flat on the grass- and
wildflower-covered ground.

"Thank you for catching me." She put the palms
of her hands to the ground and tried to push herself up, but Jake didn't let go.

"My pleasure, Red." His mustache twitched. "It
wasn't one of my best catches, though. You rather
took me by surprise, I'm afraid."

"Took me a bit by surprise, too."

"Are you hurt?"

She felt his hand rubbing her back, her spine.
Was it a rub? she wondered. Or was it a caress?
Whatever, it felt awfully good. Laying against him
felt awfully good, too. "I'm fine, Jake. Could you
help me up now?"

"You're not the least bit heavy." The mustache
twitched again. Somehow she knew he was smiling, and for some reason she wanted to touch the

silkiness of the hair that hugged the edges of his lips and descended downward at their sides. At that very moment, she realized Jake McAllister had *hero* plastered all over him.

"Wouldn't you like to rest here awhile, make sure you're feeling better?"

She reached behind her back and grabbed for his wrists, pulling them away from her waist, knowing full well he wasn't going to offer any resistance. "No, I would not," she lied.

Easily pulling his wrists from her grasp, he raised his head and shoulders from the ground, his elbows and forearms braced against the grass and dirt. "Is that better?"

Oh, my! Somehow she found herself in a sitting position, straddling his hips. She felt the heat in her chest, felt it climbing quite rapidly up her neck until it hit her cheeks and turned them the brightest crimson. How many years had it been since she'd straddled a man's hips? Too many, and she'd forgotten how good it could feel.

"Have I told you yet how pretty you are when you blush?"

"No, but I can well imagine."

It wasn't easy, but she managed to push herself to a standing position, took a quick look at her scraped and rope-slashed hands, then shoved them behind her back. That was the moment they started to ache, but she wasn't about to wince in agony, or let him see her in pain. "Did you come here for a reason?"

Jake brushed off the seat of his jeans as he stood, picking up the crumpled rose that had fallen from behind her ear and now lay on the ground. He absently tucked it into the pocket of his old and faded blue workshirt. "Only to tell you to be careful around here." He grabbed the broken end of rope and unconsciously tied it into a knot. "Falling swings aren't the only things you need to watch out for."

He had her full attention now. "Care to show me what else so I don't find myself in trouble?"

"Come on. I'll show you the old well." He sauntered away and she felt compelled to follow, her legs barely able to keep up with his infernally long, ambling gait.

He stopped in an area where Queen Anne's lace grew in profusion with thick clumps of purple lupine and an abundance of ferns. He pulled away a stray strand of barbed wire and pushed through the vegetation to reveal an old rock well, covered over with cracked and splintered two-by-sixes.

"It's beautiful." Laurie pushed around Jake for a better view.

"It's dangerous," he stated flatly, grasping her arm and pulling her to a stop before she could get any closer. "I boarded it up when Jacob was born. Didn't want him accidentally toppling in someday."

"It looks safe now. I didn't even know this place was here." Laurie pulled out of his grasp and moved closer to the well. "Why did you want to show it to me?"

Jake stood next to her, leaning over the moss-covered rocks, and applied the brawn of his arms and shoulders against the planks to test their strength. "Didn't want you stumbling on it by accident and getting hurt. If you're gonna be making more repairs to the place, you might add this to your list. You'll never get any water out of it, but I always thought it could be a nice area if someone had the time and inclination to clean it up."

It was more than nice, Laurie thought, as she surveyed the overgrown copse. It was beautiful. A garden tilled and planted by God and nature. "You know," she said as she picked a handful of wildflowers, "I can just picture this place with a white wrought-iron table and chairs. It's a perfect spot to sit quietly and read."

"You're too much of a romantic."

"Come on, Jake. Can't you picture it? Wouldn't you like to laze about in a hammock strung from those trees?" She nodded to two thick pines.

Jake turned around, resting a hip against the rock well. "Yeah, I suppose." He broke off a dark red rose and stuck it behind Laurie's ear when she came near.

She shivered at his touch, at the intimacy, the sensual way his fingers grazed her cheek and whispered over her ear. "I like red roses." The words barely squeezed from her throat as she attempted to breathe.

"You know," Jake said, squinting now as he stared at their surroundings. "I could swear the roses around here used to be yellow."

"Yellow? Are you sure?"

Jake studied the massive wall of red, the thorny stems long and twisted, one entwined with another, like lovers bound together forever. "I thought they were yellow," he said, shrugging his shoulders. "But guess not."

Laurie turned a complete circle and everywhere she looked were roses—dark red roses, with no trace of yellow in sight. Maybe someone had heard her wish. Maybe Merry? No, she told herself. That wasn't possible.

"I'm glad they're red. I never cared for yellow roses."

"Well, they'd look a hell of a lot better if they weren't tangled in barbed wire. I'll get over here in a day or two and clean it up a bit, maybe fix that swing, too."

Laurie smiled, forgetting all about red and yellow roses. "Thanks, Jake. Y'know, until that rope broke, I was beginning to enjoy myself, even began to think I didn't have a care or a worry in the world."

"What kind of worries do you have, Laurie?" he asked, as if he were really concerned.

"It's not important."

She didn't want to think about it, and didn't want to talk about it. It was easier to walk away.

"Don't leave yet." Jake grabbed her arm, then released it when her muscles tensed. "What's wrong?"

"Why? You feel like analyzing me?"

"No, but I learned a long time ago when someone says it's not important it means there's something serious going on, something they might like to share."

"It really doesn't matter, Jake. I left all my problems behind in New York."

"You mean you ran from there just like you did from Bunch Gulch?"

"Yeah, Jake," she snapped. "I ran. Again. Haven't you ever run from anything?"

"No. I believe in facing my problems."

Her emerald eyes blazed. "Then you tell me how I'm supposed to face a man in a mask who's threatened to fuck me to death? You tell me how I'm supposed to face a phantom who leaves yellow roses at my doorstep along with letters describing in minute detail every sadistic and perverted thing he'd like to do to me? You think I should have stayed there, Jake? You think it's fun to go to bed frightened, to wake up frightened, to walk down the street wondering if someone's going to stick a yellow rose in your face and a knife in your gut?"

He didn't move toward her, didn't take his eyes from hers, but she could see the way he gritted his teeth, the way he swallowed, hard, forcing down a bevy of mixed emotions—sympathy, anger, fear. "I'm sorry. I didn't know."

"No, and you didn't want to take the time to find out. Well, now you know. I ran here to get away, and I don't plan to go back until it's safe, and that might never happen."

"Are you safe here?"

"I don't know," Laurie stammered, looking down at the stems of wildflowers she'd crushed in her hands. "I don't know if I'm safe anywhere. I can only hope he doesn't find out where I am and follow me."

"You shouldn't be alone."

"I've got a housekeeper. I've got locks on the doors."

"But they didn't keep out my kids. You really think they'll keep out someone who's bent on getting in?"

"I can't hide, Jake. I had a bodyguard and I hated it. I don't like feeling trapped, I like to do what I want when I want. I just have to believe I'm safe."

"Well, I'm only a few minutes away. If you need me . . ."

She covered his mouth to silence him. He owed her nothing and she expected nothing from him. If she wanted anything at all from Jake McAllister, it definitely wasn't protection. "Don't worry. I'll holler."

"Better use the phone." He winked, then nodded with his head for her to follow as he headed back to the clearing and the broken swing. He swept his Stetson up from the place where it had landed when she'd sailed into his arms, and pulled it tight on his head, once again covering his eyes.

"I've got a great baseball bat you can keep at the side of your bed."

"I've got a .380 automatic under the mattress."

His look of shock was priceless. "You know how to use it?"

"Yeah. Aim for the chest and pull the trigger."

"You really think that's necessary?"

"You ever been stalked like an animal?"

Her words hit him with all the power of the baseball bat he'd wanted to give her. "No. Look, I'm sorry. I've got rifles for hunting. Guess I never thought of needing one for protection."

"Yeah, well, I never thought I'd need one either. But this guy, as far as I can tell, isn't your basic upstanding citizen, and trust me, if he finds me here, I plan to use it."

"What about the police?"

Laurie shook her head. "My entire life has been analyzed by the police. My friends, acquaintances, and business associates have been questioned, and it's done no damn good. Look, Jake. I don't want to talk about it. Okay? I left all that behind in New York, and I'd like to forget it ever happened. Very few people know where I am, and there's no way he's going to find me."

He wrapped his hands around her shoulders, drawing them slowly down the length of her arms. "If you get the urge to talk—"

Laurie winced and pulled away.

His eyes followed the sudden motion of her

hands thrown behind her back. "Let me see your hands."

"Why?" He gave her *the* nod, that eyebrow-raising glare.

"Sure." She shrugged. "Why not." She held them out for inspection. "Just a few scratches."

"Why didn't you say something earlier? Dammit, Red, you're worse than a little kid. They need to be scrubbed and soaked in peroxide."

"No way. That hurts."

"Either you do it, or I'll do it. If you don't have any peroxide, I've got bottles at my place. Seems I bathe the boys in it once or twice a week."

"I'll take care of them, Jake," she growled.

With his hat tilted back she could see the twinkle of his eyes, tender and loving and warm. Even the scraggly beard and the sweat-stained hat couldn't hide the gentleness wrapped around him.

Absently, he brushed a stray tear from the soft skin just below her eye, a tear she didn't even realize had fallen, a tear she didn't understand.

"I've got fences to mend today, but I'll try to get over here in a day or two, see if I can get that swing back in order."

"You think you might be able to rig up a hammock, too?"

"Make a list," he said, softly stroking her cheek before backing away. "But don't get any notions about making me a better neighbor."

"I wouldn't think of it, Jake," she whispered, her smile turning to a grin as her slim-hipped hero walked away. No, making Jake a better neighbor was not what she had in mind.

Jake stood in the mid-afternoon sunlight, sweat dripping down his back and chest as he stirred cement in an old dented wheelbarrow. The screen door slammed and he looked up to see Jacob running toward him.

"Your brothers in the house?"

"Yeah. I made them take a nap. They were getting awfully cranky."

Jake laughed and ruffled Jacob's hair. His eldest son, only six, going on twenty, loved his younger brothers with the same passion Jake loved all three. Jake couldn't see any reason to have a wife, or his sons to have a mother, when he had Jacob around, but it didn't seem right for a six-year-old to take on so much responsibility.

"Can I help?" Jacob asked.

"Sure. Hold this post steady while I pour in the cement."

"Okay." Jacob wrapped his rapidly growing hands around the four-by-four and locked his gaze on his dad's face.

"Don't think Sue Ellen will be able to knock this one down."

Jake shoveled cement into the hole and tamped it down with his boot. "No. I don't think so either."

"Did you tell Laurie about Sue Ellen?"

A grin flashed across Jake's face and he shook his head. "Didn't even think about it."

Jacob grinned, too, then shrugged his shoulders. "You like her, Dad?"

"Who? Sue Ellen?" Jake winked as he teased his son.

"No, Dad! Laurie."

"S'pose so."

"You gonna marry her?"

"Don't think so."

"Why not? She makes great cookies."

"I told you last night that cookies don't matter. Besides, it's her housekeeper who makes the cookies."

Jake grabbed the handles of the wheelbarrow and moved down to the next post. "Here, son. Hold this one, too."

Jacob followed his dad and straightened the fence post in its hole. "You gonna see her again?"

"Yeah."

"You gonna take her on a date?"

"No. I'm gonna do some work around her place, fix up that old well."

"When?"

"Couple of days maybe."

"Why not now?"

"Got my own work to do."

"Oh." The boy's shoulders dropped and for the first time Jake realized just how much Jacob wanted a mom. How could he make him understand that he didn't want another wife?

In silence, they finished setting that post, and a third. Jacob helped his dad clean up the wheelbarrow, then Jake took his son's hand and led him to the shade of an old spreading pine. He pulled the boy down into his lap, pulled up a blade of grass, and twisted it between his fingers. "You miss your mom?"

Jacob watched his dad playing with the grass. "Heck, Dad. I don't even remember her."

Unfortunately, Jake did, and things were a damn sight better the way they were now, just Jake and his boys.

"Well, kiddo, she was pretty," Jake finally told his son. "Blond hair just like yours, and big blue eyes. She liked fancy clothes and expensive perfume and looked mighty nice when she was all dressed up. She liked to go dancing and to the theater."

"Can't do that much around here."

"No. That's part of the reason she left."

Jacob tilted his head up to look at his dad. "Didn't she love us?"

How could he possibly tell his son the truth? Jake had never heard Amy mention anything about love when she talked about their boys. She made sure they were fed and bathed and clothed, but that's about as far as her mothering went. There hadn't been much of a bond, not like the one Jake had instinctively formed with his kids.

"Your mother was unhappy living here, Jacob. She didn't much care for ranching. Didn't like the dirt or the cows or the chores. I guess that's part of the reason I don't want to get married again. Not many women want a life like that."

Jacob scratched his head. "I don't think Laurie minds."

Once again they'd gone in a complete circle, he trying to explain, Jacob failing to understand.

"Don't set your heart on Laurie. She's from New York, son, and she'll be going back again soon."

"You really think so, Dad?"

"Yeah."

"Maybe you should ask her to stay."

He'd asked Amy that once, and she'd left anyway. "No, son. If she stays, she'll have to make the decision on her own."

Laurie sat at her computer and stared at an empty screen—again. She hadn't written a word in two hours although scene after scene flitted through her brain. But the scenes weren't taking place on a barren and deserted prairie in the old west, they were taking place next to a broken swing, amidst roses and wildflowers surrounding an ancient, moss-covered well.

"My, my, my. That heroine of yours is going to be in a sad and sorry state if you don't get her out of that prison pretty soon."

Laurie swirled around in her chair and looked at Merry standing at the door, her arms folded and shoved underneath her bosom. "Mental block," Laurie moaned.

"Pish posh! You're too busy thinking about that neighbor of yours."

"Jake McAllister? Why would I think of him?"

"Oh, my. If it wasn't for my Nicky, dear old soul that he is, I'd have my eyes set on that young fellow myself. My, my, my, if it wasn't for that beard, that boy could make a woman's heart flutter."

Laurie followed Merry as the old woman bustled to the open window and looked out. The sun had gone down, a trillion stars lit up the blackened sky, and a lone, dim porch light cast a mellow gold across the cabin in the distance.

"Such a shame. That dear man taking care of three little ones all on his own. Oh, my. No wonder he's such a mess."

"He's not a mess, Merry. He just needs a shave, maybe some clean clothes."

"Yes, I suppose you're right." Merry shoved her spectacles higher on her nose. "Suppose we should help him any way we can."

"I already offered. He's not interested in money—mine anyway."

"No, no, no, Laurie dear. He's a man and you just can't go around offering money. It's that pride thing. Such a problem."

"It's more than that, Merry. He's stubborn, too.

I've been accused of having a stubborn streak, but he carries it to the extreme. And since you've mentioned pride, well . . ."

"Yes, dear. You suffer from that ailment also. That's what makes you perfect for each other."

"Perfect?"

"But of course. The tension between you crackles. Isn't that what makes your books so good?"

"That's fiction, Merry."

"Yes, and to be perfectly honest, we could all use a little more fiction in our lives, a little less reality, and a few more dreams."

"I don't need a dream in my life. I've got everything I ever wanted. Oh, I'll be the first to admit I like men. They serve a purpose on occasion, and they're great for plunging toilets and taking out the trash. But Jake McAllister isn't my type."

"My, my, my, child. It's obvious you don't know a good man when you see one. You take my Nicky, now. Goodness me. There's a man to make your toes curl. To me, he's the handsomest man in the universe. Others might see nothing more than a round little belly, that, well, to be perfectly honest, shakes like a bowl full of jelly. But it's what's underneath, child, not what's on the surface."

"I know that, Merry. And I'm sure Jake's a good man. But—look, I'm just not interested in hooking up with a man. Besides, I've done awfully well without one." Of course, she thought, her crazy, romantic wish on that star last night had been a total contradiction to her words. So had all those strange little feelings that crept into her mind when she got anywhere close to Jake McAllister. Hell! She didn't need a man. "A good man every now and then can be rather enjoyable, Merry, but," she continued adamantly, "I'm not looking for anything permanent, so, please, don't try to convince me I am."

"I wouldn't think of it, child."

Laurie eyed Merry suspiciously, noting that infernal twinkle in her eyes that could mean nothing but mischief. "I came to Bunch Gulch to get away from problems, I don't need another one in my life. I definitely don't need four."

"No, no, no. Of course you don't."

Merry was agreeing much too readily, Laurie thought, as she spun around to her computer and placed her fingers on the keys, staring once again at an empty screen. "And don't come up with any schemes to get me over to his place, Merry."

"My, my, my, child. I wouldn't think of it."

"Gosh, Dad. Your lap's just not big enough for all of us."

"I don't recall it ever being a problem before." Jake adjusted Joseph and Joshua in his arms and Jacob scooted up close to his dad's side as they sat together in the wooden swing on the porch and looked at the stars in the clear summer sky.

"Sure would be nice if we had a mom. Then we'd all have somewhere to sit."

Jake sucked in a deep breath and tried to ignore his son. He'd just about had his fill of talk about moms. "A year or two from now you won't want to be sitting in anyone's lap."

"Yeah. I s'pose you're right. Just thought it would be nice to see what it was like."

Wrapping his arm around Jacob and pulling him closer, he pointed out the North Star, the Big Dipper, and Andromeda, steering the conversation away from Laurie, although he knew the boy was right. He had been cheated out of a mother's love.

But damn! Until Laurie showed up, the love he'd given the boys had been enough. He didn't want anyone interfering, even if that someone had Betty Boop lips, soft curvy breasts, and just a whisper of a waist.

He'd touched all those things today, felt them burning through his shirt, through his skin and bones and right into his heart. He didn't want to feel anything, didn't want a woman coming between him and the boys, didn't want someone infringing on his territory. Laurie had already stolen his house, he didn't want her stealing his heart, the boys' hearts, then walking away. Once in a lifetime was more than enough for that.

But hell! He'd thought about her all day. And he was having a helluva time staying away from her.

Absently, he reached into his pocket and pulled out the rose he'd picked up off the ground, the blood red rose that had crushed under his weight and Laurie's when he'd held her close.

"What's that, Dad?"

"A rose."

Jacob yawned and pressed his head closer to his dad's side. "Laurie smells like roses."

Jake held it close to his lips, twisting it between his fingers—remembering. "Yes, son. I know."

6

Laurie rolled over for at least the thirteenth time to look at the digital readout on the clock next to her bed. 4:02. She smacked her pillow with her fist and tried to bury her head in its softness, but all attempts at sleep were absolutely useless. Once again she'd spent another restless night.

Gingerly pushing the covers away, she shifted in the bed and groaned, suddenly remembering why she'd taken three Extra-Strength Excedrin and coated her body in Ben Gay right before going to bed. She ached from the nail on her little toe to the hair that sprung from the top of her head, and she realized flying without benefit of airplane was not all it was cracked up to be. She tried to sit, but her ribs ached from smacking into Jake's tree trunk of a chest, her palms smarted from the rope burns, and her neck and shoulders had tightened up from too many days' worth of tension. Physically and mentally she was a wreck.

Grabbing one edge of the mattress, she managed to pull herself to a sitting position, then inched her legs over the side of the bed. Slipping into her bunny slippers, and hunched over like Grandma Moses, she shuffled across the floor, opened the door, and hollered for Merry.

No one answered.

"Where is that woman when I need her?" Laurie moaned, wishing for nothing more than a cup of Merry's steaming cocoa to soothe her insides, and a hot bubbling bath already prepared by the time she crept downstairs.

She grabbed hold of the banister with raw fingers, groaning again. She shook her hands and blew on the chafed and tender spots and those already scabbing over.

Lovely, she thought, absolutely lovely. Her hands ached, her body ached, and her mood was turning black. All she needed now was a call from her editor or agent asking how the book was going. What could she possibly say? *"The book? Oh, well, I don't have time to think about it now. I'm too busy dreaming up plots for my own life."* They wouldn't buy it, and they wouldn't appreciate it— never in a million years.

Slowly, she descended the stairs, shuffling across the hardwood floor of the living room till she finally reached the bath. She pushed open the door and flicked on the light. The scent of roses and lilac simmered from the bubbling water in the white porcelain claw foot, and a forest-green lacquered tray sat on the end on a tile ledge, a cup of steaming cocoa and what looked like a warm, buttery, berry-filled croissant in the middle.

"Oh, bless you, Merry," Laurie whispered, instantly taking back all her other horrid thoughts. Having Merry around, a woman who seemed to know her thoughts long before she knew them herself, was trying at times, but a wonderful diversion from what had been a miserable year, and she'd so easily become an extension of her life.

A note from Merry was propped up next to the

cup, and Laurie plucked up the holly-strewn stationery and read Merry's words. *"Relax and enjoy. Must run errands. Be back this afternoon."*

It didn't take much more than a moment for Laurie to obey, and dropping her nightshirt to the floor, she stepped into the enveloping suds.

The warm water lapped at her breasts as she relaxed. Eyes closed, she tried to remember a dream, or was it one of the crazy plots she'd been hashing out in her mind as she attempted to drift off to sleep?

She rolled her head, stretching the muscles of her neck and shoulders. Lord, she thought, it felt good to just sit and relax, and think of Jake, the sexiest hero she'd ever met this side of a computer or book. How easy it would be to plant him inside a novel, naked, maybe, with a gunbelt strapped around his slim Olympian god hips, astride a horse, astride—her.

Laurie sighed and reached for a fluffy purple sponge. She gently stroked her arms and breasts, pretending Jake was beside her, caressing her with those wonderful callused fingers, kissing her and letting the mustache tickle her lips, her nose, and— she sighed—other places as well. Once upon a time she'd created a hero with a mustache, a wicked mustache, who did absolutely wonderful things to the heroine.

Oh how she loved the power of imagination. She let her thoughts drift away, escaping into a dream that seemed so real, so right.

He was beside her now. She could feel his breath on her chest, hot and close.

She knew she should open her eyes, knew she should return to reality, but she didn't want the dream to end, didn't want the feelings to go away.

His hand dipped into the water and stroked her arm, her shoulder.

The magic of her dream was powerful. Pure magic, yet oh so very real.

He caressed her chest, her neck. He licked her face.

Licked her face?

Laurie cracked open an eye.

And screamed!

The most pitiful-looking brown-eyed cow she'd ever seen let out a blood-curdling moan that reverberated against the walls and through Laurie's ears.

Sue Ellen. It had to be Sue Ellen.

"Get out of here!" Laurie yelled, slapping at bubbles and water, slipping and sliding as she rushed to get out of the tub.

Sue Ellen stumbled back, her big brown eyes wide, frightened, and startled. Her immense black and white rump butted the sink as her hooves lost traction on the tiled floor, jarring it loose from the wall. Cold water spewed forth from a loosened pipe, spraying Laurie as she attempted to keep her balance and shut off the valve, trying to keep her legs from tangling with Sue Ellen's as the bovine stormed from the room.

Laurie snatched up her nightshirt, shoved her feet into her slippers, and took off in hot pursuit. She ran into the kitchen, pulling her knee-length Mickey Mouse pajamas over her dripping body, her feet sloshing in the fluffy pink bunnies on her feet.

Sue Ellen stood in the middle of the kitchen investigating Merry's poinsettia, which had been knocked to the floor. Dirt littered the planks and red petals and stems lay in broken and crushed clumps next to a red platter of fresh chocolate chip cookies.

"Out!" Laurie cried. "Out of my house. Now!"

Sue Ellen tore her gaze from the poinsettia, turned sorrowful eyes to Laurie, and mooed. She lowered her head again, sniffed at the cookies, and scooped one up with a fat pink tongue.

"Didn't you hear me? I said get out."

Moooo.

Flinging open the pantry door, Laurie grabbed a long-handled broom and smacked Sue Ellen across the butt, giving a quick thought to the .380 under her mattress.

Sue Ellen continued to chew, her jaws rotating as she savored each morsel. She flicked her tail, swatting Laurie across the face. It was more than obvious Sue Ellen hated to be bothered when she was eating.

"Dammit!" Laurie swung again and missed, hitting instead her antique crystal vase, which flew from the table and shattered against the wall.

Tears of anger streaked Laurie's burning cheeks.

Sue Ellen mooed, victorious once again, and lumbered across the kitchen, through the wide open door, then slowly, cautiously, made her way down from the porch, headed directly for Laurie's precious roses.

"Oh, no you don't." Broom in hand, Laurie sidestepped the dark green pile of goo lying just outside the door, and ran after the cow, chasing her from the roses, down the well-worn path, strategically avoiding the trail markers Sue Ellen had left in the dirt.

Laurie swung the broom.

Sue Ellen bellowed.

And Laurie's choicest street slang flowed like prose from her mouth.

Sue Ellen ran through the gate separating Laurie's property from Jake's, and once on the other side, she slowed, no doubt aware she was home, and possibly out of danger.

Laurie slammed and latched the gate, and shoved her fists into her hips. "Don't you dare think about coming back into my house ever, ever again," she yelled at the cow, as if Sue Ellen could understand.

Mooo!

Laurie leaned against the gate and, for the first time, wondered how Sue Ellen had gotten into her house in the first place. Had Merry accidentally left the door ajar when she left to run errands? Damn! She'd have to have a talk with the woman. Maybe Laurie had left the stalker behind her in New York, but that was no excuse for leaving the house wide open for just any old person—or cow—that decided to saunter in.

But how had Sue Ellen gotten out of the pasture in the first place? Laurie looked at the gate she'd been leaning against, realizing it hadn't been latched. Had Jake left it open? One of the boys? Well, she'd just have to have a talk with them, too. She wouldn't put up with this kind of nonsense again.

Sloshing through the dusty dirt, Laurie headed for the cabin with Sue Ellen following behind like a puppy starved for affection. Not even the evil eye Laurie inflicted upon the poor, trusting cow would make Sue Ellen turn away.

Laurie trudged up the stairs in her bedraggled and muddy bunny slippers and knocked on the door, giving serious thought to just barging in and giving Jake McAllister a piece of her mind. But her black mood eased the moment the door opened and a fresh-faced child with a half-inch jagged scar on his chin peered through the crack. She couldn't help but smile at the sight, wanting to caress her fingers over the softness of his still-babyish pink cheeks. "Morning, Joseph. Is your father home?"

"Daddy!" Joseph yelled.

A moment later the door opened wide and Laurie stood face to chest with a god who smelled of soap and aftershave.

She nearly lost her breath as her gaze drifted down to the faded Levi's that hugged Hercules' slim hips and strong, horse-hugging thighs, and only then did she realize they weren't completely zipped, they weren't even snapped at the top.

Red inched up her neck, and Laurie wished she had a fan.

A towel was slung over one bronzed shoulder, blond hair, damp and tousled, clung to the back of his neck where thick, wet strands twisted and curled. His face—oh, Lord, his face—was smooth, and dimples dented his cheeks just a fraction of an inch from where his thick mustache drooped over the corners of his mouth. It was heaven, absolute heaven, seeing that face without a scraggly, ugly, lifeless coating of hair.

He cleared his throat, and Laurie's gaze shot to eyes radiating with laughter and an immeasurable amount of warmth.

"Staring again, huh, Red?"

"I wasn't expecting a naked man to answer the door."

"Well, I wasn't exactly expecting you either." He inspected her close to nonexistent attire, her soap-matted hair, and the blotches of mud on her legs, his eyes full of humor. "What happened?"

"Your cow happened."

Jake couldn't help but laugh as Sue Ellen's immense body lumbered up the last porch step and nudged Laurie's behind, pushing her close to his ready and waiting arms. *Damn*! Laurie Langtry was a sight in that clinging shirt. It stuck to every curve, every sweet, luscious mound.

"Well, Red, I sure owe that cow of mine a big favor. Haven't gotten out of the shower to such a pretty sight in a helluva long time."

Laurie ground her teeth together and glared, while Jake prepared himself for a blow to his stomach. He couldn't tell if it was anger with Sue Ellen or anger with him that made Laurie's face as red as her hair.

Laurie glanced down at her nightshirt and pulled the clinging knit fabric from her breasts and stomach, only to have it sucked right back against her skin. She folded her arms across her chest, unable to hide any other portions of her anatomy, and glared directly, furiously, at Jake. "Did you let her out of the pasture on purpose?"

"Would I do that?"

Jacob pulled on Jake's arm. "Tell her, Dad. Tell her."

"Tell me what?" Laurie fumed.

Jake's throat tightened as he tried to hold back his laughter, but he couldn't keep his damnable mustache from twitching. "Guess I forgot to mention she's rather fond of your place."

"Forgot!" Laurie's eyes narrowed as she studied his grin. "Do you realize she broke into my house, broke a vase, a planter, the bathroom sink, and a plate full of chocolate chip cookies, not to mention leaving a pile of crap at my back door?"

"Sounds like Sue Ellen, all right."

"You mean this isn't the first time?"

Jake shook his head.

"She did it to Grandma and Grandpa, too," Jacob stated.

"Sorry, Laurie," Jake said in between snorts of laughter. "I spent most of yesterday fixing the fence and the blasted gate just so she wouldn't get out. Unfortunately, she has a mind of her own."

"She's a cow!"

"Yeah. Stubborn, too."

Jake could see Laurie's knuckles turning white as she tightened her grip on the handle of the broom, and he had the distinct feeling she wanted to swing the thing at his head.

He watched her chest rise and fall, her heavy breathing started to slow, and the red drained from her face, down her neck, and slowly disappeared. God, he loved the way her emotions showed so distinctly in her ever-changing facial color.

"Look," he said, "I'll take care of whatever Sue Ellen broke or messed up, but she doesn't like being fenced in, and I can't promise it won't happen again."

Laurie just stood there and glared.

"She likes your roses," he added as an afterthought.

"I found that out," she snipped.

Sue Ellen nudged Laurie again.

"I think she likes you, too."

Jake wiggled his brows.

Laurie rolled her eyes.

And everyone but Laurie laughed.

"You must be cold." He tried not to stare at the hardened nipples that showed so distinctly through her damp and clinging shirt. But he couldn't help himself. He attempted to swallow, but his throat felt as dry and useless as the old rock well. "Why don't you come in," he finally managed to say. "I'll give you something dry and warmer to put on."

She crisscrossed her arms more tightly over her chest. "Thanks, but I should get home and clean up the mess."

"It's early, Laurie, and the mess isn't going anywhere. Come on," he urged. "Have breakfast with us."

"Please, Laurie," Joseph and Joshua begged from behind their father's legs.

"Well, maybe, but I don't want to be any trouble."

"Trouble?" Jake wrapped his arm around Laurie's shoulders and led her into the house. "I have three hungry boys to feed every morning of the week, so one more mouth won't be trouble."

"Then you'll have to let me help."

Jake gave her a halfhearted smile. "Thanks, but you already told me you can't cook. You also said you make just about the worst cup of coffee this side of the Atlantic."

"And what about you? You burn hot dogs."

His eyebrows twitched in time with his mustache. "I never said breakfast would be any good."

Laurie rubbed her feet with the threadbare towel Jake had pulled from a small linen closet in the hall when he showed her to the bath. Somehow she'd managed to rinse them clean, although from all appearances, half the pasture had stuck to her legs and oozed between her toes when she'd sloshed along the path, and it had taken several scrubbings before the dirt disappeared from her flesh and washed away down the drain.

She'd rinsed the soap from her hair too, squeezing the water out before tossing the wet towel over the chrome rack, right next to the damp one that had earlier draped over Jake's shoulder. She slowly turned around, surveying her surroundings in the confining space of the rustic bath. It felt so intimate standing in this room that smelled of Old Spice and Irish Spring, where a few remnants of a scraggly blond beard still clung to the edge of the sink. Laurie shut her eyes, memorizing the scents, realizing these were a few of the things she'd missed in life, a few of the things that made this old cabin a home.

Opening her eyes, and careful not to make any noise, she cracked open the medicine cabinet and found a can of Right Guard, shook it well, used it sparingly, and put it back exactly as she'd found it, the lid setting off to one side. A half full bottle of Corn Huskers lotion sat on the edge of the sink and she wondered how often Jake used it. Not often, she imagined, given the rough feel of his fingers as he touched her skin. She thought of that touch, imagining Jake's strong, masculine hands coated with lotion, rubbing over every square inch of her body. A quiver raced from her heart, to her stomach, to the tips of her toes, then straight to that part of her anatomy that hadn't quivered from a man's touch in a very long time.

Laurie jumped at the knock on the bathroom door, her hand flying to her rapidly beating heart.

"How do you like your coffee?" Jake asked through the thickness of pine.

From the deepest recesses of her brain she sought the words she needed to answer his simple question. "Two big scoops of sugar and half a cup of milk."

No sound came from the other side of the door, but she could tell Jake hadn't walked away. Finally, he spoke. "Did I hear you correctly? Half a cup of milk?"

Laurie leaned against the door, as if doing so would bring her that much closer to the man on the other side. "Yes, please."

She heard a faint laugh, then muttered words as she listened to the pad of his bare feet moving away from the door. "You're a strange woman, Laurie Langtry."

His words, the laughing tone of his voice, made her smile.

Minutes later, she slipped into one of Jake's light blue work shirts and rolled up the sleeves, which extended nearly a foot past the tips of her fingers. The tails hung to her knees, and she was naked as a newborn babe underneath.

Lifting Jake's comb from the edge of the sink, she pulled it through her curls, watching a blond strand entwine with her red. Oh, Lord, the man had power over her. It felt so strange, so terribly intimate using his comb, his deodorant, his bathroom.

Opening the door, she stood in a short hallway and looked for a moment into the bedroom that had to be Jake's, a queen-sized bed filling a big portion of the room, its heavy, carved oak headboard and footboard finely-sculpted works of art. Tall pines and snow-capped mountains had been etched into the wood, their form and dimension perfect in every detail, the handiwork of a true craftsman. The same detailed work bordered the top of a dresser, and Laurie wondered if Jake had carved them himself.

A pair of scuffed but mud-free boots sat next to the bed, white socks draped over the side of one, neat and tidy, just like everything else in the room. A patchwork quilt in blues and reds and greens graced the mattress and pillows, and another blue workshirt hung over a post at the end of the bed. Nothing else was out of place. She saw no dust, no clutter, no mess, as if the room had been decorated and cleaned for a photo shoot. She expected something completely different from Jake McAllister. Where were the piles of dirty laundry, the unmade bed, the ashtray full of half-smoked butts?

She saw nothing out of place, except the book on the nightstand next to the bed. Her book, *My Captain*, opened somewhere in the middle, spread out face down, ready to pick up and read. Her heart thudded at the thought of him perusing her words. She wondered what he thought, if he liked it, hated it, if he wanted to read more. It was the same thing she felt every time someone she knew read her words.

"Your coffee's ready." She jumped again at the sound of Jake's voice, and turned to find him standing just a foot away, a mug of milky brown coffee in his hand.

"Like what you see?" Jake asked.

Laurie wrapped her hands around the mug and took a sip, studying the intricacies of Jake's beardless face, just as she'd studied his room. Like the oak carvings, Jake was nothing less than a work of art. "The carvings are beautiful."

"Thanks. It's something I started tinkering with a few years back when my nights got rather lonely."

Laurie sighed. "You must miss her then?"

"Amy?"

Laurie nodded.

"No. Not even in the winter when it would be nice to have someone warm in bed."

The red crept up her neck and was working its way toward her cheeks. She could feel the heat, and wished there was some way she could control it.

"I bought an electric blanket a few years ago. Not quite the same, but it helps."

"I've got an electric blanket, too," Laurie admitted, never before realizing how lonely and solitary the use of one could be.

Jake led the way down the hall and entered the kitchen. He pulled out a chair, waited for Laurie to sit, then took a seat at the opposite end, sliding the carton of milk across the table.

The boys hadn't said a word, just sat still in their seats, their hands in their laps, waiting, Laurie was certain, for Jake to bless the meal.

"Would you like to say grace, Laurie?"

Her eyes flashed at him across the table. "Me?"

"We take turns around here. Nothing fancy, just a few words of thanks."

Laurie folded her hands and lowered her head. "Dear Lord," she hesitatingly began, giving herself a moment or two to think of something more to say. "Thank you for snoopy cows, for dry clothes and hot oatmeal, and, most of all, for good neighbors." She opened one eye, peeking at Jake, and caught the halfhearted exasperation in the shake of his head, his slow smile, and finally his approving wink. "Amen."

She poured milk, spooned sugar, and didn't feel a bit self-conscious that four pairs of eyes watched her every move. She shoveled a healthy bite of oatmeal into her mouth. "You make a breakfast fit for a king," she said with a more than gracious smile.

"Thanks."

"Daddy?" Jacob stabbed at his oatmeal, digging out faces in the sticky mush.

"Yes?" Each time Laurie heard Jake speak to his sons, even one simple word, the love he felt for them came across loud and clear. Tolerant. Eager to listen. Willing to understand. Never in her life had she met a man as good as Jake McAllister, and she had the distinct feeling she never would ever again.

Jacob chewed quickly and swallowed his cereal with a gulp. "Are you going to fix the things Sue Ellen messed up in Laurie's house?"

Laurie grinned, negatively shaking her head. "There's no need. It probably isn't nearly as bad as I imagined when that cow of yours and I were slipping and sliding all over the tile."

The smile Jake flashed across the table could easily melt hardened lava. "What's the problem, Red? Got something to hide inside that house of yours?"

"No, but you're busy and it won't hurt me to clean up the mess."

"What about the broken sink? Do you have plumbing skills you haven't told me about?"

"No plumbing skills. No cooking skills."

"If I didn't know better, Red," he teased with a wicked grin, "I'd swear you made up that entire story just to come over here and have breakfast with us guys."

"If that's what I'd wanted, Jake, I wouldn't have come over half-naked and dripping wet."

"Maybe there were other motives behind that little gesture." He wiggled his brows.

Laurie shot him an angry frown. "Have you forgotten there are children present?"

Jake scratched the back of his head as if he didn't understand what the children had to do with the conversation. "Okay, Red." He winked. "Next time you want to get half-naked and dripping wet, we'll do it in private."

Laurie groaned.

Jake's mustache twitched.

And her heart did a back flip.

7

Jacob planted his hand firmly in Laurie's and pulled her out the cabin door toward the well-trod path. Jake followed just a few feet behind, Joshua firmly ensconced on his shoulders, with Joseph running along at his side, picking up stones and tossing them into the wind-whipped grass as he'd seen his dad do time and time again.

Jake rather liked the view from behind, contemplating Laurie's backside as she marched along the trail. She took long, easy strides with her short, shapely, freckle-coated legs, as if she had spent many a year trying to keep up with a much taller populace. She had a winning, high-class style, and pure, unadulterated grace, even wrapped in an old and faded workshirt.

Jacob and Laurie were engaged in an animated conversation, Laurie's gaze constantly following Jacob's pointed finger and turn of head. With a touch of sadness, Jake easily remembered that Amy had never shared that with the boy, with any of them—motherly things, like the pretty, sweet smell of roses, the drops of dew sliding down thick blades of grass, the softness of a woman's hand tucked into a child's.

They were things that could make a boy want a

mom, someone just like Laurie. And that thought frightened him. Laurie Langtry could easily inch her way into all of their hearts, then rip them out and run. She didn't belong in Bunch Gulch, she belonged in New York. Maybe she was being stalked, but she could have run anywhere—to Europe, to some far-away island. Why, then, had she returned to a place where she'd been snubbed and frowned on for so many years?

"So, Red," Jake called out as he ran to catch up with the pretty redhead and his son. "Why *did* you buy *my* old farmhouse?"

"You'll laugh."

"I doubt it. In the last four years I've done a lot of thinking about why a stranger would buy that house, and believe me, none of my thoughts has made me laugh."

Laurie dropped Jacob's hand and picked a stone up from the hard-packed earth. She rubbed her fingers over its dirt-crusted surface, smoothing away the soil to reveal its deep purple shine. "I used to collect stones like this when I was little."

"They're just plain old rocks. There's millions around here."

She shook her head. "Mine were special. I had one for every birthday party you ever celebrated. You'd invite me, but I couldn't afford a present, and even if I could, I doubt my grandmother would have let me go. So I'd sneak away and hide somewhere near your house and watch, pretending I was having fun right along with everyone else. And I'd find a pretty rock to take home as my souvenir."

"Was it always so lonely for you?"

"When I was younger, I guess. But I had a vivid imagination and if I wasn't happy, I'd just pretend to be someone else. I still do it when I write my books."

Jake lifted Joshua from his shoulders as they neared the white picket fence, and he put a comforting hand on Laurie's shoulder to keep her at his side. "You boys go up and play on the porch. We'll be right there." He watched them stampede through the gate and charge up the stairs, already involved in a game of their own.

"You still haven't told me why you bought the house."

Laurie gripped a pointed picket on the fence and looked at the three-story white farmhouse with wide shutters, all trimmed in forest green, trellises at each side woven with red roses planted decades before. "It wasn't just birthday parties when I'd sneak over here. It was anytime I was sad, or lonely, and wanted to see what happiness was really like. There was always something going on at this house. Parties and barbecues, football games." Laurie drew up her shoulders and turned around, bracing herself against the fence. "I thought if I lived in a house like this I'd have all the love in the world."

Jake swept a rock up from the ground, rubbed off the dirt, and put it in Laurie's palm, folding her fingers tightly around it. He'd never given much thought to the rocks on his property, figuring God put them in the ground to give man a reason to swear, and he'd done his fair share of that every time he hit a blasted stone with a shovel or pick. Yet walking beside him was little Laurie Langtry, admiring their colors, their smoothness, pretending they were precious gems. Did she see everything in that light? Did she see his old farmhouse that way, too?

For years Jake listened to his dad swear at the place—in the same manner Jake swore at the rocks. The plumbing had needed new fixtures and new pipes; the electricity needed complete rewiring. The floors needed sanding, the outside needed fresh paint and a new roof, but there'd been no money for any of those things, and so the house began to age, showing signs of neglect.

Jake had never figured out how he could give the place new life, but he'd always thought he'd be given the chance to try. And then his folks up and decided to move, and needed money to get away. They'd wanted to get rid of everything, but when Jake refused to leave the land, they sold the biggest headache on the thousand acres they owned. Jake had raged at them. He'd sulked. He'd gotten drunk. Then Amy disappeared and he grew up fast—the rage disappeared, but not the bitterness.

Now, he took a good hard look at the house, and saw what he'd wanted. Perfection. Laurie had given it what he couldn't. A new life.

"What are you thinking about, Jake?"

He looked away from the house that had mesmerized him, into the emerald eyes that could easily do the same. "I've seen all the work going on around here in the last few years, but never took a close look. It's changed. Probably looks like it did back in 1880 when my great-grandfather built the place."

"When I was making plans to buy it, the agent told me it would need a lot of work, but I didn't care how much money I had to spend. I wanted it. That's all that mattered." She smiled as she looked at her home. "Guess I just always thought it was special."

"Yeah, me too. I grew up in this place," he said. "My dad was born here, so was my grandfather, and God knows I want it back. I've got too many good memories associated with it. Family memories. But we couldn't keep it up. It was falling down around my folks, and it probably would have collapsed if I'd been given custody." Jake took a long look at the pristine white and green farmhouse, then turned and looked across the pastures to the old cabin where he'd moved when he married Amy. The place where he'd raised and loved his sons. "You're right when you say there was a lot of love here, but the house wasn't responsible."

"My housekeeper's already given me this lecture," she interrupted. " 'A house isn't a home without loved ones,' " Laurie said, mocking Merry's know-it-all-stance of arms pushed firmly under her bosom.

"She's right. That old cabin that should have been torn down years ago is as much a home to me as this place was."

"Okay, so I bought it for all the wrong reasons, but at least now you know why I did. I wanted everything I missed out on as a kid."

Jake cupped her face and thought about kissing her lips, but it wasn't the right time, or the right place, and he wasn't even sure if the gesture was right for him, no matter how much he wanted to do it. "Then I'm glad you bought it," he said, withdrawing his hand and plowing it through his hair. "If it had been for any other reason, like you just wanted a big old place in the middle of nowhere where you could hide and write, I might not be so thrilled."

"Well," Laurie managed to laugh, "it could be a

good place to hide and write if I ever sat down at the computer."

"Or if little boys would leave you alone."

"I hope they never do. I like having them around."

"I'll remember those words a month from now when they've broken half your crystal and eaten you out of house and home."

"Food and crystal can be replaced."

"And what about the bathroom Sue Ellen destroyed?"

Laurie's shoulders sagged. "I'd almost forgotten."

"Come on," Jake said. "Let's take a look."

"Why don't you guys go watch TV," Laurie suggested, as she led them through the living room door. The boys scrambled off, and she and Jake headed for the demolished downstairs bath. She put her hand on the knob, and looked at Jake. "Prepare yourself. It isn't a pretty sight."

"I live with three boys. I can take just about anything." He laughed, and Laurie shoved open the door.

"Well, I'll be." Jake stared at glossy green tile and cold white porcelain, at potted ferns and glistening gold fixtures. But nowhere did he see a mess.

"I can't believe it. It's not possible."

"You're sure this is the right bathroom?"

"Of course."

"You're sure you weren't daydreaming?" Jake teased, relaxing against the doorjamb and watching Laurie's reddening face. "Maybe you were plotting some crazy idea for your next novel, or, as I suggested earlier, just trying to lure me into your web for something more exciting?" He

crossed his arms across his chest and wiggled his
brows, and his mustache twitched for a little extra
added effect.

"Be real, Jake. Cows don't wander into bathrooms in my novels, and you know I'm too forth-
right to dream up some crazy scheme. Besides, you
said she's done this before."

"Then I suppose your housekeeper's a miracle
worker."

Laurie shook her head and walked away from
Jake and the bathroom, heading toward the kitchen
with Jake on her heels. She shoved through the
swinging kitchen door and stepped inside. The
kitchen, like the bathroom, was spotless. Laurie
threw up her hands. "I don't believe it. Merry must
have been here. That's the only explanation I can
think of." She sank into a kitchen chair and stared at
the perfectly potted poinsettia setting on the
counter, the same one that had earlier lain in a heap
on the floor. She clinked her fingernail on the crystal
vase, listened to its distinctive chime, and remembered the way she'd knocked it across the room
with the broom when she'd been aiming for Sue Ellen. She looked at Jake, whose mustache twitched in
time with the infernal twinkle of his smirking Montana blue-sky eyes. "Okay, so you want to know the
truth. Here it is. My housekeeper's magic. She does
this all the time. I make a wish," she said, snapping
her fingers, "and it comes true."

"Magical housekeeper, hmmm?" Jake's eyebrows raised. "Think she can whip up some horses
and a herd of cattle to fill my pastures?"

Laurie finally let a smile ease the discomfort in
her tightened jaw. "I'll put in a good word."

"I'd appreciate it. Magical housekeepers don't
abound here in Bunch Gulch."

"No, I don't imagine they do. Look, Jake. I'm sorry you had to come all the way over here on false pretenses." She apologized, but she didn't mean a word of it.

"I was going to clean irrigation ditches in the south pasture. I don't think a slight diversion's going to hurt much."

"Would you be interested in seeing my library?"

"Any etchings?"

"Not a one. Just books, and a desk heaped with notes and papers."

Jake scratched the back of his neck, wanting to stay, wanting to be far away, not only from Laurie, but from the house he still wished was his. "I don't know. Maybe I should just go out and fix that blasted well."

"It won't take long. It's my favorite room in the house. I'd really like you to see what I've done."

There was a web somewhere up in that room, he knew it, sensed it, and she was luring him nearer, tempting him with hints of something sweet. "Well," he dragged the word out with a sigh. "I suppose."

"Good. I promise you won't be disappointed."

She filled a plate with Merry's special chocolate chip cookies, oozing with chocolate and nuts with one side dipped in dark, sinfully delicious fudge, and poured three glasses of milk for the boys. They stopped in the living room before heading to the third floor, and found the boys sprawled on the floor in front of the TV, bellies down, scuffed boots knocking together and waving in the air as they watched Walt Disney's *Aladdin*.

"Does your housekeeper live in a bottle?" Jake whispered in Laurie's ear as he leaned over and set the glasses of milk on the table next to the plate of cookies.

"She lives up north somewhere with a jolly old husband named Nicky. That's about all I could get out of her on that subject."

"Damn! I was hoping to get an eyeful of some pretty little genie with a great belly button floating around this place."

Laurie just laughed. "Fat chance."

She grabbed Jake's arm and pulled him away from the boys and toward the stairs, but not before he'd grabbed three cookies and shoved part of one in his mouth. "Not bad. You know, I'm beginning to wonder if this housekeeper you keep referring to is really you, that you're a great cook and an even better housekeeper."

"No, no, no." Merry's words slipped out of her mouth as if she'd been using them for years. "Trust me on this one, Jake. Little Suzy Home-maker I'll never be."

Laurie opened the door to her office, her favorite room in the house, a room that felt more like home than any other, and when Jake stepped inside, its warmth grew into a burning flame. He belonged, as if he'd just stepped out of the pages of one of her novels, an Olympian god with a touch of roughness around the edges. Jake McAllister was everything she'd ever dreamed a man should be, he was everything she'd want in a man, if she wanted one around on a permanent basis.

"Doesn't look quite the same as it did when I lived here," Jake said, stepping inside and checking out the bookshelves. "Who did the wood-work?"

"I'm not sure," Laurie said, trailing her hand

over the highly polished oak. "I hired a decorator and she took care of all the details."

He inspected the edges of the shelves. "I would have done some carving on the cornices. Maybe some sprigs of holly, a pine bough, something to dress it up. Otherwise," he rubbed a finger over the smoothly routed edge, "he did a halfway decent job."

"If I'd known you were into woodwork, I would have asked the decorator to hire you for the job."

"No. Don't do it for money, just for fun."

"That's crazy, Jake. I've seen your work. It's beautiful. You should take advantage of your skills, advertise, make some money."

Jake shrugged. "Probably, but I've had enough of a load taking care of the ranch. I lease out most of the pasture at the far end of the canyon, but I've got hay to bale, fences to keep up, ditches to clean out. Takes time." He turned his head to the door as if listening for sounds downstairs, and smiled. "And then there's the boys." He shrugged again. "Yeah, I need more money, but I need time with them a helluva lot more."

"Guess I've done nothing in the last few years but concentrate on making money. I've pretty much forgotten what it's like to have fun. Being back in Bunch Gulch is the closest I've come to a vacation in a long time."

"Yeah, but look what you've gotten for all your efforts." He skimmed his fingers over the spines of the books on the shelves. "Pretty impressive," he said, tracing the letters of her name on one book after another until he reached *My Captain*. "I've been reading this one." He pulled it from the case. "Not bad."

"That's all? Not bad?"

His mustache twitched. "Let's see." He flipped through pages. "Where was that? Ah, yes. Page 237."

Laurie yanked the book from his hands. "Is that all you found interesting? The love scenes?"

He laughed. "No. I liked the story, too. Stayed awake most of the night reading the thing. Couldn't sleep, but couldn't put it down, either."

"You always read when you can't sleep?"

"No. I usually pace."

Laurie went to the window, pulling aside the curtain, and looked out across the pasture to the cabin in the distance. "I know. I don't sleep much, either, so I write, and sometimes I stand at this window and watch you walking back and forth, and wonder what's troubling you."

"You really want to know?"

Laurie nodded, leaning against the windowsill.

Jake spun Laurie's desk chair around and straddled the seat, crossing his arms over the back. For a moment, he wondered why he found the need to share his deepest thoughts with Laurie. "I could tell you all day long that my money problems don't matter, that I don't think about it, but I'd be lying. I think about it constantly. I make enough to pay the taxes and utility bills. We don't eat steak seven nights a week, but we're not starving or walking around naked. There's just not much left over for luxuries. I used to think I could make the ranch work again, make it pay for itself, be able to put some money away for college educations, but no matter how hard I work at it, that hasn't happened. I've been accused of being lazy because I don't have a job that pays real money. Ah, hell! I don't mind working, Laurie, but I swore when

Amy ran off that I'd never leave the boys, not like she did."

Laurie pushed a stack of papers to the center of her desk and sat on the edge. "Why'd she leave?"

He raked his fingers through his hair, then laced them together behind his neck, and stared at the ceiling. He'd never told anyone, yet he found it easy to pour it all out with Laurie. "She hated it here, and I refused to leave. She didn't like ranching, didn't like living in the middle of nowhere. Of course, we were too stupid to know any of those things when we got married. She was from California and came up to visit a friend, met me, and within a week, well . . ." He shrugged his shoulders. "I wanted kids, she didn't. I got what I wanted and one day she left. I'd gone into Hamilton to buy some feed and when I got back, her car was gone, her clothes, everything that belonged to her except the boys."

Laurie frowned in disbelief. "She didn't leave them alone, did she?"

"She knew I'd be home."

"That doesn't make it right. How could she do it?"

"She wanted out. That's just about what she wrote in her note, too. Took her two months to get in touch and let me know where she was, and in four years she's only written once more. I don't even know where she is."

"You must have hated her."

"I did, but not because she left. I hated the fact that she'd left the boys alone. Hell, Red, the twins were only three months. Jacob was just barely two." He looked away from Laurie, through the window to the blue, cloudless sky. "That's when I swore I'd never leave them alone. Meg watches them occasionally, but most of the time they're never so far away I can't see or hear them."

"You can't be with them every second."

"No, but I make damn sure I know where they are, unless they sneak off, like the other morning when they showed up here."

"They're welcome here any time. I like them, Jake. I don't mind having them around, and if I can help you out . . ."

"Yeah, well," he cut her off, "I appreciate the offer, but they can be a handful. Sometimes I think it might be better for them if I got a job and stuck them with a baby-sitter during the day, but I don't want to give up my time with them. Maybe later, when they're older, I'll get a job, but not now."

She understood completely. She'd probably feel the same way if she had children. "You're doing the right thing."

"Tell my mom and dad that. I get lectured at least once a month about the craziness of trying to make a go of the ranch. Gotta admit I'm getting tired of mending fences to keep in my one and only cow, a crazy old mule, and someone else's herd."

"Someday you'll have more. Soon as that genie with the delectable belly button appears."

Jake laughed. She had a way of lightening his usually black mood. No one had done that before, except the boys, and Meg. But Meg didn't take his breath away like this redheaded spitfire. "You think you can write a genie into my life?"

"I would if I could. Afraid fantasy's not my style, though."

"You mean bulging biceps and heaving bosoms aren't fantasy?"

Laurie shoved his chair with her foot and dared

him to say another word. "Maybe we'd better get out of here before you put your foot in your mouth."

"Yeah, I should check on the boys. Seems awfully quiet downstairs."

"They're watching TV," Laurie remarked. "How could they possibly get into trouble?"

"They're my sons, Red. Trust me. They get in trouble in their sleep."

Jake slid the book back into its place on the shelf and pulled out another. "Mind if I borrow this?"

"*Torch Song*? No." She shook her head, grinning.

"What's so funny?" He ran his fingers over the flaming gold torch embossed on the midnight-blue cover. "Something in here you don't want me to read?"

"Thousands already have, you might as well, too." She felt the unmistakable flush creep up her neck and blaze across her cheeks. "My first and only attempt at a bit of erotica."

"You mean that wasn't erotica I was reading in *My Captain*?"

"Far from it."

"Hell, I just might learn something." He chuckled, shoving the book under his arm. "I've gotta go check on the boys. You gonna splash some cold water on your face, or come downstairs looking like you've been practicing some of the stuff in your books?"

Laurie made a great show of fanning her face, all to no avail. "I'll be down in a minute. I think it's about time I got dressed. Running around half-naked isn't my normal style."

He absently studied her form, his eyes landing on the mud-caked bunny slippers and sliding up her bare legs to the old and faded shirt, to her freckled pixie nose, and the springing red curls on the top of her head. "You look good running around that way, Red." His mustache twitched as he sauntered across the room, stood in the hallway and tilted his head to look at her over his shoulder. "Don't be too long. Those kids of mine look forward to seeing you a lot more than they do me lately."

He bounded down the stairs two and three at a time. Joseph and Joshua hadn't moved an inch, laying side by side, their heads propped up on pillows stolen from one of Laurie's chairs. They looked perfectly at home, comfortable and happy. He didn't want Laurie to steal them away, but he didn't want to deny them all the things she could offer.

"Where's your brother?" Jake asked, swiping a half-eaten cookie from the plate and popping it into his mouth.

"He had to go home," Joseph offered without moving his head or taking his eyes from the television.

"I told you guys to stay here."

"We told him that, Daddy," Joshua stated, looking at his dad over his shoulder. "He said he had work to do."

Jake shoved his hands into his hair, grasping hold of a hunk at his temples.

"Is something wrong?" Laurie asked, walking slowly up behind Jake and putting a comforting hand on his arm.

"Jacob decided not to listen to orders. Not the first time," he laughed, "probably won't be the last."

"Come on you guys." Jake grabbed Joseph by the waist, lifting him easily and standing him on the floor. "Let's go home and see what trouble your brother's getting into."

"But the movie's not over, Daddy."

"Let them stay, Jake," Laurie implored. "I'll take them home when it's through."

"You're sure?"

"It's no problem at all. Besides, if I'm left on my own there's no telling how many of those cookies I'll devour and"—her voice turned seductive as she inched her fingers over her waist, her hips, her thighs—"I really don't need any excess inches."

Her hips, like her breasts, curved rather nicely, he thought, as his eyes followed the slow, seductive movement of her hands over an emerald knit tank dress that hugged those curves he was growing to like a helluva lot more than he should. God, was she trying to unman him right then and there? Was she doing it consciously, or did her sensual dance come natural, totally unrehearsed? "Okay," he finally managed to croak, "but don't let them get in your way."

"You forget, Jake. I've dealt with some of the biggest egos in New York. I rarely let anyone or anything get in my way."

With one more look at the boys, and another leisurely, visual stroll down Laurie's delectable anatomy, he headed out the door and down the well-worn path.

By the time he reached the gate, a strange, nagging sensation was eating at his insides. Jacob preferred outdoors to in, just like his dad, so it had never been easy to keep him cooped up inside. Jake couldn't blame him for deserting his brothers and the TV, but he had expected to find him outside, climbing a tree, throwing rocks, or shoving stones down ground squirrel holes. Never would he expect to hear that his oldest son had gone home because he had work to do.

Jake heard no laughter, no cries, no noise at all coming from the house as he drew near. The nagging sensation turned to fear, and he started to run. He shoved through the screen door. "Jacob!" he yelled, his voice bouncing off the silent walls.

It took only moments to search the great room, the bath, the bedrooms. No clothes had been taken from the boy's closet or drawers, none of his toys seemed out of place. No food sat on the counter, no carton of milk, no traces at all that Jacob had been in the house since they'd left with Laurie just an hour before.

Where? Where had he gone?

Outside, Jake ran along the irrigation ditches, checked the rocky wading pool dammed up in the creek, their favorite fishing hole, and finally climbed the rickety ladder leading to a tree house he'd built as a boy. Nothing. Grabbing on to an ageless branch, he gazed across the pastures looking for any signs of his son, but all he saw were a cabin, a farmhouse, brown dots he recognized as someone else's herd in the distance, a lop-eared mule, and Sue Ellen in the tall green grass in a far-off pasture.

"Please, Lord," he prayed, eyes filling with tears. "Please, let me find him."

Skipping the last few rungs of the ladder, Jake jumped to the ground and ran again up the path, hoping, praying, that Jacob had returned to Laurie's, that he wanted to see the end of *Aladdin*, that he felt bad about running off and leaving his dad and his brothers. He hoped, prayed, that Jacob was safe, that he'd once again be able to hold him in his arms.

He didn't knock, he just slammed into the kitchen and shouldered his way through the swinging door to the living room. Laurie looked up from the floor where she sat between the twins, her eyes narrowing in worry at Jake's sudden return.

"Is Jacob here?" he panted, his chest heaving from despair.

"No."

Jake grabbed Laurie's hand and pulled her up from the floor. "You boys stay here and finish watching your movie." They didn't turn around and he thanked the good Lord that they didn't sense his panic.

"I can't find him." Jake gripped Laurie's shoulders as they stood in the kitchen, his fingers digging through fabric and flesh. "I've been through the cabin, the pastures, down by the creek. I just don't know where he could be."

"Would he have walked into town? Does he have friends there, someone he might have wanted to visit?"

Jake shook his head. "Meg, maybe. But he's never gone to town alone."

"Have you looked around this place?"

"Joe said he'd gone home. I didn't think . . ." His fingers loosened on Laurie's shoulders, and suddenly, violently, he slammed his fist against the wall.

He ran from the kitchen, Laurie behind him. He missed the stairs completely, running along the edge of the picket fence past the tumble of roses and the swing he hadn't yet had time to fix.

In the clearing the vine-covered rock well sat as it had for years, lonely and forlorn, but one thing had changed. The boards Jake had nailed across the top had been pried off and lay on the ground next to Jake's best hammer. His heart came close to stopping as he leaned against the rocks and looked down into the dark abyss. "Jacob!" he cried, his voice echoing back.

Laurie touched his arm, little comfort when he felt as though his world might be coming to an end. "I can't see anything down there. Do you have a flashlight?"

"Yeah. Do you need a rope?"

"I don't now. Just get the flashlight."

"Jacob," he called out again, and when all was quiet he listened, but heard no movement, no sound, no light or labored breathing. No whimpering of a small child who'd been hurt.

Time seemed to drag on as he waited, and then Laurie was at his side, the light already beaming from the long black flashlight. Jake held it over the edge, moving the light in circles, searching the pit for a child, but he saw nothing. He turned the light toward the sides, toward the jutting ledges carved in granite and dirt.

Only emptiness stared back at him.

Jake flicked off the light, turned and rested his hip against the well. "He's not down there."

"Thank God."

"Where do I look now?" He wiped a tear from his face with the back of his hand. "Dammit, Laurie. Where could he be?"

"Hey, Dad!"

Jake's head jerked around at the sound of his son's voice. He was walking through the profusion of tall wildflowers toward his dad, his smile as big as the wheelbarrow he was pushing.

Jake rushed to the boy, grabbed him up in his arms and nearly squeezed the breath out of him.

And, just as quickly, he stood him on the ground, gripping his arms, and knelt before him. "Where the hell have you been? You scared the living daylights out of me."

"Gee, Dad. You said you wanted to fix this place up for Laurie and you hadn't gotten around to it so I figured I'd do it for you. Heck, I figured I had to do anything I could to make this place nice."

"Why would you do that?" Laurie asked, standing at Jake's side, her voice soft and low.

Jacob looked at Laurie and shrugged his shoulders. "Dad said he wouldn't do anything to make you stay, but Joe and Josh and I want you to."

"I don't plan on leaving, Jacob," Laurie said as she bent over and kissed his forehead. "I appreciate all you want to do, but next time why don't you ask me or your dad to help. It's dangerous around here, and the last thing we want to happen is for you to get hurt. We thought you'd fallen down the well."

"Nah! I was careful, but those boards were the devil to get off of there."

"Careful or not, Jacob," Jake stressed, shaking the boy gently to get his attention, and to get his point across, "this place is off limits for you and your brothers unless I'm with you."

"What about Laurie? Can we come here with her?"

Jake tilted his head to look at Laurie. She was smiling, those Betty Boop lips of hers plump and kissable and turned up just a bit at the corners. No wonder his sons had fallen in love. "You have a problem with that?"

"No." She turned from Jake to Jacob. "But you're not to come over here unless you tell your father first. I don't ever, *ever* want to see him worried like he was just a little while ago."

"Yes, ma'am."

"Run on inside and get your brothers, Jacob. I want you to take them home and I want you to stay put. I'll be there shortly."

"But I've got to put the wheelbarrow away. You told me never to leave tools outside."

"It can wait," Jake admonished.

"Yes, sir." Jacob's eyes and head turned down to the toes of his scuffed-up boots, dejection evident in the slump of his thin little shoulders.

Jake stood, gently stroking his son's cheek with the palm of his big, callused hand. For too many terrifying minutes he thought he'd never see the boy again, never hold him. He'd never felt so empty, and wondered if that's how he'd feel when the boys grew up and left home. "Thanks for wanting to help out, son. I'm sure you would have done a wonderful job."

Jacob nodded, his eyes raised to meet his dad's. "I'll go get Joey and Josh now."

Jake watched Jacob head down the path, slow and easy at first, then a light skip was added to his step, and finally he picked up a rock and tossed it at a pine. Hurt and rejection mended quickly for some in the McAllister family, Jake realized. Why couldn't he be one of the lucky ones?

"The boys are getting awfully attached to you." Jake averted his eyes from Laurie as he lifted the boards from the ground and once again covered the hole of the well. "I don't think it's such a good idea."

"Excuse me?" Laurie grabbed Jake's arm, forcing him to look her direction. "I don't see any problem. I like their company. They seem to like mine. What is it, Jake? You afraid they might adopt some of my old wayward ways?"

"No." He spoke soft and low and didn't turn around to face her. "I'm afraid they'll fall in love and you'll run away."

"Like their mother?"

"Yeah, just like that. They've been hurt before, I won't allow it to happen again."

Laurie put her hand on his arm and forced him to turn her way. "You plan on intervening in everything that happens to them the rest of their lives? They're going to get hurt someday, Jake. By me—maybe. By you—more than likely. Hurt's all part of growing up. You can't keep it from happening."

His blazing eyes bore down on her. "When you have kids of your own, then you can preach. Until you do, do me a favor. Don't go out of your way to steal their hearts."

Jake threw the last board on top of the well. "Don't go near this thing till I get it fixed."

"And don't give me orders," she stated to his stiff, proud back. "It's a waste of your time, Jake. I don't listen to them and I sure as hell don't follow them."

"Please, Laurie," he begged, sweeping the hammer up from the ground and twisting its wooden handle between tightened fists. "If you care anything at all for those kids, don't hurt them. They want a mom." He looked at her with reddened, anguished eyes. "I don't want another wife. I know in my heart I'll never leave them, but I can't say the same thing about someone else. I know I can't protect them from everything, but that's the one thing I do have control over."

"Is it the boys you're worried about, or yourself?"

The heat of her eyes beat against him and he knew she had every right to ask that question. He only wished he had an answer. He wanted to protect the boys, but they acted as a buffer for him, too. Laurie Langtry was inching her way into his soul and his heart, two places he'd kept sealed for a very long time, and he wasn't sure if he wanted her there or not.

He tossed the hammer into the scarred and beaten wheelbarrow, the hollow noise reverberating through the copse like an Oriental gong. He grabbed the wooden handles, lifting the end of the wheelbarrow as he straightened. "Y'know, Red. You're pretty. You're rich. Any man in his right mind would want you."

"I've never known anyone saner than you, Jake McAllister."

"Yeah, that's the hell of it, Red." He pushed on the wheelbarrow and headed toward the well-worn path connecting his place to hers. "That's the hell of it."

8

"I want to build a castle."

"You what?"

"A castle." Laurie sipped Earl Grey and picked at the remaining crumbs from Meghan's blue-ribbon carrot cake as they sat across from each other at the table in Meghan's sun-brightened country kitchen. "I got the idea looking at all your art work."

"There's not a castle in the bunch."

"Maybe not, but you've painted cottages that would make Thomas Kinkade jealous." Laurie pushed away from the table, taking her plate and Meghan's to the sink and rinsing off the sticky cream cheese frosting. "Don't you think you could sketch out a castle?"

Meghan rested her elbows on the table and scratched her temple. "Do me a favor and start at the beginning, Laurie. A moment ago we were talking about Kurt and how you planned to get us together, and suddenly you launch into some silliness about building castles."

"It all fits together, Meg," Laurie said, taking her seat once again. "Kurt may be the minister of your church, but he also builds log cabins."

"Oh, yes," Meghan grinned, her eyes pools of

humor mixed with confusion. "I can see perfectly how this fits together."

"It's simple. I want to build a castle; well, not really a castle, but a play structure with towers and drawbridges and slides and ladders and swings."

"Why?"

"Because Jake wants me to stay away from his boys and I absolutely refuse. He's being stubborn and pigheaded and thinks I'm trying to steal the kids away from him."

Meghan shook her head. "And this is your way of endearing yourself to him?"

"I have no desire to endear myself to him. He either likes me the way I am or he doesn't have to like me at all."

Meghan laughed. "I don't think liking you has anything to do with it. Sounds to me like he's scared."

"Of me? That's crazy."

"Is it?" Meghan raised her eyebrows, sounding more like the advice-for-the-lovelorn expert than Laurie. "I watch the kids every so often, and he's never accused me of trying to steal them away. And you know why? Because he's not interested in me as anything more than a friend, and the boys sense it. I'm not a threat, like you."

"But I'm not a threat."

"Would you like me to tell him that? He's coming over later."

"No. Then he'd accuse me of being paranoid." Laurie downed a sip of tea, and wondered why Jake planned to visit Meg. For two people not interested in each other, they sure spent a lot of time talking. Maybe she *was* paranoid after all. "So, why's Jake coming over?" she asked, the curiosity driving her crazy.

"I'm going to watch the boys for a few days while they go to Vacation Bible School."

"Well," Laurie remarked, a little perturbed, "he gave me the impression he rarely lets them out of his sight."

"It was my idea, definitely not his. He thought I'd lost my mind. Took me nearly half an hour to convince him he needed a break, and that it wouldn't hurt the boys, either. Might be good for the two of you, too, now that I think of it. He needs time to realize you're not a threat. And you need time to think about why you're going all out for those kids. It is the boys you're wanting to please, isn't it?"

Laurie shrugged her shoulders. She was doing it for the boys, she told herself. Just for the boys.

Meghan grabbed hold of a hunk of her hair and began to weave it into a braid. "So, are you ever going to tell me how Kurt fits into your castle plans?"

"You got me so far off the subject, I almost forgot what I came here for," Laurie said, easily drawn back to the subject of Kurt, and castles, and ways to drive Jake crazy. "If you can draw up some sketches, I'll talk Kurt into building it for me."

"But he builds log cabins."

"And I bet he can build the sturdiest play structure around."

"I'm sure he can, but why would he want to work with me?"

"Because, I'll tell him you're the designer and he needs to work with you through every step, start to finish."

Meghan's skepticism showed in her curious frown. "You think this will work?"

"It's the basic principle of writing a romance novel. One person's interested, the other might be. You get them together and keep them together long enough, sparks are bound to fly—good, bad, indifferent. And, believe me, bad and indifferent are sometimes just as delightful as good."

Laurie walked across the soft layer of wood chips, inhaling the sweet fragrance of redwood and cedar and pine, her ears filled with the sounds of chain saws and heavy mallets pounding against wood. Scattered about the yard were several log homes in various stages of construction, some just the frames of outer walls, rough-cut and jagged-edged, others nearing completion, each log marked for that day when it was ready to be shipped.

She stepped onto the office porch, and smelled the fragrant honeysuckle spilling from dug-out log planters. She had expected to find a rustic place, dirty and dusty, but when she opened the door and stepped inside, the same homey, comfortable feeling she'd experienced at Meghan's assailed her. Kurt Elliott's office was warm and inviting, with Native American paintings in hand-carved and naturally stained wood frames hanging on the carefully fitted log walls. A brightly colored Indian blanket was draped over the upstairs railing, and overstuffed buckskin leather couches and chairs sat around a massive, brightly polished knotty pine table.

"Can I help you?"

Laurie looked up to see a tall, burly man casually walking down the stairs. A thick crop of black hair, salted with silver, topped his darkly tanned face, and a black and red plaid shirt tightly hugged his powerful logger's body and firm stomach that looked as though eating fine food and drinking good beer—even if he was a man of God—agreed with him.

She walked towards him as he stepped onto the parquet floor. "I'm Laurie Langtry."

"Kurt Elliott," he said, taking her hand.

"I half-expected to see you with a cleric's collar under that plaid shirt."

"Well, I'm a big believer in looking at the inside of a person, not the trappings on the outside."

"Pretty nice trait for a minister."

"I hear you have some pretty interesting traits, too."

Laurie felt an ounce of red creeping up her cheeks. "Oh, dear."

"I suppose the *oh dear* would be justified if I believed half of what I'd heard." He laughed, his deep voice booming off the log walls. "Fortunately, I don't."

"I appreciate that. I have an old reputation that's probably not easy to wipe out of peoples' memories."

"I like to think most of the people in this community are fair and decent. Give them time, Laurie. They'll come around."

"My housekeeper's used words quite similar to those a time or two." She quickly glanced around the room, and sized up the man, seeing perfectly well why Meghan was hooked.

"You've got a lovely place here." She ran her hand over the smooth, round timber of the banister.

"It's my best-selling tool, but I have the feeling you're not here to look at log cabins."

"Actually, I did want to talk to you about a building, but not exactly a house."

"Too bad. I build the best log home this side of the Mississippi." He walked into the kitchen area and took two pottery mugs off a wood peg rack. "I also make a good pot of coffee. Would you care for some?"

"Yes, please. Lots of sugar and half milk, if you have it." She ignored his laughter as she had so many other peoples' in the past, and sat on one of the couches and flipped through a thick photo album on the coffee table. Kurt Elliott's homes, she decided, after looking at page after page of contemporary and rustic creations, were indeed masterpieces.

He set the mug next to her hand and sat across from her, crossing thick tree-trunk legs encased in dark blue denim. "I've watched you on TV a time or two. It's nice to finally see you in person. Mildred Adams tells me you're on vacation and you'll be going back to New York soon."

Laurie grinned. "Interesting. I haven't said one word to Mrs. Adams since I came back."

"Word spreads fast around here, whether it's right or wrong. Of course, one would think you'd have an awful long commute if you planned to stay here permanently. Aren't too many network shows filmed around Bunch Gulch."

"No commute." Laurie laughed. "My contract's up, and I haven't yet decided to re-sign."

"Their loss, our gain, I'm sure."

Out of anyone else's mouth Laurie might have thought he was flirting, but she sensed a great deal of honesty and sincerity in Kurt Elliott. He was definitely a perfect match for Meghan.

He took a sip of coffee and studied her over the brim of his cup. "So, what were you hoping I could build for you?"

"A castle." She waited for his look of shock, but he just smiled and waited. Damn! It wasn't fair for one man to have so much patience and faith.

"Ever build a play structure?"

"No, but I've been known to put together some pretty crazy ideas for log homes. If you've got an idea, I can probably come up with a design and build it—if I had the time."

"Oh." Laurie sounded dejected. "I hadn't given time and labor too much thought."

"Before you lose hope, give me some idea what you have in mind."

"Nothing as big as you've seen in parks, something smaller for just a few rambunctious boys."

"I didn't realize you had children."

"Not mine. Jake McAllister's."

"I see." He nodded his head, his fingers drumming against his mug. "Does Jake know about your plans?"

"He's not paying so I don't exactly see the need to consult him, do you?"

"Suppose not." He set the cup on the table between them and steepled his fingers as if he were ready to pray, for deliverance from crazy women, Laurie supposed. "I can't give you any figures on time or cost until I see some kind of design."

"Money's no problem. Whatever it takes is fine. As for the design, I have a friend in town who knows what I want. She's promised to draw up some designs, and if you're the least bit interested in doing the work, I think it would be best if you work directly with her."

Kurt's thick salt-and-pepper eyebrows knit together and Laurie had the uncanny feeling he saw right through her scheme. "Who's the friend?"

"Meghan O'Reilly."

Kurt's frown left his face, replaced by a hint of sadness. He picked up his cup and walked to the window, looking out at the work being performed. "I don't know if I can do this job for you."

"And why not?"

"What do you know about Meg's husband?"

"Not much. I know he died a few years ago, but she hasn't gone into detail."

Kurt leaned against the windowsill, continuing to look at the logs being pulled and shoved and lifted and lowered in his yard. "He was working for me when he died." Kurt rubbed the back of his neck, and Laurie could see the tension building in his jaw, his shoulders. "The crane operator was lifting the main beam for a house we were working on and Steve was guiding it into place. Something we do all the time, but that day, the chain snapped, and . . ." Kurt took a deep breath, and let out a ton of frustration and remorse. "I was standing right here. I saw it snap. The crane was new. It never should have happened, but it did. I ran out, but there was nothing I could do. Steve was gone by the time I got to him. I'm the one who had to tell Meg. And I'm the one who held her when she cried, and officiated at his funeral. I'm her minister, that's all there should be between us. I see her at church, but anything more than that wouldn't seem right."

"Is that what your Bible tells you?"

He stared at Laurie for the longest time before he spoke. "I haven't forgotten what happened, and in spite of my belief, my faith in God, I feel guilty, like I should have been able to prevent his death."

"She doesn't hold anything against you."

"She wouldn't." He smiled. "Not Meg."

The man was in love. Laurie had seen it before, over and over again. But he was frightened, and she wanted to help.

Laurie put her hand on Kurt's arm. "You know what you need, Pastor?"

He cocked his furry eyebrows. "A dose of my own preaching?"

"Close. You need a lecture from me on what you should do to overcome your fears."

Kurt faced her again. "They're not fears, Laurie. Meghan's the prettiest, sweetest woman I ever encountered. But I'm her minister."

"Yeah, that's right. You're a man of the cloth and you know how to lead your flock toward righteousness, but you haven't got a clue about women."

"I know about Meg."

"And just what is it you think you know?"

"I saw her through some tough times, and I've got the feeling she sees me as some kind of saint. Well, I may be a man of God, but I've got my faults, and I don't think I could ever live up to her expectations."

Laurie rolled her eyes. "What is it with the men in this town? Are you all afraid a woman's going to clap you in handcuffs if you smile, or say a kind word, or, God forbid—" Laurie caught her words a little too late, and tossed Kurt a brief, begging-for-forgiveness smile before continuing. "Excuse me, but what's the harm in having a cup of coffee together, or going out to dinner, or designing a castle for a couple of kids?" She took a deep breath. "I learned a long time ago to face fear head on. So—" Laurie scrunched up her eyes and gave the situation a good hard thought, just the way she did when she ran into a difficult situation while writing. "Here's what you're going to do."

"I don't think I'm going to like this."

"Hush! Meghan's designing my castle, you're going to build it. And when it's done, I'll donate matching costs to your church and you can do whatever you want with the money. But, you've got to go over to Meghan's, you've got to work with her on the design, you've got to let her assist you every step of the way on the play structure. A cup of coffee or dinner together wouldn't hurt either."

"Matching funds?"

Laurie nodded.

"Could you double that? The hymnals are a mess and we lost our stained-glass window in a bad storm last winter."

"You drive a hard bargain, Pastor."

"You should see me on the pulpit. By the way, have you ever considered my line of work? You've got a definite knack for making people open up."

"Oh, no, Kurt." She raised her hands, warding off his thoughts and words. "I'm a romance writer. I don't heal. I don't console, and to be perfectly honest, I haven't seen the inside of a church in a very long time."

"Well, I tend to believe in miracles, Laurie. I'll work with Meghan, maybe break a little bread and share a little wine. I'll build you a castle, and maybe"—he winked—"I'll see you in church one of these days."

"I had it drummed into my head at a very young age that that's one place I didn't belong. Haven't gotten over it yet."

"You belong, Laurie, just as you belong right here in Bunch Gulch. Whatever happens, don't let anyone tell you differently."

* * *

Laurie pushed the wobbly-wheeled cart through the junk food aisle and absently tossed a package of Oreos into the basket next to a bag of Cheetos and a six-pack of Diet Dr Pepper. As she pushed, she continued to scan the shelves for other interesting delicacies to stave off hunger during the marathon writing session she planned for the next few days. She loved Merry's cookies, her gingerbread, her pot roasts, and the wonderfully rich and wholesome turkey, stuffing, and cranberry sauce sandwiches she made, but days in front of the computer screen called for junk food and sloppy sweat suits. It had been her routine for years, and she didn't want to ruin a great thing.

She turned the aisle and nearly collided into Tom Harrington. "Good afternoon," she said with a smile.

His eyes darted to the items in the basket, and Laurie guessed he was taking a quick tally, just to make sure she didn't rip him off when she left. Nothing, she decided, had changed about Tom Harrington over the years.

"I'm Laurie Langtry," she said, sticking out her hand. "Remember me?"

"Of course I remember. Most of the people in town do. What are you doing back here?" His voice was just as gruff as it had been when she was a youngster sweeping dirt under the cabinets instead of picking it up in the dust pan and throwing it away.

"This is where I was raised, Mr. Harrington, and I'm thinking about sticking around permanently."

"What's wrong with New York?"

"Nothing. Nothing at all." Gently, she patted his upper arm and smiled. "I just missed the warmth and friendship of Bunch Gulch. That's all." She pushed the cart away from Tom, hoping her words had pierced maybe an inch of the armor he wore.

She grabbed a bottle of Tom's best chardonnay, some locally grown huckleberry preserves, and pushed her cart up to the checkout counter. She helped bag her groceries, remembering just how she'd been instructed to do it over and over again when she'd worked there as a teen, only this time she made sure to put heavy items on the bottom, light on the top, the opposite of what she'd done as a kid to get Tom's goat.

She scratched out a check and Tom inspected every detail. "You sure this is good?" he questioned.

"Look, Mr. Harrington. Couldn't you pretend I'm new in town? Couldn't you pretend I never worked for you? Couldn't you forget that you didn't like me when I was a kid, and try to like the me who's living here now?"

"No. Don't think I can do any of those things." He opened the cash register and slipped the check under the bin. "I know where you live, just in case it bounces."

Laurie tried to remain calm, she tried not to wad her fist and shove it into his soft, protruding belly. There was nothing to prove by getting angry. "You've really fixed the store up nice over the years." She struggled to find something pleasant to say. "I sure prefer shopping in places like yours. Never could stand those big supermarts."

"Can't get everything here," he grumbled.

"Maybe not, but if you don't mind me coming in, this is where I'd like to shop. Besides, we'll never build up any kind of friendship if I shop somewhere else."

Tom let out a huff of air and shook his head, then went back to sweeping the floors.

Kurt Elliott had told her she belonged in Bunch Gulch, but it still didn't appear everyone else in town felt the same. However, she had made up her mind to move back, she was thinking she might never leave, and when Laurie set her mind on something, she let nothing and no one stand in her way.

"Damn fool woman!" Jake muttered to himself as he stomped out of Meg's house and headed for the store. He'd told Laurie to steer clear of his boys, so what in the hell was she doing building a castle in her yard for them to play on? Didn't she have anything better to do than meddle in other people's business?

He shook his head as he walked, his hands clenched at his sides, his strides long and determined. She was almost as bad as she'd been in high school, he decided, as he left the side street where Meghan's old Victorian sat amidst a profusion of yellow daisies, orange marigolds, and purple and pink Sweet William. He turned onto Main Street where he'd left his Jeep, recounting all the things about Laurie that had driven him crazy fourteen years ago, things that hadn't changed a bit. She was headstrong, unruly, and didn't give a damn about anything, from outward appearances anyway. But, God, he had wanted her. Age fifteen. Age sixteen. Age seventeen. As far back as he could remember she'd been around, taunting him, laughing at him, calling him Mr. Goody Two Shoes. He'd wanted her desperately, wanted to have half her guts, half her determination. Like all the boys, he'd wanted to kiss her lips and explore that belly button she showed off like a gold medal when she strutted around in her tattered, hip-hugging blue jeans, and those tank tops that clung to her braless body and made all the boys drool. But he wanted more than a kiss, more than a feel, he wanted to hold her, and protect her, like he would an injured animal. But he'd kept his feelings secret. What would his friends say? His parents? She was nothing but poor white trash, and she had a reputation that would make a call girl look pristine. He didn't believe a word of it, but damn, she'd never done anything to disprove the rumors. Apparently she hadn't cared, and, unfortunately, he'd cared too much.

"Ah, hell!" He kicked the tire of his battered and bruised Jeep to relieve just an ounce of frustration. He wanted her still, but now it wasn't friends or parents standing in his way. He'd come a long way from the boy who'd worried what other people thought. It was his sons, and his own stubborn fear of losing her if he gave away his heart.

"Bad day?"

Jake jerked around at the laughter in Laurie's voice. "Bad week," he barked. "Started right about the time you drove up in that flashy Corvette and decided you should change the lives of half the people in Bunch Gulch."

Laurie's eyebrows raised, but not her voice. "If you're good at changing lives, you might as well do it. Some lives aren't worth a plug nickel, but if I can make 'em shine, you bet I will."

Jake was in no mood to listen to her damn fool talk. "You got any perishables in that bag?" he growled.

Laurie stared down at the overstuffed brown paper bag she held in her arms. "Probably."

"Too bad." He yanked it out of her hands and dropped it on the front seat of the Corvette, grabbed her hand, and ushered her into the passenger seat of his Jeep. "Put your seatbelt on."

"You're giving me orders again," Laurie snapped as she pulled the belt across her lap.

"You're damn right." Jake hopped over the driver's side door and snapped his seatbelt into place. He cranked the key, revved the engine, and shoved the Jeep into reverse, jerking out of the parking spot. He slammed to a stop, ground the gears into first, and tore up Main.

"Where are we going?" Laurie wrapped her hands around the edge of the seat to keep from sliding into Jake as he sped around the corner and turned off on a dirt road that looked like nothing more than an ancient wagon trail, now strewn with rocks and weeds and old discarded beer cans.

"Hold on tight."

"I am, dammit. Where are we going?"

"Somewhere where I can give you a piece of my mind without half the town hearing."

The wheels spun in loose, shifting sand. The Jeep twisted and turned, then straightened as Jake struggled with the steering wheel, floored the accelerator, and headed for parts unknown.

"You're going to kill us, Jake."

He wanted to wrap his fingers around her pretty little neck, but killing wasn't what he had in mind, he only hoped driving at breakneck speed and yelling at the top of his lungs would wipe out some of his frustration, rip the strange feelings he had for her from his head.

"Stop this car, Jake!" she screamed. "Now!"

He drove out of the ruts into tall green grass splattered with wildflowers at the edge of a creek, slammed on the brakes, and jerked the Jeep to a halt.

Laurie unlatched the seatbelt, fumbled with the handle, and shoved her shoulder into the door until it finally jolted open, but Jake was at her side before she could move even two feet away from the car.

Her pixie chin jutted up in the air. "You going to yell at me now?"

"Yeah. I told you to leave well enough alone, and then I find out you're building some silly-ass castle-slash-play structure on your property so my boys will have someplace to play."

"So"—she shrugged—"what's the problem?"

"The problem, as I've stated before, is I don't want you trying to win them over."

"You afraid they'll leave you?"

His finger was pointing at her face. "Don't even . . ." He shook his head and shoved his hands into his back pockets, turning around so he wouldn't have to face her. "Yeah, I'm afraid of them leaving me."

"Where's your confidence, Jake? You had tons of it in school. Valedictorian. Class president."

"Every ounce of confidence I had walked out the door right along with Amy," he shouted, walking away from Laurie and tromping down to the creek. He picked up a stone and threw it into the gently rolling water.

"My folks left and sold what should have been mine to a stranger," he began again in a much softer voice when Laurie's shadow mingled with his. "My marriage failed, my ranch started dwindling, I had to sell my livestock. Yeah, Red, I lost my confidence."

Laurie pressed her hands against his back. He

could feel her heat through his shirt, radiating
through his body, as her fingers inched their way
around him toward his chest. "You're the most
successful man I've ever known, Jake."

"That's nonsense." He pulled away, afraid of
what he might do if her breasts touched him, if she
got much closer.

"It's not. You're the best father I've ever known.
You give all of yourself to those boys. I can't think
of any greater success."

"I do it because I love them. Success has nothing
to do with it."

"Dammit, Jake! What's gotten into you?"

His muscles tensed. He could feel them tying
into knots in his shoulders, in his neck.

"It's me, isn't it?"

He raked his fingers through his hair, and his
stomach clenched when he felt her hands circle his
body, reaching upward to his chest in slow, delib-
erate motion. "You're the most maddening woman
I've ever met, Laurie."

He could feel the soft fullness of her breasts
against the small of his back, and all he could do
was close his eyes and try to catch his breath.

"Did you like me when we were in high school,
Jake?"

His head shook in denial. He was afraid to let
her know the truth.

"You used to come into the Mercantile when I
was working. I remember how you pretended to
buy gum or soda, but I thought you were looking
at me, laughing at me, because I was working to
pay Tom Harrington back for a pack of cigarettes
one of your friends had stolen."

Jake pulled away and turned around. "I wasn't
laughing, Laurie. I wanted to tell him the truth. I

wanted to tell everyone the truth. But you'd already admitted it. Sometimes I got the feeling you wanted everyone to think you were bad."

"It was easier to go with the flow than fight it. No one would have believed me anyway."

"I would have believed you."

Laurie's eyes misted. "You would?"

"Yeah, I knew the truth. I always knew. You put on a good show in front of everyone, but I saw you crying a time or two. I never had the guts to tell anybody. Like you, it was easier to go along with the crowd. I should have stuck up for you then. Now you don't need anyone. You've proven to this town that you're a success, that you outshine everyone else. There's nothing left to prove anymore."

"You think that's why I came back? You think I should leave since I have nothing to prove? You think I have no long-lasting reason to be here?"

He shrugged his shoulders. "You're going to do what you want no matter what I say. But no, I don't want you to go back to New York now and face that asshole who's stalking you. But you don't belong here, Laurie. There's nothing here for you. No theaters, no fancy restaurants, no nightlife."

Even from a foot away Jake could feel the depth of Laurie's sigh. "Are we going back to square one again, Jake? Aren't we ever going to get past your fears that I might get tired of Bunch Gulch and run away?"

"You forget I've seen it all before." He plowed his hands through his hair. "Dammit, Red. Why did you have to come back? Why?" He looked down at her pixie face, at Betty Boop lips, into the depths of emerald eyes that were filling with tears.

"Ah, hell!" He grabbed Laurie's arms and pulled her hard against his chest. Reaching low, he cupped her bottom, tight and firm and a perfect fit in his hands. The Levi's could easily have been nothing more than denim blue paint the way they hugged her hips and thighs and legs, and he slid her up his body till her mouth was just an inch away. And he kissed her, hot and furious. Her lips parted, from instinct, from desire, and his tongue delved inside, tasting for the first time the burning passion of a hellcat with flaming red hair.

He felt the hot brand of her fingers on his face, searing his skin, sliding across his cheeks, plunging into his hair, pulling him closer, closer to her heart. She wrapped her legs around his waist like a vice, and he freed one of his hands, no longer needing it to hold her against him, and slowly inched under the t-shirt toward the thin strap of her bra. He wanted to take her, now, to feel the sweetness of her legs around him when they weren't encumbered by the fortress of her clothes. Lord, he wanted her.

Somehow he pulled his mouth from hers, wanting to taste the sweetness of her cheek, her ear, wanting to feel the tightening of her limbs, wanting to hear and feel the deepening of her breath, the hard beat of her heart when he kissed the base of her neck, savoring it with the teasing tenderness of his tongue.

"Don't stop, Jake. Please, don't stop."

He jerked away, her words a bucket of ice thrown against his face. What was he doing? What was happening?

"What's wrong?"

He lowered her to the ground, holding her for a moment till her legs steadied, till his breathing eased. "This is wrong, Laurie. You. Me. It's impossible."

"It's not, Jake. You want me. I know it. And, oh God, Jake—I want you, too."

"For how long, Red? For how long?"

Were those tears he could see at the corners of her eyes? Was she crying? Damn, he didn't want to hurt her. But he didn't want to fall in love, either, and if he allowed her to get that close ever again, there'd be no controlling his heart.

9

Laurie stuffed a piece of dark chocolate fudge into her mouth and swigged a gulp of milk, then flopped back on the sofa and stared at the ten-foot-high ceiling. "He kissed me, Merry, but I don't understand him." She sighed, remembering the depth of Jake's kiss, the way her stomach clenched, the way hidden parts of her anatomy tingled and throbbed and begged to be touched. "I've never been kissed like that before."

"So what, pray tell, is it you don't understand?" Merry asked, rocking back and forth in her maple rocker, a lacy red and white afghan flowing over the side as she spun it out of clicking knitting needles.

"He starts to get close, then he pushes me away. He's afraid I'll leave, yet he's afraid I'll stay. He's repeated the same litany to me a dozen times, and I'm getting sick and tired of his moaning and groaning and his ridiculous contradictions. I swear, Merry, he's more confused than the heroes in my novels, and I'm getting nowhere with him."

"And where is it you want to go with him, child?"

"I don't know. I liked him when I was a kid.

Maybe I'm just trying to relive my teenage years, make them better than they were."

"Yes. That's a possibility, child."

"Who am I kidding?" Laurie felt like she was lying on a psychiatrist's couch, talking about nothing, and paying through the nose for words that were of no help at all. "That's not what I want at all."

"Then what is it?"

"I care for him. I like his kids. I like Meg and Kurt, and that old fart Tom Harrington isn't any worse than half the people I've done business with in the past." Laurie twisted onto her side, propping her head up on her arm, and watched Merry as she knitted. "I don't miss a thing about New York, Merry."

"Not the theaters? Not the stores?"

"I prefer the stars in this big old sky to the ones I've seen on the stage. And I don't need to dress up when I write, and that's the part of my career I've really loved—not the glamour. I thought I'd miss that, but I don't."

"That might change."

"I was pretty successful at changing my life once, Merry. I could do it again."

"And you'd like Jake to be part of that change?"

Laurie thought about Jake's temper, his blustering. She thought about his gentleness with his kids, his fear at losing them or their love; she thought about the rough calluses on his fingers that felt like fine velvet against her skin. She thought about his Olympian god body and his Montana blue-sky eyes. And she thought about his kisses, and how his voice and their conversations warmed her insides.

"You know what, Merry? I want to marry him."

Laurie surprised herself at the strangeness of the words. She hadn't given marriage much more than a moment's thought in thirty-two years, so why, she wondered, was she doing it now? The answer was simple. She'd fallen in love.

"Marriage. Oh, my."

"Don't say it that way, Merry. This house isn't a home—not yet. It needs kids, a family, and love. You've said that over and over. I didn't think that was necessary, but now I do. I've spent every night I've been here looking out that window, wishing I could be part of what's going on in that cabin. I write love stories with happily-ever-after endings. I want what's in my books, Merry. I want what I've never had. And I want Jake."

"Jake McAllister swore a long time ago he'd never marry again. I just don't know if that can be changed."

"I changed my life, Merry. I'll change his, too. My mother told me all I had to do was believe. And I do. I do believe, and if you believe hard enough, and have faith, your wishes come true."

Laurie pushed herself off of the couch and planted a kiss on Merry's plump cranberry cheek. "I've got work to do, Merry. No more sitting around and moping for me. I've got a book to write, and Jake McAllister to catch." She winked and ran halfway up the stairs, then stopped and turned back to Merry. "Think you can whip up a pot roast for dinner tonight? I know it's not Sunday, but it sounds awfully good."

"If that's what you wish for, child."

"Thanks, Merry. Don't know what I'd ever do without you."

Merry's eyes twinkled at Laurie's words, and when the redhead disappeared from sight, Merry looked toward the ceiling and smiled. "Did you hear that, Nicky. She believes. She really and truly believes."

Laurie's eyelids grew heavy as the glowing numbers on the clock changed to 3:30. She'd lain awake for hours thinking of Jake, his kiss, the strong, unrelenting desire she felt for him. He felt the same for her. She knew it, felt it, sensed it, but there was one major difference. Laurie was at peace with the feeling; Jake was actively, strategically doing battle.

The tick of the pendulum on the wall clock downstairs vibrated through the studs, echoing behind her headboard, and in her ears. The wind outside rustled the leaves of the trees and shrubs, scratching against the wood paneling of the house. In the distance, a lone coyote cried, and on the night stand, the digital clock clicked to 3:31.

She forced herself to close her eyes, to push thoughts of Jake from her mind. Even with all his contradictions, thoughts of Jake were so much sweeter than the thoughts she'd been plagued with, haunted by, in New York. She closed her eyes and snuggled into the downy comfort of her pillow, praying that pleasant, wonderful dreams would soon envelop her.

And then she heard a slow, muffled grind. Her eyes popped open and she stared into the darkness of her room. She held her breath, quiet, listening. It came again, that unmistakable grating noise she knew instinctively was the old brass knob at the front door. Had she forgotten to lock one of the doors? Had she felt so secure in Bunch Gulch that she'd let that routine slip her mind? Had she been thinking of Jake to the exclusion of everything else? Or had Merry come back? She said she'd be visiting friends and would return in the morning, but maybe she'd changed her mind.

She heard the grinding noise again, and gripped the edge of the comforter, unconsciously wringing the fabric in tightened, white-knuckled fingers.

"Please Lord," she prayed in silence, "let it be Merry."

The latch clicked, and she heard the whispery creak of antique hinges as the heavy oak door opened those first few inches.

She tried to slow her erratic breathing, tried to calm the fast beat of her heart, tried to control the panic that raced through her brain, but for the first time in weeks the fear she'd known in New York returned, with a vengeance, and all she wanted to do was run away. But tonight, there was no place left to run.

Somehow she forced her fingers from the comforter and reached out for the phone beside her bed, and in the dim moonlight that cast eerie shadows across the room, she steadied her fingers enough to press the numbers.

One ring.

Two.

Please, please answer.

Three rings.

Four.

Dammit Jake! Where are you?

Five.

She heard light footsteps on the stairs. Someone was coming to her room, someone who didn't want her to know. Someone who wanted to be silent and stealthy.

Six rings.

She slid her fingers under the edge of the mattress and pulled out the automatic she'd purchased for protection. She knew how to use it. She'd taken lessons, and practiced, and she was a deadly shot. But could she really use it?

She heard the rattling fumble of the phone on the other end. The receiver had been picked up, dropped, lifted again.

"Hello."

"Jake." Her voice was a whispered plea. "He's here."

"Oh, God!"

The receiver clanked loudly in her ear as if it had been dropped on the floor, crashing against the wooden planks. She listened, heard the sound of a slamming door, then silence.

Except for the footsteps on the stairs.

She released the safety and tightened her grip on the cold steel. Slowly, quietly, she hung up the phone, gripped the weapon in front of her with both hands, aiming, steady and sure, at the door.

Someone was on the eighth step. She recognized the distinctive squeak.

She was too frightened to hide, too afraid to move. She felt her heart thundering in her chest, felt her muscles stiffening. How could he have found her? she wondered. Why was he doing this to her?

He was in the hallway. He was coming toward her. She heard the intruder just outside the door. She could hear breathing. Heavy. Deep. And menacing.

"I love you, Laurie," he whispered, but the words pounded through her ears like the thundering of canons.

Every muscle in her body shook. Her lips quivered, but she kept her elbows locked, kept the gun pointed at the door.

"I know you can hear me Laurie. Why don't you answer? Are you frightened? Are you holding the gun you bought?"

Oh, God. He knows.

"Why are you afraid of me, Laurie? I'm not coming in. Not tonight. But I'm leaving a present. A gift to show you just how much I care."

She heard the distinct brush of denim against denim, the rustle of leather, as if he were bending down, and she knew what he was doing. He was leaving a yellow rose at her door.

"I love you Laurie," he whispered. "And soon— very soon, you'll be mine."

Footsteps, loud and fast, moving away from the door. Down the hall, down the stairs, through the living room.

Gravel crunched in the drive.

Then, all was silent.

She lowered the gun to her lap, closed her eyes and listened.

The front door slammed again.

Her head shot up, eyes wide, horrified. *Oh, God. Don't come back. Please. Leave me alone.*

Again, she aimed the gun at the door. Again she heard footsteps on the stairs, the creak, then pounding on her bedroom door.

"Laurie!"

The knob turned.

"Get away! I have a gun!" she screamed.

"Laurie! Put the gun down. It's me. It's Jake. Unlock the door."

"Jake?" Her voice wavered.

"I'm here, Laurie. Put the gun down."

Slowly, with shaking hands, she lowered the

gun, fastened the safety, and lay it on the bed.

Her body ached from shock and fear, but she flung back the covers and raced to the door. Somehow she managed to turn the old brass skeleton key she'd forgotten she'd used before climbing into bed.

She threw open the door and Jake stood before her, a bouquet of long-stemmed yellow roses clutched in his hands.

She screamed.

The flowers fell from Jake's fingers, and he caught her, pulling her into his embrace, before she could scream again. "It's all right, Laurie. I'm here. I'm here."

She wept against the strength of his chest, her fingernails digging into the flesh of his arms. And then he picked her up, cradling her like a baby, and carried her to the bed, holding her tight, cuddling her close as he sat on the edge.

Tenderly, he smoothed tear-dampened curls from her temples, soothing her nerves, caressing away her fright. "Does he always leave roses?"

She only nodded, burying her head deeper into his protective comfort.

"I didn't see anyone," he stated, and reached for the phone. "I'm going to call the sheriff. Maybe the guy left fingerprints or something."

"It won't do any good." She shook her head. "He's never left fingerprints. Only roses, and messages."

"He's got to slip up sometime, Laurie."

"He won't. I know it." She clutched him tighter. "He's gone. Please," she begged, "don't leave me."

Gently, he rubbed his hands over the lengths of her arms, desperately trying to return some warmth to her body, but still she continued to shake, still she continued to fear for her life, and she didn't want to be alone, and vulnerable.

Jake stood, pulling her tightly against him, never letting go as he steadied her on her feet at his side. He wove his fingers through hers. "I didn't lock the door behind me. Come on. Let's make sure it's safe downstairs."

She looked into his eyes for reassurance, then back to the bed. "Take my gun."

He shook his head. "We don't need it, Laurie."

She thought about arguing, but changed her mind. Somehow, she felt safe at his side, the first time she'd really felt safe in years.

Standing in the doorway, he peered down the hall, clutching Laurie's fingers as he looked at the row of closed doors. "You okay?" he asked, and when she nodded, he stepped into the open, and down the stairs.

The wind gently played with the lace panels covering the glass panes of the front door which stood open, like an invitation for visitors, welcome or not. Jake closed the door and turned the lock. "Tomorrow I'm installing deadbolts," he said. "And chains. Maybe you should get an alarm system."

She pulled her hand from his and combed her fingers through her hair. She looked into his face with tear-filled eyes. "I had all that in New York and I felt like a prisoner. I don't want to live that way again."

He smiled with a warm gentleness, and wrapped an arm around her shoulder. "Deadbolts for sure. And chains. We'll discuss the alarm system tomorrow."

He examined each window, turned on lights in bathrooms and pantry and closets, and ended in the kitchen, the door wide open, just as it had been when Sue Ellen sauntered in.

"How about some coffee?" he asked, pulling out a chair at the table and insisting Laurie sit down as he closed and locked the door.

"There's wine in the pantry, and glasses in the hutch."

"I don't normally drink this early in the morning." His voice had lightened with a tinge of laughter.

"I don't usually have intruders at four a.m., either. Fix yourself some coffee if you'd like, but I'll polish off the wine. Might as well give me the whole bottle."

"Don't think so, Red. I've seen drunks before, and it ain't a pretty sight."

"I'm not concerned about being pretty right now."

Jake watched Laurie's head sink into her folded arms which rested on the table, grabbed the phone, and stabbed the buttons.

"You calling the sheriff?" Laurie mumbled, never raising her head.

"Uh-huh. Might be awhile before he gets here."

"Won't do any good."

Jake ignored her as he waited for an answer, gave all the information, hung up, and began to pace.

"You going to get me that wine?" Laurie asked.

"After you talk to the sheriff."

He paced some more. He rubbed Laurie's shoulders. He held her when tears began to pour from her eyes, and he opened the kitchen door and welcomed the deputy when he heard gravel crunch in the drive and saw the headlights.

"I already called New York," the deputy advised Laurie and Jake when he stepped into the kitchen, clipboard in hand. "They've got a thick file of reports, but no leads. No fingerprints—"

"I told you that," Laurie interrupted. "There's nothing to go on. I don't think anyone ever believed me."

"They believed you, Miz Langtry. But this guy's no different than half the other stalkers people are bothered by. They're crazy, but they're smart."

He pulled a pen from his pocket. "Feel like telling me what happened tonight?"

Laurie closed her eyes and started at the beginning, at the moment she heard the grind of the doorknob. Her voice wobbled and cracked, and she stumbled a time or two when she told the deputy what the stalker had said, when she told him about the yellow roses.

"You need to be more careful about locking those doors, Miz Langtry," the deputy stated, glancing up from his writing just long enough to survey the door. "You need better locks."

"I'm putting deadbolts on tomorrow," Jake said, wrapping an arm around Laurie when it looked like she might collapse and slip from the chair.

"We'll make a point of checking the area. We don't spend much time at this end of the valley, but I'll talk to the sergeant about switching the patrols around, see if we can find this guy. Town's too small to hide a stranger."

"You won't find him," Laurie insisted. "But I appreciate you trying."

"You gonna check for fingerprints?" Jake asked.

The deputy shook his head. "Not tonight. We'll send somebody out tomorrow when it's light to look around, give you some suggestions about security." He shrugged, tucked his clipboard under his arm and his pen into his shirt pocket. "I'll check out the florists. See if I can find out who bought yellow roses. But it's a crap shoot. Wish there was more we could do."

"It's okay," Laurie said, still sitting at the kitchen table, her fingers woven through the curls on top her head. "I know the routine." She bit her lower lip and sniffed back tears, wondering if she'd ever feel safe again. She had nowhere left to hide. He'd found her in the middle of nowhere— it was useless to try to run again.

Jake closed and locked the door behind the deputy. "You want that wine now?"

"More than ready."

He removed two long-stemmed crystal goblets from a cupboard, and for the first time since he'd come to her rescue over an hour before, she noticed he wore no shirt, no shoes. A baggy pair of gray sweat shorts, his only attire, hung loose about his hips. His legs were long and lean, with pronounced, heavy muscles in his thighs, the skin fair, as though it rarely saw the sun, and sprinkled with a light coating of curly blond hair. Slim hips and waist tapered upward to broad, muscular shoulders which she remembered so vividly, but were the perfect diversion right now. When he turned, she stared at the ripple of muscle at his stomach, at the taut, smooth, nearly hairless skin of his chest, and finally, found his eyes, cloaked in a fine gauze of embarrassment.

"Y'know, Red, you're the only woman who's ever stared at me that way."

"I like what I see," she said, her words wobbling, as tears flowed again.

"Go ahead and cry, Laurie. That and the wine's about the best thing for you right now."

He held the bottle before him, working the cork with his thumbs, the muscles of his arms flexing as he struggled to remove it from the bottle. The cork popped, and Jake beamed, his mustache twitching, as he filled her glass to the brim, and poured an inch in his. He was trying to lighten her mood, ease her tension, but he was failing. Tonight she felt nothing would work but total oblivion.

He stood behind her and gently kneaded her shoulders, her neck, trying to ease the tension as she drank the wine and tried to relax. "Have you ever seen the guy, Laurie?" he asked.

She nodded her head, applying her fingers to her temples and massaging the throbbing that had started moments before. "Once. In the winter," she said, balancing her elbows on the table to support her heavy head. "He was tall and slender. He was all in black—ice skates, slacks, his leather jacket and gloves. And a ski mask. That's what I see in my dreams. Always that ski mask, and his eyes. I couldn't see his face, only his eyes, and his smile. I knew he was mad even before he spoke."

"How long's this been going on?"

"A year and a half. It was just every few months in the beginning, then it became more frequent. Things showed up at work, were sent to my publisher. I'd be in a restaurant and he'd have the roses delivered to me. And then he found out where I lived. That's why I left. I got scared. I felt watched all the time." She began to sob again, uncontrollable tears flowing down her face. "I couldn't take it anymore."

Jake poured more wine into her empty glass, as her tension eased, as her muscles loosened under his rhythmic touch.

"I hired a bodyguard who followed me every-

where. Into stores, theaters. He sat just outside my
office at home while I worked, and slept in my
extra bedroom. He ate in my kitchen, even checked
under my bed and in the closets every time I went
back to the flat. It's been hell, Jake. Absolute hell.''

She took another gulp of the chardonnay. Her
body relaxed as Jake rubbed her shoulders, her
arms. He tenderly massaged her temples with the
light touch of his fingertips. She closed her eyes
and felt the warm tingle flowing through her body,
partially from the wine, partially from Jake's pul-
sating but tender caress.

"I thought I'd be safe here," she continued, her
words slightly slurred. "I thought I could escape.
But now I know I can't. I might as well have stayed
in New York."

She put her hand on Jake's as he lifted the bottle
to again fill her glass. His fingers were strong,
long, and when he set the bottle down, she drew
his hand to her lips, kissing his fingertips. They
were callused and rough, but she'd never felt anything so perfect.

He took control now, drawing his fingers along
the fine line of her jaw, to the soft skin of her neck.
She trembled at his touch, and he knelt down behind her, wrapping his arms around her chest,
resting his beard-roughened cheek against hers.

"I won't let him hurt you, Laurie," he whispered, kissing her ear, sending a new sensation
through every pore, every nerve. "That's a promise."

"I wish he'd disappear. I wish he'd end up in
prison, on a chain gang, pounding rocks for the
rest of his life." She giggled. "Can't you see him
Jake, all dressed in stripes with a ball and chain
around his leg?"

The wine had gone to her head. She sensed it, felt every muscle relax to the point of being useless. Jake scooped her up from the chair and carried her through the kitchen, up the stairs, and into her room. He kicked the bedroom door closed, laid her down on the bed, and pulled the comforter up to her chin.

"Don't leave me, Jake."

"I won't. Try to sleep."

"I can't. It's too hot."

Jake opened the windows, letting in the freshness of early morning.

"My head's spinning, Jake. Lay down beside me. Hold me."

Through the haze of the wine, she watched the flicker of doubt on his face, and knew in her heart what she wanted, knew without a doubt that it wasn't the alcohol making her say those words. She wanted and needed him near her, wanted and needed to hide within the strong barrier of his arms. He cared for her, maybe not enough to commit to a lifetime, but enough to be at her side, comforting her, when she needed him the most.

Slowly, he moved toward the bed. She sat up and pushed the comforter away, kneeling now, facing him, watching the heavy rise and fall of his chest with each labored breath.

She wanted him. Her hands slowly glided over her breasts, her stomach, enticing him, making him want her. She gripped the hem of her nightshirt and gradually, seductively, pulled it over her head, and dropped it to the floor.

He watched her, not moving, not making a sound, totally mesmerized by her spell. She stretched out her arms, beckoning him to her with the come-hither curl of her fingers, inviting him, tempting him, to sample her warmth.

The first traces of morning light glinted into the room and over her body and she saw him watching the play of light, his gaze roaming across her breasts, to her stomach, to the hidden place between her legs. She wanted him desperately and he was taking too much time.

Slowly, he loosened the tie at his waist and his shorts fell to the floor. He was taking control now, she sensed it, and she didn't care if he wanted to dominate her forever, just as long as he hurried now. He reached out then, touching the tips of her fingers, tracing circles in her palms, slowly, slowly. She trembled and fought to breathe.

The wait was painful. She throbbed uncontrollably at the sight of his body, at the warmth and longing in his eyes. He casually inched his fingers and hands up the lengths of her arms, teasing her, taunting her, every inch of her skin sensitive to his touch.

His rough fingers slid over the soft flesh of her breasts, the calluses like velvet as they gently stroked and caressed, and at last brushed over her nipples until they pebbled, hard, needing so much to be kissed.

She dug her fingers into his hair when his tongue set her breast on fire. She pulled him closer, forgetting everything in life but the warmth of his mouth, the heat coursing through her body, till the center of her being swelled and throbbed with need.

She felt the shift on the bed, felt the soft coating of hair on his thigh brushing against her leg as he moved closer, sliding one hand over her thigh, over her hip, and circling her waist as he pressed her into the softness of the bed. His hands cupped her cheeks, holding her close, and she saw a mixture of confusion and desire in the blue pools of his eyes.

And when she could wait no longer, when she wanted to take control, his mouth covered hers, slowly parting her lips, searching for what had once been sampled in anger and frustration, but never fully tasted. Their tongues met and explored, and time no longer mattered. She was lost in a whirlpool of sensations, drowning in a torrent of desire.

His hand trailed the length of her, lingering for a moment over the hollow of her stomach. She arched her back at his touch, and with an instinct as old as time, opened herself to the gentle, probing warmth of his fingers. She clutched his arms and moaned, pulling him over her, her strength immeasurable, his body weightless, fluid. The time would come to touch him, to hold him, to explore every part of his body, but not now. This was her moment, this was her time to accept his gifts. She wrapped her legs around him, and as she gave herself up to the power of his kiss, he buried himself deep inside her warmth.

Breathing heavily, he withdrew, and slowly he reentered, beginning a smooth, skillful rhythm, like a master violinist drawing his bow back and forth over the strings of his Stradivarius, building momentum as the music crescendoed to a feverish pitch.

She writhed beneath him, gasping, clutching at his arms, at the brass rails of the headboard, at the sheets at her sides, until he took hold of her wrists and imprisoned them above her head. She was his at that moment, totally and completely, trapped in a rush of wonder and exploration.

Kissing away the perspiration at her temples, he lowered his hot and slick body until it melded with hers, and she looked into eyes that captured her heart just as surely as his hands had captured her wrists.

"I love you, Jake," she whispered.

And he drove deep, straight for her heart, and wrapped her in an embrace she hoped would never, ever end.

Laurie woke to the warmth of morning sunlight shining directly through her window and into her eyes, and to the heat of Jake's glorious brawn melded against her skin. He casually stroked her stomach in slow, easy circles, as he rested at her side. "Good morning," he said with a wink.

Her head throbbed, and she pressed the heels of her hands to her temples, burying her fingers into her hair as if pressure would ease the dizzying ache. "I'm not too sure, but I think I might have imbibed a bit too much."

His mustache twitched. "Wine, or me?"

"Wine—I'm positive." She eased her hands from her head and rolled to her side. "You're a much nicer intoxicant, but ten times as addictive." Facing him now, she pushed the comforter low, caressing the hard, flat planes of his belly, and fondly traced the jagged three-inch scar at his hip, remembering the story he'd told her, as she'd drifted off to sleep, about his first and last tangle with a rodeo bull. Never before had she fallen asleep in the midst of such a well-told story. Never before had she slumbered so peacefully as she did in his arms.

He kissed her forehead, pressing his lips gently

to the bridge of her nose, to her eyes, settling at last on her lips, parting them gently with his tongue. Early morning, Laurie thought, had never tasted or felt so good.

Other thoughts of early morning suddenly returned. She kicked the covers off her legs and his, sat up, not the least embarrassed about her nakedness, and grabbed his ankle, pulling it onto her lap.

"What are you doing?" he asked, unable to hold back a laugh.

"Your feet. You ran over here without any shoes."

"Hell, Red! I ran over here almost buck naked."

Tenderly she stroked the soft soles of his feet, pink and plump like a baby's. "You've got cuts all over the bottom." She looked up and scolded. "Dammit, Jake. Why didn't you put shoes on?"

"I wasn't thinking about my feet," he fired back. "A madman was in your house. What would you have done if I'd called you for help? Fixed your hair? Put on makeup?"

"No, I would have done the same as you, only . . ." She dropped his ankle and shoved her fists into her hips. "I would have answered the phone a damn sight sooner. Where were you?"

"Outside."

"In the middle of the night?"

"I couldn't sleep. It's been a curse lately, and it's worse when the boys are gone."

She changed instantly from battleaxe to coquette, batting her eyes with a tempting, seductive air. "Did you sleep well with me?"

"Not a wink. You snore."

She gently pounded a fist into his chest. "I do not!"

He nodded. "Like a fog horn." He grabbed her

wrist and yanked her over his chest, into his embrace, capturing her mouth and kissing her long and hard and deep, wiping away all pretense of righteous indignation. Was he losing his heart? she wondered. Did he feel the same need and desire and want? Did he feel anything other than lust? She prayed that he did, and prayed that what they had shared during the night, what they were sharing now, would last.

"You tempt me too much, woman." He laughed, rolling her onto her back and straddling her thighs. "Great line, huh? Picked it up from that book of yours."

"I hope you found other redeeming qualities in it, too."

"I rather liked the way they devoured that platter of roasted chicken, right smack in the middle of his bed. Which reminds me . . ." He kissed her lips, hard and fast, swung his legs over the side of the bed, and pulled on his shorts. "I'm starved. Want some breakfast?"

"I don't think I've got the strength to get out of bed."

"Then don't. Stay put right where you are and I'll rummage."

Laurie watched him walk out of the bedroom, a study in contrasts—the fair skin of his legs against the bronzed tan of his back and arms, his slim hips just a fraction of the width of his cow-lifting shoulders. She wanted him as surely as she wanted the sun to continue to rise and set in her life.

She inched her way out of bed, grabbed her Yosemite Sam nightshirt from the floor, and forced her aching legs to propel her to the bathroom. She glanced in the mirror and moaned. She looked a sight, her hair springing more unruly than ever at the top of her head, her eyes puffy, dark circles, like smudges of coal, sweeping under her lower lashes. Grabbing her toothbrush, she scrubbed away the taste of wine and morning, but not the lingering reminders of Jake's mouth and tongue and flesh. Those were forever embedded in her mind.

After splashing cold water on her face, she dabbed on moisturizer, slipped the shirt back over her head, and hoped to be back in bed before Jake returned.

But he was sitting atop the flowery chintz comforter in the middle of her king-sized bed, a lacquered tray filled with an assortment of goodies beside him. "I didn't see your housekeeper, but I have the strangest feeling she knows we're here. All of this," he said, sweeping an arm in the air over the tray, "was waiting when I got downstairs. Food's still hot, too. I'm beginning to think you were telling the truth about that genie."

He held the tray steady while Laurie crawled onto the bed. "You think she knew I spent the night in your bedroom?"

"More than likely." Laurie groaned. What would Merry think? she wondered. She tucked her shirt between her as she sat cross-legged facing Jake. "I've never known a woman like Merry. She seems to know what I'm going to think and do long before I know myself. It's scary."

"So, you're trying to tell me she thinks last night was destined to happen?"

"The you and me part," Laurie nodded. "I don't think she had an inkling about the stalker."

"Personally, I'd like to forget about him, at least this morning. This afternoon we'll deal with dead-bolts and alarm systems."

Laurie's hand shot out and covered Jake's mouth. "Hush! You said we could talk about that later, so please, let's skip it for now. At least the alarm system. I'd feel like a prisoner."

"You need protection."

"What I need is food." Laurie ignored his scowl, and effectively dropped the subject, lifting the tray from Jake's lap and setting it between them. "Let's see what Merry's prepared this morning."

"Not exactly roast chicken." He handed a blue pottery mug to Laurie. "How about hot cocoa and marshmallows?"

"Mmm. The drink of the gods." Laurie sniffed the heavenly aroma, as steam rose above her like a halo. She sipped the chocolate, and lifted a cinnamon and raisin bagel, slathered with cream cheese, crushed pineapple, and pecans, and held it out for Jake. "Give this a try."

He touched her wrist, entwining his hand around hers, and guided it to his lips. "A man could get used to this, you know." He took a bite, and she raised up on her knees, leaning toward Jake to sample the other side.

"Do you smell bacon?" she asked.

"Under here." Jake lifted a blue linen napkin from a white china plate layered with curly bacon and juicy sausage links. He snapped a slice of bacon in half and waved it under Laurie's nose. "Smells good. Care for a piece?"

She nodded and opened her mouth, graciously accepting his offering.

"Tell me about your TV and radio jobs," Jake asked, licking the salty, smoky grease from his fingers before flicking open and using a pink linen napkin formed in the shape of a rose.

"The TV show was sort of a fluke." She cupped

her hands around the mug and sipped cocoa, remembering that day long ago. "*My Captain* had been adapted for television, and the studio asked me to do some talk show promos the week it was going to air. It all seems so unreal now. I was nervous the first two shows I did, but by the time I did *America Today* I was feeling like a pro. Everything went perfectly, at least that's what the producer told me. A few weeks later I had lunch with her and she asked if I'd be interested in doing a segment a few times a week. They were looking for a gossip columnist. Of course, I didn't fit that bill, but they said they'd change the format if I'd consider it. I didn't have a clue what I could do, but we hashed out ideas, and within just a few weeks I was dishing out advice for the lovelorn."

"You still like dishing out advice?" he asked, stretching out on his side, his head propped up on his fist, and Laurie was leery of the sudden change in topic, and cautious in how she answered.

"Only when I have a good answer, only when I think I can help."

"Like you're doing with Meg and Kurt?"

"Meg asked for advice, I didn't volunteer." She felt an argument coming on, and she wasn't prepared.

"You enjoy meddling in peoples' lives, don't you? It's sort of like writing a novel, maneuvering your characters around to suit your whims."

Laurie took a deep, cleansing breath, fighting back anger, yet wondered why she should hold it in when every word he spoke called for a defensive attack. Somehow, she forced an innocent smile. "I am what I am, Jake. A writer. A fairy godmother who makes wishes come true. A woman who's honest—" She picked up a sausage. "And open—"

She put it between her lips, circled it with her tongue, slowly, very, very slowly, and pulled it out again, savoring the hot, spicy taste.

Bit by bit by bit.

"And very attracted to the man in her bed."

Jake grabbed her wrist. "Don't do that, Red."

Her eyes widened in feigned innocence. "Don't do what?"

"Slide that sausage in and out of your mouth like—like . . ." He dropped her wrist and flopped back on the bed, his hands clasped behind his neck, staring up at the ceiling. "Just don't do it, okay?"

Laurie crept toward him on hands and knees, and looked directly into his befuddled and bewildered eyes. "Sorry," she cooed. But she wasn't. She'd known exactly what she was doing. She knew by the way his chest rose and fell, hard and labored, knew by the way he adjusted the uncomfortable fit of his shorts, knew by the way he averted his gaze that she'd disturbed his peace, and thwarted a fight.

"So, did you enjoy it?" he muttered, and she had no idea whatsoever what he was talking about.

"If you mean the sausage," she said as she straddled his hips, wiggling, adjusting herself against his body, "it was delicious."

He rolled his eyes. "The job on TV."

She shrugged, then braced her hands against his chest, moving them slowly upward till they touched, and kneaded, the tightened muscles around his neck. "My book sales soared. Two more were optioned for TV. I liked the money, but

I didn't like sitting in front of the camera, or giving up my privacy."

"What about the radio show?"

At that she could smile for real. "It was a kick. I never could understand why people would call *me*, Laurie Langtry, queen of the high school dropouts, and ask for advice about their love life. It's sort of scary helping out strangers, never knowing who you're talking to or how they might react. I tried to keep it light, we even had a disclaimer saying I wasn't a professional."

"You think Rush Limbaugh has credentials to do what he does?"

Laurie's fingers tightened, her eyes and mouth scrunched into a sneer. "I prefer the subject of disclaimers to Rush Limbaugh, thank you."

He grinned.

She wiggled.

And Jake squirmed.

She sat up again and reached for a bagel, offering him a bite as he attempted to calmly lay beneath her straddled legs.

"As I was saying, I had a disclaimer because I didn't want people with serious problems thinking I could help them. If someone called and sounded really distressed, I didn't get the call. My staff screened everything thoroughly, but . . ." Her smile disappeared as she recalled the conversation that changed her life. "One call got through that never should have."

Laurie put the bagel back on the tray and moved away from Jake, sitting on the edge of the bed, her arms clutching her stomach, her hands shaking.

Jake was behind her immediately, pulling her between his thighs for comfort and nothing more. He covered her hands with his, pulling her close.

"The stalker?" he asked, his voice little more than a whisper in her ear.

"I don't know for sure. It was some guy who wanted to know how he could get closer to the woman he loved. He told me he was shy, and afraid he wouldn't be good enough. She was rich and sophisticated, he said, and he was a laborer. He was afraid she'd laugh at him."

"What did you tell him?"

"To give her a gift. He had a heavy accent, like he was from Texas, and all I could think of was yellow roses."

A tear slid down Laurie's cheek and Jake caressed it away.

"I was in Central Park the next day, watching the skaters. It was winter, and the snow was just starting to fall, so I didn't think anything about it when a man skated up to me in a ski mask. But then he handed me a yellow rose. And ... well, I told you before what he said." She pulled one hand loose from Jake's comforting grasp and wiped her eyes. "I thought it would stop, but it didn't. My writing's suffered. I didn't renew my TV or my radio contracts. All I wanted to do was run away and leave him and everything else behind."

"You did the right thing. And I promise, Laurie, I won't let him hurt you."

"Don't promise, Jake. It's not something you have control over." She pushed out of his arms, away from the bed, and went to the window, brushed back the curtain, and stared across the valley where she'd once thought she'd be safe. "If he found me here," she explained, "he could find me anywhere."

Remaining on the edge of the bed, Jake's shoulders slumped, elbows resting on his widespread knees while his hands hung limp between. Laurie sensed his helplessness, a feeling she'd lived with for too long a time, and wished it hadn't become a part of his life, too. "Thank you for being here for me."

He raised his head, slowly smiling. "Any time, Red."

One moment passed, and another, and finally he moved, standing behind her, absently caressing the flesh of her arms in slow, circular motions, following her gaze out the window. "Think I could interest you in doing something fun and exciting with me today?"

A touch of humor filled his voice, light and distracting. If only Jake knew the power of his words, that they gave her more strength and comfort than a million bodyguards. "And just what is it you have in mind, Mr. McAllister?"

"I need to work on my pump. Care to help?"

Laurie stifled a laugh, wanting to tell him there was nothing the least bit wrong with his pump, that it had worked very well in the wee hours of the morning, but she bit her lip and held back her words. Somehow she managed to turn around in his arms and keep a straight face when she looked into his eyes. "Thanks for asking, but I already have plans."

"Plans or no plans, I think you should stick with me."

"Wish I could, but I promised Meg I'd meet with her and Mrs. Adams about the Fourth of July party. You could join us."

He scratched the back of his head and appeared to give her words some thought, then slowly shook his head. "Think I'll skip the visit with Mrs. Adams."

She had hoped he'd stay by her side, for more reasons than just protection. She wanted him desperately, but it was obvious their morning, and their lovemaking, was over. She'd offered herself to him so easily. She'd given all she had—her heart and her body—without asking anything in return, and now he was going to leave. Could she or should she have expected more?

Weaving his fingers into hers, he drew her knuckles to his stubbled cheek, and slowly, tenderly, kissed her freckle-coated skin. "You going to Meg's right away?"

"As soon as I change."

"Well, Red," he said slowly, thoughtfully. He slid his fingers across her cheek to cup her chin, tilting her face. "I've gotta get those deadbolts in town. Might as well keep you company, at least as far as Meg's."

Her heart rejoiced once again. He wasn't going to leave her after all. "I've got to shower first." Her next thought was crazy, but she was going to ask anyway. "Care to join me?"

He shook his head, and she knew she'd hoped for far too much. But at least his eyes lit with longing when he told her no. His thumb gently caressed her lips, and he contemplated them, as if he wanted to kiss her once again. "You'd never get to Meg's if I climbed into the water with you."

His chest rose and fell heavily while she backed away from him, and at that very moment, she knew she'd offer herself again and again and again, asking nothing in return, until he was ready to accept all she had to give.

* * *

What had he done? Jake wondered, as he sat outside her bathroom door listening to the water flow over the pixie who'd lain in his arms just hours before.

How many times had he told himself he didn't want to get attached, didn't want to fall under her spell? But his iron will had been useless against her early that morning when she'd knelt on her bed and seduced him with her smile, her fears, and with every ounce of her petite little body.

He had to pull away from her before it was too late—for both of them. She'd already said she loved him—he'd heard the words much too clearly, escaping quietly from her lips just shortly before he lost all control and delved deeply into that body of hers that had been all too willing to accept him. But those words had to be a mistake, spoken in the middle of the best time he'd ever had with a woman. He remembered each moment. He'd had a good time, a great time, but it wasn't going to happen again. There was too much at stake: Laurie's heart, his heart, his boys' hearts. She'd probably hate him when he told her he didn't want her in his bed again. Hell, he was going to hate himself. But he had to do it—and soon.

10

"I know it's less than a week away, Mrs. Adams," Meghan stressed to the blue-haired matron in a polyester double-knit pantsuit left over from the seventies. "But again I'd like to suggest we do something a little different."

"Nonsense, Meghan," Mrs. Adams stated with her nose slightly in the air. "I've lived in this town well over half a century and the Fourth of July party is a ritual. It just wouldn't be right to make any changes."

Laurie had listened to Mrs. Adams' imperialistic nonsense far too long. It was time she did what Meghan had wanted—interfere. "Change is good, Meg. What did you have in mind?" Mrs. Adams jerked her head around at the intrusion, pursed her lips, and glared.

"Not a lot," Meghan said sweetly. "The music, maybe some of the games for the kids."

"Absolutely not." Mrs. Adams' back stiffened as she glared from Laurie to Meg. "Bert Ramsey's been bringing his stereo and record collection for the last forty years. His feelings would be hurt if we did something else. As for the kids, it's sack races and apple bobbing—period."

"Those things are fine," Meghan said, her voice

low and sweet and not the least bit ruffled, "but I think we should expend a little more money this year, put up a volleyball net, something the kids can enjoy on the Fourth and all year, too."

"Yeah," Jacob piped in, peeking his head around the corner, obviously tired of being relegated to a quiet spot in front of the TV with his brothers. "We like volleyball *and* softball."

"Young man," Mrs. Adams snapped. "Children should never, ever interrupt their elders. Now," she shooed him away with a wave of her hand, "go back where you belong."

Instructions given, Mrs. Adams ignored the child, fully expecting him to obey, but when she turned away and took a sip of tea, Jacob stuck out his tongue and wagged his finger at the brick wall of Mrs. Adams' back.

Laurie tried not to laugh, and forced herself not to invite Jacob to sit beside her and join in the planning session. Instead, she winked at the boy and nodded toward the door, gently urging him out of the room.

"As I was saying, Mrs. Adams," Meghan began again, gracefully sitting on the couch, legs crossed ladylike with her hands on her knees, while her Birkenstock-covered foot wagged in the air, her only sign of impatience and frustration. "We have very little for the children, and nothing for the teenagers. They'd like to dance to some rock and roll. I'd like some oldies."

"Wouldn't the twist be fun?" Laurie added, doing her best Chubby Checker routine from her sitting position on the couch, ignoring Mrs. Adams' frown.

"I'm sorry, Meghan. It's already planned and we're not changing a thing." Mrs. Adams turned toward Laurie, sizing her up and down for at least the fifth time in an hour. "And we don't need you interfering and causing trouble."

Laurie smiled sweetly, innocently, trying to follow Meghan's lead, but failed miserably when she looked at the elderly woman who regarded her with so much undeserved contempt. "I've been interfering in things since the day I was born, Mrs. Adams. Surely you don't expect me to sit back and be quiet now?"

"I most surely do. So does Mrs. Tenney. Isn't that right?" She looked at her forgotten and overlooked friend for confirmation.

"Well," Mrs. Tenney added, fidgeting with the handle of the black patent leather purse she clutched in her purple-pantsuited lap. "It would be rather lovely to hear some big band. I haven't done the jitterbug in years."

"Nonsense!" Mrs. Adams interrupted. "You can barely walk let alone do the jitterbug. Besides, you're serving punch."

Laurie leaned forward, resting her folded arms on her knees, wishing Mrs. Adams would adopt a bit of Mrs. Tenney's grace and charm. "Most people prefer to serve their own punch, Mrs. Adams, and I bet there'd be half a dozen men at the party who'd love to give Mrs. Tenney a shoulder to lean on, or a hand to hold, if she wanted to give the jitterbug a try. What about you?" She reached out and put a friendly hand on Mrs. Adams' knee. "What dance would you like to do?"

Mrs. Adams' head didn't move, only her eyes, and Laurie could almost sense an ounce of bitterness draining out of the woman as she looked at the hand on her knee. "I haven't danced since Mr.

Adams passed on and that's been a good twenty years ago."

"I've seen Bert Ramsey watching you at church," Meghan commented as she filled the dainty flower- and vine-painted china cups with another round of tea. "If I'm not mistaken, I think he'd like to get out from behind that old stereo of his and dance—with you."

"Bert Ramsey's as old as the hills and he needs a new set of dentures." Mrs. Adams lifted her cup and took a sip, leaving a thick smear of cherry red lipstick on the china. "And," she added, "I'm not the least bit interested."

Laurie tossed a conspiratorial wink at Meg. "Of course you're not. Maybe he does enjoy spinning those old records every year and standing back and watching all the fun." Laurie's shoulders theatrically sagged and she let out a long, deep sigh. "Maybe we should just forget the idea of getting a DJ."

"I suppose you're right. He's expensive anyway," Meg added.

"Well," Mrs. Adams cleared her throat. "If you insist on having other entertainment, you can take the money out of the party fund." She relented, her pursed lips softening just a tad. "But none of that rap music. It's repetitious and annoying, not to mention violent. I've read stories about some of the rappers—they like to stir people up, cause trouble." She glanced at Laurie, eyed her up and down, frowning at the tight black leather skirt and matching black vest. "I just don't like it and I won't have it at *my* party."

"No rap, Mrs. Adams," Meghan said. "That's a promise."

"Very well, then." Mrs. Adams gripped Mrs.

Tenney's arm. "It's time to go Muriel."

Meg ushered the ladies to the door, and she and Laurie followed them onto the porch. "Thank you for coming," Meg said, while Laurie gripped the banister, prepared to offer assistance or catch either lady if they miscalculated their steps while wobbling down the stairs.

Mrs. Adams turned when she reached the end of the cobblestone walk. "Make sure your decorating gets done early, Meghan. I live in fear of something going wrong at these parties. So difficult to trust others."

"Don't worry, Mrs. Adams. Everything will be perfect." Meghan kept the smile on her face till the ladies were out of sight, and she and Laurie were safely inside. She shut the door, leaned against it, and sighed. "I've nicknamed her Attila the Hun. Pretty appropriate, don't you think?"

"Even Attila was conquered." Laurie slumped down in the couch and leaned her head into the overstuffed tweed. "She's old and lonely, and I'm bound and determined the same misery's not going to follow us. So, what's happening with Kurt?"

A smile fluttered across Meghan's lips. "He had breakfast with us this morning."

"Good start. And how did it go?"

"He wasn't a bit like he is in church. I've never seen him so nervous."

"And which do you prefer?"

"Nervous. Unsure. It makes him seem more human."

"Letting all his faults show, huh?"

"Oh, Laurie." A dreamy, faraway look captured Meghan's face. "He doesn't have any faults."

Meghan, Laurie decided, had fallen hopelessly in love over one simple breakfast, and for just a moment she wondered if she had done the right thing pushing the two together. Jake had put doubts in her mind, made her think her desire to help others was a simple case of meddling, sticking her nose where it didn't belong. For Meghan's sake, she fervently hoped he was wrong.

"So, what did he think of your designs?"

"He was surprised I could work something up so quickly when I had just a few ideas to work from. I have to admit, he preferred the pencil sketches of the fortress-type castles to the pastel, Sleeping Beauty ones."

"That's a man for you. Suppose he's right, though. I can't picture Jake's kids playing in anything pink."

Meghan laughed, then ventured off into never-neverland again. "He told me he could use someone with my talents in his business. Can you believe that? I told him that's the craziest thing I've ever heard. I'm an artist, not a building designer. Besides, I do okay selling my paintings at art shows, and I don't want to be confined to someone else's schedule."

"And how did he react?"

"He just smiled and asked me out to dinner next Sunday."

Laurie grinned, realization dawning that she'd been right, Jake wrong, and pushing the two together was a stroke of brilliance.

Behind her, Laurie heard the heavy stomp of a boot on the porch, the creek of the screen door, and her shoulders tensed, drawing up like a frightened cat. Would she ever get over her fear of unexpected sounds? She jerked around, and her shoulders sagged, relaxing when she saw Jake's familiar form in the doorway.

"You sure took your time getting back here," Meg said, catching the screen door before it had a chance to slam.

"Planned it that way. Figured I'd just be in the way while you were entertaining Mrs. Adams."

Jake shook his head and laughed. "I got in her way one too many times when I was a kid. No need dredging up the past now." Jake winked at Meg, then turned his heated gaze to Laurie. "Got the deadbolts." There wasn't anything sensual about his words, but as far as Laurie was concerned, he could have told her she was his sun and moon and stars. Looking at him standing in the middle of Meghan's living room, she was once again mesmerized by the man whose blond hair, long past due for a cut, curled over the collar of a faded blue workshirt. He was so very different from the men she'd grown accustomed to in the last few years. None of them warmed her with a smile, none of them teased her with the twitch of a droopy Wyatt Earp mustache, and none of them had Montana blue-sky eyes that could look straight into her emerald ones and easily read her betraying thoughts. Looking at Jake McAllister, she experienced a tremor in her chest that felt like Cupid had struck her heart dead center with one of his arrows, and she hoped one had been aimed in Jake's direction, too.

"Daddy!" The twins raced into the room and tackled Jake's legs, nearly toppling him to the floor, Jacob grabbed his dad's best Stetson and shoved it on his head, and she fell even more in love with the man when she saw his look of desire turn to a look of unquestioning devotion.

"These guys give you any trouble, Meg?"

"You know they never do." Meghan busied herself picking up tea cups. "Would you like some coffee?"

"Thanks, but no. Just wanted to check on the boys before Laurie and I head for home."

Laurie's breath caught in her throat again, and she wondered if anyone could see the heavy beat of her heart against her chest. *Home.* He'd said the word so easily, right along with *Laurie* and *I,* as if the three belonged together. The words sounded lasting, and loving, and they were words she wanted to carve in granite, or in a deed to the farmhouse that she wished she could share with the man who'd become so much a part of her life.

"Can we go home too, Dad?" Jacob asked, tugging on Jake's arm in an attempt to draw his unwavering attention away from Laurie.

"Not on your life," Meg chastised, as she tweaked Jacob's chin. "We're finger painting in Bible school tomorrow, and I'm sure you don't want to miss that."

Jacob looked up at his dad, his eyes begging for a reprieve. "I could miss it."

"No. Don't think so, son. I had to do it myself when I was your age."

"That doesn't make it right—or fun."

Jake gave his son that look, that tilt of his head, and Jacob shrugged. "Guess painting's okay. Sure not as much fun as chasing Sue Ellen, though."

Grabbing the child up into his arms, Jake hugged him tightly, and Laurie could sense his turmoil at leaving the boys behind. If he hadn't been so adamant about protecting her, he might have whisked his kids away from Meg's. It didn't seem right, or fair, for them to be separated, and she wondered, anew, how much Jake regretted her intrusion into their lives.

"It's only for a few more days," she heard Jake telling the boys as he hugged one after the other, trying to say goodbye amidst halfhearted explanations of why he couldn't drive them into town every day for Bible school.

Feeling like an eavesdropper, Laurie escaped into the kitchen, giving Meg a helping hand with the dishes before she, too, said her goodbyes, with a promise to Meg to come again the next day to add her ideas to the castle renderings.

Jake took Laurie's arm and led her down the steps, and, sitting side by side in the Jeep, they waved goodbye to Meghan and the boys, then rode home in near silence. Laurie knew something weighed heavily on his mind; she only hoped it was the boys' absence, and not her presence.

They reached the farmhouse, and while Laurie worked in her office, Jake changed the locks. It seemed so domestic, so right, and so very, very comfortable, but the sheriff's late afternoon visit made her remember why Jake was at her side, why he'd been with her during the night, and she prayed there was more to his attention than a friend offering protection.

"Thought I'd fix up that well this afternoon, too," Jake said after the sheriff left without offering any more reassurance than Laurie had gotten in New York. "Feel like keeping me company?"

For the rest of my life, she wanted to answer, but instead grabbed his hammer and smiled. "Lead the way."

Two hours later, when the scraps of barbed wire and many years' accumulation of thistles and weeds had been cleared from around the well, Laurie sat in the grass and watched Jake, his muscles refusing to tire the way hers had. The thicket

of roses and wildflowers was fast becoming her
favorite place on the property. It was beautiful, not
unlike the play of sinew in Jake's shoulders and
back, and intoxicating, like the smile he flashed
when he plopped down beside her, stretching out
in the cool carpet of green. "You like watching me
work?"

She nodded. She liked watching him sleeping,
playing, and thinking deeply, as he seemed to be
doing now, and she wished she could read his
mind.

Jake couldn't take his eyes off the subdued firebrand who sat next to him, picking one dandelion
after another, puckering those sweet and wonderful Betty Boop lips and blowing lightly, scattering
wishing dust into the air. She looked so perfect
sitting there in her too tight jeans, and too skimpy
purple crop top that clashed with her flaming red
curls. But the damned diamond studs in her ears
and that zillion-carat bracelet radiated in the sun,
and he knew she belonged in New York, that high-
caliber world of money and fame. She might like
the beauty of his valley, but she loved the lights of
Broadway, the theater, and opera. And she loved
her radio show, the power to make people feel
good, and coming up with ridiculous solutions to
God only knows what kind of romantic problems.
He could never ask her to stay. She'd tire of the
freezing winters, the long distances to town. She
might even tire of him, and the boys, and heaven
forbid, he didn't want to live through that ever
again.

All afternoon he'd been thinking of gentle ways
to tell her that making love had been a mistake.
He had to tell her, to end what never should have
started. But she was like the center of gravity, and

he was drawn toward her, unable to resist as he rested his head in her lap. For just one moment, he closed his eyes and breathed in her scent, the remains of raspberry soap and lotion, and a trace of some expensive perfume that he'd never be able to treat her with. He opened his eyes again, and watched her drop the dandelion stems, then felt her hands slide into his hair, her fingers unconsciously stroking his skin, setting his body ablaze, his breathing rapid, his brain a mass of confusion.

"Tell me about this marriage of yours that didn't work." Her words brought him back to reality, to the reason he didn't want to fall under her spell.

"Bad idea."

"I don't think so. Did you love her?"

This was territory he hadn't wanted to discuss with anyone, but with Laurie, everything seemed so easy. "I thought I loved her, but sometimes I'm not too sure. I was twenty-five, she was eighteen and just—well—too damn young. Only good thing to come out of the marriage was the boys."

"What happened?"

He stared at his hands as he picked the petals off a dark red rose he'd earlier tucked into his shirt pocket, letting them fall to his chest. "In the beginning we went out a lot, took some weekend trips. Things seemed to be fine as long as we were having fun, but that got old. I wanted to settle down and have kids. She kept saying she wasn't ready. I was persistent, and I got my way." He looked up into Laurie's eyes, fearing he might see a look of repulsion, but he saw only understanding. "I've never claimed to be perfect, Red."

"I've never thought you were."

He scowled.

She plastered her face with a grin.

"Everything went downhill between us when Jacob was born. She felt tied down, she felt I wasn't around enough to help her. When my folks left, there was no one to help me out around the ranch, and I didn't have time to help her with the house, or the baby. Maybe I wasn't supportive, maybe I didn't understand what she was going through. I don't know." He sat up then, and stared at the setting sun he could see through the thick forest of trees.

"I thought she would have a breakdown when the doctor told her she was pregnant with twins. I had to help her then—there wasn't any choice. I couldn't afford a housekeeper or a ranch hand, so I sold most of the livestock. I put the money aside, hoping I'd be able to use it someday to buy more stock. But nothing I did seemed to be enough, and then she left. Took her car, most of our money, and left the boys." He turned saddened eyes to Laurie. "Heard enough?"

She stared at the ground, deep in thought, thinking, he was positive, of another question to ask that might hurt him to answer.

"You said she never writes, but do you hear from her at all?"

He shook his head. "We talked a few times when I filed for divorce, but that's about it."

"What about the boys? Don't they miss her?"

"The twins don't know her at all, and Jacob remembers little. I guess it's for the best."

"I'm so sorry." Laurie put a hand on his beard-roughed cheek and he couldn't believe the overwhelming tenderness he felt for her at that moment. Her simple words, her gentle touch, soothing the pain of the long-buried wound she'd coaxed him to dig up.

"I never missed her," he offered, knowing the words might sound harsh and cruel, but he was glad he finally had someone to tell. "If she'd taken the boys, it would have been different. I would have chased her to hell and back for them. For me—well—she only hurt my pride."

"And soured you on women."

Yeah, dammit. Maybe Amy had planned it that way, he thought. Maybe it was her way of getting back at him for forcing her into a domestic life she hadn't wanted. "I don't claim to have been the best husband, and I can't blame everything on Amy. I wanted kids and she didn't. She made that plain from the very beginning and I wouldn't listen. Y'know," he began, taking a deep breath, "she gave me a hell of a lot more than I ever gave her."

"You're too hard on yourself. She could have stuck it out, tried to make things work, but she didn't. She deserted you, and she deserted her babies. That's the thing I can't understand. How could she just pack up and run away?"

Jake studied Laurie's face, the sadness in her eyes, and wondered if Amy's eyes had looked the same right before she left. "It's easy to run, Laurie. It's harder to stay and face things. You should know that better than anyone."

Her gaze dimmed, dropping to the hands folded in her lap. He hadn't meant to verbally slap her face, but it had happened. It was the same slap he'd wanted to mete out to Amy over and over again, but he'd never had the opportunity. Somehow, though, it didn't seem right hitting Laurie with those words.

He touched her cheek, gently sliding his fingers to her chin, tilting it up to see the dampness in her eyes. "That wasn't fair. The situations were different."

"It doesn't matter. Running away is running away." She stood, going to the old rock well, and leaned against the moss-covered stones. "Most men would have run away if they'd been in your shoes," she said. "Weren't you frightened?"

"Maybe a little. I didn't get much sleep the first two years, and I changed a helluva lot of diapers, but I'd do it again. Only thing I'd do differently is try to hang on to the livestock. I've got the land, but it's not much of a ranch without the animals. Haven't got much to give my boys, now, or in the future."

"You've given them more than most kids get. They'll appreciate that a whole lot more in the long run than some big inheritance."

"Yeah, well, I'd always hoped to give them both." He pushed up from the ground and stood beside her, his thigh lightly touching her hip, as he, too, leaned against the well and stared at the wall of roses till they became nothing but a blur of red. He had nothing to give his boys, and nothing to give Laurie. That might never change. The boys would accept it, but he'd never ask her to—it wouldn't be fair.

He needed to end things now, but how could he? She needed his protection. Or was that just an excuse to keep her close a little longer? "It's getting late. I've got briquettes and a freezer full of wieners. Care to join me for dinner?"

"And then what?"

Another painful question.

Tell her now, Jake, he told himself. *Tell her now.* "And then maybe you should spend the night. I don't want you here alone where I can't protect you. The boys are gone, and, well, you could sleep in Jacob's bed until they come home."

"Jacob's bed? Why not yours? Or have you already forgotten last night?"

"I haven't forgotten." He plowed his fingers through his hair and looked to the heavens, hoping for divine intervention, for something to make the moment easier. "I haven't forgotten last night. And I don't regret it, not one moment. But . . ."

"Please, Jake," Laurie interrupted, her voice broken, on the verge of tears. "Don't give me any more buts. I've heard enough."

"Hear me out. Please. I can't let it happen again. You'll get hurt, the boys'll get hurt, and so will I. There's so much more involved than just you and me."

"Such as?" she interrupted indignantly.

"I have nothing to offer you except a zero bank account and a run-down cabin. I've got three kids, and a history of being a lousy husband. I can give you protection, and my friendship. But that's all." Red crept up her neck and tinged her cheeks, but this time it wasn't embarrassment that made her freckles disappear. She was mad, and, oh Lord, he was glad. He could accept that so much easier than her tears. "You do understand, don't you?" he asked.

"The only thing I understand is that you're a stubborn, pigheaded fool, and if you think I'm the least bit interested in your cabin, your zero bank account, or the fact that you might have been a lousy husband to a lousy wife, you've got another think coming."

"Dammit, Red! I'm not stubborn or pigheaded."

Her anger turned to frustration, her words slow, whispered. "Then what are you?"

It didn't take long for him to calm, or to think of an honest answer. "I'm scared."

He watched her take a deep breath, and watched a tear slide down her cheek. "So am I. You're not the only one who's had someone rip your life apart. I've been there, too. There's just one difference. I accepted it, I dealt with it, and I know it can happen again. It's part of life, and I'm not going to give up anything just because I could get hurt again."

"There's more than one difference, Laurie. You don't have three kids to protect."

"The hell with the kids, Jake. We're talking about you. Don't hide behind the boys."

He turned away, his chest heaving with hostility. How dare she throw his love for his sons in his face? He never should have gotten involved with her, never should have let his emotions get out of control.

"I'm sorry, Jake." She put a hand on his back, her touch like a branding iron, searing her imprint through his shirt, through his skin, straight to his heart. "I shouldn't have said what I did about the boys. That wasn't fair. If they were mine, I'd fight the devil himself to keep them from any kind of harm."

"I'd fight the devil, too. But I don't want to fight with you."

"Then tell me honestly. What do you want with me?"

Honesty couldn't be part of his answer. If ever a lie was needed, it was now. She wasn't the devil, she wasn't a nymph from the bowels of hell, but she was an enchantress who was stealing his soul, and he had to reclaim his life. For his boys' sake, and not his own, he had to lie. "I want to pretend last night didn't happen. I want to be friends." He took a deep breath, regret heavy on his chest. "Just friends."

She stared into his eyes, studying what lay behind them, and he hoped he'd cloaked his true feelings.

Slowly, she extended her hand, calling a truce just as she had the day she'd almost run him down in the middle of Main Street, only this time he gladly took her hand. "Friends," she said, as tears raced down her cheeks and over Betty Boop lips that tried to smile.

"Friends." He forced his mustache to twitch, and wondered how long the truce would last this time.

11

Sleep abandoned him, so he sat on the porch swing throughout the night and watched for any strange movements around Laurie's house. She'd wanted to be alone, to sleep, behind the protection of her deadbolted doors, and nothing he'd said could change her mind. But the lights burned in her third-floor office till well after three, and in her bedroom till nearly four, and he wondered if she was as afraid for her safety, and as disturbed by their truce as he.

At five in the morning he stood under an ice-cold shower and tried to rid himself of his fear for her safety, of his overwhelming and disturbing need to be with her, and of the fatigue that plagued his body.

Daylight came, and he worked long past the fall of the sun, thinking his labor would ease his anxiety, that he could sweat away his frustration. But it hadn't worked, it had only made his arms and back ache, and his stomach growled for the meals he'd forgotten to eat.

Taking another cold shower had done little to lighten his mood, smoking his grandfather's pipe had made his throat burn, and he knew the only thing that would soothe his mind and body was being near Laurie again. It was a crazy, insane mistake, but one he'd deal with later.

He grabbed his best Stetson, shoved it on his head, and headed for the well-worn path. He'd told Meg the boys had been gone long enough, and he had an hour to kill before picking them up. It was enough time for a friendly chat, a neighborly cup of coffee, maybe a cookie or two, but not so much time that he'd make another foolish error and take Laurie in his arms.

No one answered when he knocked on the door, yet all the lights were on inside. He tried the knob, and the door opened easily. Why wasn't the deadbolt locked? She'd promised. She'd sworn not to take any chances. Had she forgotten? Or—

He stalked into the kitchen, peaceful, quiet, and serene, the aroma of fresh-baked bread, perking coffee, and apple pie filling his senses. But he saw none of the treats that smelled so delectable, only the lone petal of a yellow rose lying in the middle of the floor.

"Laurie," he cried, frightened, afraid, straining his lungs as he raced through the swinging doors. At the foot of the stairs rested another petal. He skipped three steps at a time, throwing open the door to Laurie's bedroom. A pile of petals lay in the center of the comforter where he and Laurie had played and eaten and loved just the morning before.

But there were no traces of Laurie anywhere.

He threw open every door as he ran down the hall, finally darting up to the third-floor office. Her computer was off. Her papers were neatly stacked, her chair rested squarely under the desk. Nothing appeared out of place except one novel missing from the orderly bookcase. And then he saw it. A

long-stemmed yellow rose lay over the open copy
of *My Captain*, and a passage had been circled in
red. Slowly, Jake scooped the book from the floor
and read.

*Madness distorted his face, and love pierced his
heart like a dagger thrown straight and true. Once
again she escaped him. Not even the roses he'd laid
at her feet, or his declaration of love, had made her
stay. But someday he would find her, enslave her,
and become the true captain of her heart.*

"It's true, you know."

Jake spun around at the stranger's voice. A man
stood in the doorway brandishing a gun. Tall and
slim, he had a ski mask pulled tightly over his face,
but through the slits, Jake saw the eyes of a madman. "You're insane."

"Ah, yes. Insane. Laurie has used those same
words before, and I believe her. I believe everything Laurie says."

Jake took a step forward, but the man's arm shot
out, steady and sure, the gun aimed directly at
Jake's heart.

"Laurie was to find the rose, not you."

Jake didn't think, he only reacted, diving toward
the man's legs, out of the line of fire, but the stalker
was faster, stepping aside, and Jake's head
slammed into the wall. Stunned, he lay still, shock
and pain sickening his stomach, his muscles and
flesh stinging as if a thousand poisoned needles
jabbed at his skin.

Through a blurry haze, Jake looked at the open
door, wondering if he could escape, somehow pro-
pelling his body through the opening, into the hall
and down the stairs.

He looked up once more, the slash of the man's mouth turned up in a malicious grin. "You can't escape." The man hissed, kicking the door, shutting off any route of escape. "I can keep you in, but you can never, ever lock me out. Not even with deadbolts."

The madman raised the gun, and Jake could see his finger twitching on the trigger. "Where would you like the first bullet? In your leg? In your groin?" His laughter rang through the room, but Jake swore he heard the humming of Christmas carols nearing the door. It had to be Laurie's housekeeper, and he prayed she'd stop when she heard the noise, the crazed laughter.

"Yes, I think the groin is perfect." The madman aimed the gun, pointing it between Jake's legs, and suddenly, the door burst open, smacking the man in the side, knocking him off balance, sending the gun clattering and skidding across the floor.

Jake dove for the gun, grabbed it, and rolled over, pointing it at the man as the round little woman scuttled into the room. But time seemed to have slowed. Merry tripped, and the plates of sizzling, fresh-from-the-oven apple pie and cups of boiling coffee on the tray she held flew through mid-air, aimed directly at the stalker, slamming against his face. Oozing, sugary apples stuck to the wool mask as the plate slipped away, and steaming coffee sloshed from the cups, splattering over his neck and chest before the cups crashed to the floor.

He screamed, like a banshee in the night, grabbing at the burning mask as he ran from the room.

Jake held up the gun, hands shaking, wanting to shoot, but afraid of hitting the woman, of hitting anyone or anything at all. He tried to stand, tried to move, wanting to trail the man, capture him, haul him off to jail, but another pain shot through his head, and everything went black.

Jake cracked open one eye and through a hazy blur saw a curl of red hair hanging over a woman's brow, and he tried to smile.

"Before you waste your strength asking crazy questions," Laurie said while holding a cold rolled-up towel to the top of his head, "yes, I called the sheriff, yes I'll stay at your house for awhile so we can protect each other, and I was at Meghan's having dinner. Anything else you care to know?"

"Where are we?" he mumbled, forcing a wink, wanting Laurie to know he was fine. "Is Merry okay, and could you enlighten me a little more on the answers you gave to questions I didn't even ask?"

She put her fingers to his lips. "Too many questions. Save them for the sheriff. He's checking out the farmhouse, dusting for prints—finally—and he's anxious to talk to you."

"I don't know what I can tell him. He was wearing a ski mask, just like you said. And he's mad, Laurie."

"I know." She closed her eyes and he thought she would cry. Lord, she'd been through so much, why couldn't he have captured that maniac? Why couldn't he have ended the stalking once and for all?

He watched Laurie open her eyes, the pools of emerald filled with tears. She tried to sniff them away, to wipe them away with the backs of her fingers. He knew she was frightened, for him, for herself, and he wished with all his heart he could work miracles, or magic, so she could be carefree and happy.

"You ever gonna tell me how I got here?" he asked, trying to force her thoughts away from the stalker.

"Kurt helped me get you home and into bed after the doctor checked you out and pronounced you bruised and sore, a bit in shock, but alive and soon to be well."

Laurie pulled the covers tight under his neck, and plumped the pillow around his head. "Merry called me at Meg's and said you'd been hurt, that she'd already called the doctor and the sheriff. She was so worried about you, about everything that's been going on. She was frightened, said all she wanted to do was go home to her husband for awhile, and something crazy about things weren't working out the way she'd planned, and she's never run into so much trouble before. I'm worried about her."

"And I'm worried about you," Jake interrupted, capturing her fingers and pulling them to his lips. The hell with friendship, he thought—at least for now.

She leaned over and kissed his eyes, closing them once again. "I'm fine. Honestly. Now, why don't you try to sleep."

He shook his head slightly, afraid any other movement would send the Seventh Cavalry rushing through his skull again, afraid if he moved too much Laurie might end those sweet kisses she was pressing against his forehead. "I need to take care of you," he whispered. "It's not supposed to be the other way around."

"Not tonight, Mr. McAllister. I'm on guard, and the boys are tucked safely in bed."

"They're okay, aren't they? Do they know what happened?"

"They're fine, Jake," she reassured him. "Just a little worried about you. They don't know what really happened. I told them you were doing some woodwork in my office, that the ladder broke, and you fell and hit your head." She smiled, and Jake swore he'd never seen such a pretty sight.

"It's the worst story I've ever told."

"But they believed you?"

Laurie nodded. "I did a much better job of storytelling when I put them to bed."

He closed his eyes again. God, he'd never felt so tired. "You gonna tell me a bedtime story?"

"No. You interrupt too much, and the doctor said I should try to keep you quiet."

"You gonna watch me all night? This old bed's plenty big for the two of us." He peeked through one eye to see the shake of Laurie's head.

"Not a chance. Jacob's in with the twins, and I'm doing the hug the teddy bear thing in his bed again tonight—and every night until you're better."

"I'm better now. I'd be even better if you could stick around. You're a helluva lot better than aspirin."

She shook her head, again. "You're delirious, Jake. If you woke up tomorrow and found me in bed with you, you'd never forgive me."

"I'd forgive you." His words slowed as he fought to keep his eyes open. "Honest."

"Go to sleep. We'll have this discussion some other time, when you know what you're saying." She closed his eyes again with her lips, and slowly left the room.

* * *

Sometime between midnight and six of the third day, Jake tired of staring at the stars and slowly crept into the house and down the hallway. He silently eased open the door to his room and peaked inside. The curtains blew in the gentle breeze, and he gritted his teeth, wishing little Laurie Langtry would follow his orders, at least once. Open windows, he'd told her, were open invitations to trouble, but she'd only complained that the nights were too warm, and the fresh air not only cooled her, but smelled of pine and roses, and made her sleep better. Hell, he hadn't slept since he'd given his bed to Laurie two nights before, and relegated himself to the front porch swing. But he'd sworn to protect her, and now, he also had his sons' safety to consider.

He walked across the room, hoping not to wake the woman sleeping in his bed, and pushed the window shut, locking the latch at the bottom.

"Jake?"

"Sorry. I didn't mean to wake you."

"You didn't. I couldn't sleep. I heard you pacing outside on the porch, and walking around the house." She sat up in the bed that seemed to swallow her small figure, and pulled the faded, striped sheet up to her breasts. "He's not going to come here, Jake. Please, don't worry so much."

"I want him to come, Laurie. I want him to come so I can break his neck. I blew it the other day when I had that gun. I should have shot him, then we wouldn't be living through this hell."

He sat on the edge of the bed, the closest he had come to Laurie since she'd soothed his aching head three days before. He'd wanted to touch her, wanted to hold her, but he'd kept his distance, positive that was the only right thing to do.

But looking at her now, at the sleepy eyes that bore into his soul, he realized he couldn't hold back any longer. Moving closer, he caressed her cheek, skimming his thumb lightly over her slightly parted lips. "Have I ever told you you're the prettiest thing I ever saw?"

"Not that I recall."

"Well, Red—" His fingers slid along her jawline, brushed over the tender flesh of her neck, and over the heavy knit of her night shirt. "You're not only the prettiest, but you're the most maddening woman I've ever known."

She touched his chin, grazing her hand lightly over his cheeks, his ear, combing small fingers through his thick, wavy hair, and brought his face closer to hers, and whispered, "Why am I so maddening, Jake?"

"These nightshirts you wear." He grabbed a hunk of fabric and pulled her close. "I can't untie them, or unbutton them, or pull them apart slow and easy so I can look at you, so I can touch you." He fought for breath, but nothing wanted to reach his lungs. "Lord almighty, Red. I want to touch you."

His lips captured hers, not tenderly, or gently, but with all the passion he'd stored inside for days. It no longer mattered that she would leave him, he thought. He'd deal with that later. Right now, he wanted her so badly every muscle in his body ached, every nerve tingled when she came within sight. And right now, he couldn't get enough.

His tongue sought all the pleasures he remembered so vividly from before, the smoothness of her teeth, the velvet softness of her tongue, while his hands sought the bottom of her shirt, smoothing over the slimness of her waist, the roundness of her hip, finally touching the warmth of her skin, and slipping his fingers beneath the shirt and drawing it upward so he could hold and fondle the breasts he'd found so perfect.

He touched her, and she threw back her head and somehow stifled the moan he knew she wanted to let escape.

"Daddy!" a small voice called from the boys' bedroom.

Oh, please Lord, he begged silently, *let me be hearing things.*

Laurie tensed, her fingers grabbed the bottom of her nightshirt and pulled it down, along with Jake's hand. "Someone's awake."

Jake rolled onto his back, his head pounding into the pillow, his breathing heavy and fast, his eyes closed, as he tried to calm his nerves, to ease the passion that throbbed in his groin.

"Daddy!"

He forced himself to sit and plucked a quick kiss from Laurie's sweet, swollen, Betty Boop lips. "I'm sorry. This is what happens when you've got kids in the house."

She smiled.

He sighed, and quietly walked out of the room.

12

Getting Jake to leave Laurie alone in her own home, for at least one night, had been more difficult than training rattlesnakes. He'd finally relented to her constant arguments that she'd be safe with the doors securely bolted and chained. Jake was insistent on checking everything out before he'd leave her side. He'd inspected every nook and cranny, every closet, under every bed, the attic, the cellar, and even the chimney. He was leaving nothing to chance, even checking the windows and issuing a strong warning about keeping them closed and locked before he reluctantly went back home. Of course, he'd called the sheriff asking that he swing by the place once or twice during the day and night to check the doors. Laurie protested, but Jake was adamant. She'd either have police protection, or sleep in his bed. She'd feel like a prisoner one way; uncomfortable the other. Sleeping alone in that big bed with Jake right down the hall, avoiding her, was almost as bad as being stalked.

She had work to do, and even though she'd given it a try at Jake's, he and the boys were too much distraction. She'd tried curling up with pen and paper to write, but she found herself wanting to go outside and play ball. They'd taken her to their favorite fishing hole and laughed when she cringed over putting a squirming worm on her hook. They'd hiked up a rugged hill for a picnic, looking down on the lush green valley as Jake pointed out all the boundaries of his property. And Laurie even tried her hand at burning hot dogs, and succeeded like a pro.

Over the past few days she'd grown accustomed to having the boys around in the evening, reading them stories, watching Jake sit at the kitchen table listening while he puffed on that old Meerschaum pipe that looked so right clenched in his teeth. Jake's cabin, so much more than her house, felt like home.

Meg and Kurt, arm in arm, had come to the cabin to discuss arrangements for the Fourth of July party, and to show her plans for the castle, while Jake sat outside and stewed. There were still so many areas where they didn't see eye to eye. He accepted the fact that she'd been right in pushing Meg and Kurt together, but he hated the idea of the castle. His pride got in the way much too often, and, although he'd hedged on the subject only once, Laurie knew her money, and his lack of it, grated his self-esteem.

On the second day, she'd gone by the house to pick up clothes and some work, and Merry was nowhere around. She missed talking to her, missed her guidance, and her funny ways, and she worried about her too. She had the feeling there was no reason to worry about her mystical, magical housekeeper, she'd probably show up at the farmhouse the same day Laurie returned, but she worried just the same.

Now, shortly after midnight, she sat at her desk, staring at the computer screen, and every time she typed her hero's name, Jake's face flashed through her mind. He was the hero she'd longed for, the hero she had written about in nearly thirty books, the hero who gave her life meaning. If Jake Mc-Allister didn't come around soon, didn't give in to his feelings, she was bound and determined to take matters into her own hands. She wanted him, plain and simple, and she was in the habit of getting what she wanted.

Click.

She jumped, smashing her hands on the keyboard, sending a garbled message across the screen.

And then she heard the humming, and Merry's favorite tune. *"Fa la la la la, la la, la la."* It had become so familiar since Merry's arrival, she'd begun to think of each day as Christmas, without the tree, without the snow, and, unfortunately, without the peace she thought should be associated with the season.

The door opened and Merry scurried into the room carrying a tray with mugs of cocoa. "My goodness, but you're up awfully late."

"I've neglected my work lately."

"No, no, no, that's not the reason at all. You couldn't sleep, plain and simple. And now you're staring at that silly old screen hoping some award-winning words will pop into your mind."

"That's the idea, Merry."

"Well, Laurie dear, it's just not going to happen today, so I suggest you have some cocoa and forget about your book. Besides, it's the Fourth of July."

Laurie slumped back in her chair and grabbed a cup of cocoa. "So, Merry, did you miss me?"

Merry sat next to the desk and sipped cocoa, studying Laurie over the rims of her low-riding spectacles. "My, my, my, child, if I didn't know better, I'd think you'd moved in with that young fellow of yours."

"He hasn't wanted to let me out of his sight. He's afraid I'm going to get hurt."

"Of course he wants to protect you, and he did a fine job of that the other night. I never imagined someone could sneak past me, and come close to hurting the ones I love."

"He's too tricky, Merry, and you could have been hurt. As it is, you're the hero. You saved Jake's life."

"No, no, no. I stumbled in by accident. I'm losing my touch. Poor Nicky, he thinks I should retire."

"And what do you want, Merry?"

"I want many more summers, and many more lives to change. That's what I thought I'd be doing this summer, but so far, I haven't been able to change a thing."

"But you *have* changed my life, Merry. You made me realize this big house isn't the home I always wanted, that the home I needed was any place filled with love." Laurie put her hand on Merry's and squeezed. "You've brought a lot of love into this house, Merry."

"But I won't always be here, child, and you'll need someone else's love to fill the rooms."

"I'm working on it, but, unfortunately, Jake just doesn't seem to be cooperating."

"Oh, my. Seems I've fallen down there, too. However, the summer's still young, the Fourth of July party is just hours away, and I have the feeling something miraculous is going to happen."

"Do you really think so?"

"Of course I do, child. I've put in a very special wish."

Laurie's eyes sparkled, and an ounce of skepticism made her laugh. "I take it you have connections where wishes are concerned?"

"Yes, child, I do," Merry said matter of factly as she patted Laurie's hand. "Now run along child, get back to bed, and leave all your cares and worries here with me."

Minutes later, Laurie climbed under the cool, crisp, fresh-smelling sheets, closed her eyes and yawned, and just before she dozed off to sleep, she wished her worries away. Miraculously, she thought of Jake, of three tow-headed boys, of an ornery cow, and a field of flowers.

Not once did she think of the stalker who had haunted her mind for years.

Laurie zipped up the red linen slacks, buttoned the waistband, and made sure the matching red blouse with white stars emblazoned across the front, and a flag at the back, was tucked in just right. She fastened the blue leather belt with a buckle of glittering rhinestone stars, and admired herself in the mirror. She looked like Old Glory, but felt like a million bucks.

She was almost ready to dash down the stairs when she saw an envelope with her name in bold black letters propped up against the light on her nightstand. Smiling at the thought of a surprise, maybe a wish from Merry, maybe a seductive love note from Jake, she stuck her finger under the sealed flap and pried it open, slightly ripping the heavy white paper.

Pulling out a ragged slip of lined notebook paper, a yellow rose petal slipped from inside and floated to the bed. Her hands shook, her lips trembled, but somehow she forced herself to read the words through the stream of tears falling from her eyes.

Tonight, Laurie. Tonight, at the party, you'll be mine.

"You're awfully quiet," Jake said, as they drove the short distance to the Grange in his rickety old Jeep.

"Just tired, I'm afraid." Her words were lies. She wasn't the least bit tired, just on edge, wondering if she should tell Jake she expected an unwanted visitor at the party. As much as she wanted to, she didn't want him spending the evening worrying. She wanted him to have fun—something he deserved. "Guess I got rather used to your bed and couldn't get to sleep in my own."

She forced herself to smile, and placed her hand over his on the gear shift. "I'm fine, Jake, really. We're going to have a great time."

"That's my plan." He looked over his shoulder into the back seat. "Isn't that right, guys?"

"Yeah!" they yelled in unison.

Jake pulled into the dirt parking lot of the Grange, between Kurt's Bronco and an old van sporting the words "Have Discs Will Travel." He swung the boys out of the back, before meeting Laurie at the front of the Jeep. Clutching her hand, he pulled her to his side. "You guys go in and see if Kurt needs any help," he said to the boys, then watched them dart away.

"Now, care to tell me what's really bothering you?"

"Nothing, Jake," she said in exasperation.

"You're lying. I'm getting to the point where I

can read you like a book, and I've never seen you so distracted."

"That's all it is Jake, just a little distraction. I've got a deadline I'm falling behind on and I've never missed one yet. I shouldn't have spent so much time preparing for this party, or running away from a madman. Heaven knows I shouldn't be here now."

"Well, you're here, and I'm bound and determined to make sure you enjoy it. Unlike the last Fourth of July party we attended together"—his mustache twitched—"I don't intend to heave my guts all over you."

"You mean you've got something a little more refined in mind?"

"How's this?" He pulled her against his chest, tilted her chin, and lowered his head, lightly kissing her lips.

But she pulled away, refusing to let him prolong the kiss.

"Dammit, Red. What's your problem?"

She couldn't tell him the truth. Not about the stalker, so she hit him right between the eyes with the thing that had bothered her for days. "That's the first time in a week you've made any attempt to kiss me. Why now? Is it because the boys aren't around? Are you afraid what they might think if you do it in front of them?"

He looked up at the heavens, gritted his teeth and sighed. "That's not what's bothering you today, and you know it. But if you want an answer, yeah, I care what they might think. I don't want them getting their hopes up and you know good and well why. We've been through all that before." He lightly brushed a finger across her lips, his Montana blue-sky eyes full of so many mixed emotions that she knew, instinctively, that he was in just as much turmoil as she. "Hell, Red. You just looked so damn pretty I couldn't keep my lips off you. Okay?"

Laurie lowered her eyes. "I'm sorry. Let's just go inside and have some fun."

"Not until you tell me what's going on inside that head of yours."

Slowly, she reached into her pocket and pulled out the scrap of paper. "Did you write this?"

Jake took it from her hands and looked at the words. She watched the pronounced hardening of his jaw, the way his shoulders drew up, tense, wary. He wadded the paper into his fist, slamming it into the palm of his other hand. "Damn!" He paced the length of the car then stopped, tightly gripping Laurie's arms. "He's not getting close to you, Laurie. Not tonight, not any night."

With callused thumbs, he wiped the tears from her eyes. "Trust me?" he asked, his voice soft and tender.

She nodded. Tonight she could easily put her life in his hands.

"You're not to leave my side all evening. Understand?"

She nodded.

"I was giving you an order, Laurie," Jake said, tilting her face toward his with a light touch of his fingers under her chin. "You're not arguing. Where's that fire of yours?"

A halfhearted grin crossed her face. "I'm saving it for Mrs. Adams." She forced a wink. "If she makes just one snide remark, I'm letting her have it."

His mustache twitched. "That's the Red I like." He draped an arm over her shoulders and wrapped his big hand around her arm, realizing just how comfortable and easy the gesture felt, as if she belonged at his side. "Come on. I want to have a ringside seat when Mrs. Adams sees what you and Meg have done. You don't look much like Muhammad Ali, but I've got the feeling you might pack the same wallop."

As they walked toward the Grange, she saw the volleyball net that had been strung from posts cemented into place just two mornings before, and looked forward to seeing the boys and their dad at play. A horseshoe pit had been dug, something Kurt thought might please the older generations, and, as promised, he'd set new redwood patio benches and tables in the shade of the pines.

"Looks pretty good, Red. I think the folks around town just might approve."

"It's not nearly as much as I wanted to do."

"And what was it you had in mind? A complete facelift of that old building?"

"No. I rather like it just the way it is." Laurie scanned the rustic wood exterior of the Grange with a sign over the door reading "Established 1879." Bunch Gulch had thrived for well over a hundred years, not as a mining town or a center of industry, but as a close-knit community of farmers and ranchers who knew they'd never get rich, but felt all the riches in the world were right there in their little valley hidden deep away in a canyon, surrounded and protected by high, craggy peaks. Water rushed through the streams year round, even when heavy snows blanketed the ground and ice thickened along the banks. Wildflowers and tall grass grew in profusion in the few months of spring and summer, blessing the community with a respite from the harsh realities of fall and winter.

Families still joined together for barn raisings, and the christening of newborn children. And every Fourth of July they gathered together to celebrate their independence, their love of country, to tell oft-told stories in the company of old and cherished friends.

As a child she didn't understand the significance of the Grange, or the parties, and she hadn't cared. But joining with Meg to decorate and plan this yearly affair that had gone on for well over a hundred years, she had seen the real reason behind it, and for the first time as a citizen of Bunch Gulch, she felt the friendship and camaraderie, and almost wished she'd never run away.

No, there wasn't a thing she wanted to change about the Grange. It was a tradition. The only thing she wanted to change were the things it had lacked when she was a child, the things that would keep the children happy, the things that would make the teenagers want to stay instead of seeking greener pastures when they came of age. No, she didn't want to change the institutions, she just wanted to update them a bit.

"Laurie?"

She heard her name, felt Jake's hand squeezing her shoulder, and realized she'd stopped not fifteen feet from the door and hadn't moved an inch while her mind wandered.

"You okay?"

Nodding, she wrapped an arm around his hips and wove a finger through a belt loop on his Levi's. "Just thinking how much I like this place."

"This is the first Fourth of July party I've been to since that night with you. Didn't think I'd ever go again."

"Why?"

He shrugged his shoulders. "Once I got out of school, I didn't see the need. Only came when I was a kid because of my folks. They were the ones having fun, not me, and there comes a point in time when you grow up and get tired of sneaking off to get drunk. Amy wouldn't have gone with me, and after she left, just couldn't see subjecting the boys to a day of boredom. Don't think we're going to have that problem today."

Laurie shook her head. "I hope not. Meg wants so much for everything to be perfect."

"And what about you?"

"I just want everyone to be happy."

His fingers slid down her shoulder and grabbed her hand, and he finally led her into the Grange as the first beat of music reverberated off the walls.

Grabbing her by the waist with one arm, he took hold of her other hand and waltzed around the room to the Platters' "Only You," stopping when they nearly collided with Kurt and Meg and the boys.

"We were beginning to think you had another party to go to," Kurt said, shaking Jake's hand and kissing Laurie's cheek.

"What, miss out on the party of the year? Not a chance."

Jake dropped Laurie's hand, and with his hands clasped behind his back, strolled around the room, surveying the transformation. "Looks great, ladies."

"He's right, you know." Kurt threw his arm around Meg as if it belonged there.

Laurie looked about the room that had been white-bread plain the day before. What once had been curtainless windows were now swagged with blue satin, red broadcloth, and white lace. Folding

tables, scratched and marred from years of Bingo
and cards and potlucks, were covered with white
linen, and metallic fireworks, exploding in a profusion of colors, sat at the center of each. Floating
overhead were hundreds of helium-filled red,
white, and blue balloons with curly-ribbon tails.
The backdrop of the dais set up specifically for the
DJ was covered with an American flag, and red
and blue strobes pulsed around his equipment.

All eyes turned toward the door when they
heard the gasp. Mrs. Adams stood dumbstruck,
her apple pie shaking in trembling hands. "What
have you done in here?" she ranted, shoving her
pie across a table and clutching her chest.

"Dressed it up a bit, that's all. You said you
wanted the decorations perfect, and we knew
you'd approve." Laurie put an arm around Mrs.
Adams, hoping to win her over, wanting so much
to reconcile with everyone she'd angered as a
child. "The DJ's prepared to play just about anything, and we already got Bert Ramsey's vote of
confidence. All we need now is yours."

"Well," Mrs. Adams tilted her head slightly and
ran an assessing eye over the decorations, and Laurie's attire. "I must admit, you and Meghan have
done an exemplary job."

"So," Laurie asked, smiling and tightening her
hand at the older woman's waist, "what's your favorite song?"

Mrs. Adams patted Laurie's hand. " 'Stardust,'
dear," she said, her voice taking on a condescend-
ing air. "But you kids don't know the first thing
about good music." Her lips pursed as she looked
at the DJ, his long black hair slicked back in a po-
nytail, one ear studded with seven rings, his

clothes army surplus rejects. "Oh, my. Bert won't be happy when he sees this."

"Please try to like him, Mrs. Adams." Laurie leaned closer and whispered into Mrs. Adams' ear. "Meghan's worked so hard to make everything perfect. Please, do it for her."

"Well, I don't know. He's probably never heard of Frank Sinatra."

"Can you play 'Stardust' by Frank Sinatra?" Laurie called out over the closing strains of Sousa's "Stars and Stripes," and received a generous smile and two thumbs up from the man sitting between the speakers.

Within moments, Tommy Dorsey's band rang out, Frank Sinatra's glorious voice filled the room, and for the first time in years Mrs. Adams' eyes lit up in wonder and disbelief. "It's like being young again." She clapped her hands together, and her body involuntarily began to sway. "Do you think he has more Sinatra music?"

"I would imagine so." Laurie relaxed for the first time in hours, and had the uncanny feeling she could actually like Mrs. Adams if given the chance to try.

"Would you care to dance, Mrs. Adams?" Jake asked, taking the woman into his arms.

"Well, I'm not sure."

"Oh, come on. Don't let me down. I've been waiting for this all week."

He waltzed her around the floor, one hand casually resting on her back, the other gently holding her hand, tucked protectively into his chest. Laurie's heart thumped, completely out of time with the music, and a twinge of love fluttered in her stomach. If she'd been a little braver, she would have tapped Mrs. Adams on the shoulder and

begged to dance with her man. But it was Mrs.
Adams' moment, and Laurie would never deny
the woman the happiness so obvious in her eyes
as she looked at the young man leading her about
the room.

Time seemed to fly by. Singles and couples and
families converged on the Grange, people Laurie
remembered from childhood, and new faces ga-
lore. The dessert and salad and entree tables filled
rapidly with chocolate cream pies, peach, apple,
and pumpkin, too. Fruit salads arrived, along with
hot and cold potato salads, and casseroles reeking
of tuna and cheese, ham and turkey and platters
of hors d'oeuvres.

Kids ran outside to a makeshift diamond with
brand-new balls and baseball bats that had been
stacked in a corner. One volleyball found its way
outside while another bounced and rolled around
the floor covered between a mass of legs and bodies doing the bop, and the bunny hop, or waltzing,
or boogying, or twisting the night away.

Jake caught Laurie up in his arms, holding her
close, smiling as radiantly as she did as they
moved together in perfect rhythm, watching the
teens dancing and enjoying themselves in the company of adults for the first time he could ever remember. "It's better than anyone ever dreamed,
Red."

"It is nice, isn't it."

"We have a lot to thank you for."

She rested her head against his chest, and savored the feel of his arm around her, holding her
close, protecting her from the man she'd wanted
so desperately to forget. "It was all Meg's idea, she
just needed a few extra guts and—now don't get

upset—some of my money to pull the whole thing off."

"Well, I suppose if it's burning that big a hole in your pocketbook, you might as well put it to some good use."

Jake caressed the hair at the nape of her neck, circling her skin in tender, gentle strokes, his fingers and mind lost in thought, as he searched the room for anyone unfamiliar, but he saw no one strange, no one new, no one at all who looked like he might want to harm the woman in his arms.

Suddenly, the doors burst open in a flash of light, white smoke, and glittering foil stars. A little man, not much taller than Josh and Joseph, paraded into the room, his tux a shimmering green, topped with a glorious satin cape of the same fabric, lined in Christmas red, his top hat tilted at a cocky angle on his head. "Ladies and gentlemen, boys and girls," the little man shouted like a circus ringmaster, "may I offer you the pleasure of meeting me, Elfin the Magnificent, the greatest magician ever to walk the earth and the moon and the planets of this solar system or any other."

The music came to a halt. The dancing stopped. Elfin the Magnificent strutted across the room, pulling behind him a tall, narrow cabinet painted midnight blue with gold and silver and glittery suns and moons and stars, and the children followed him, skipping merrily, as if Elfin the Magnificent were the Pied Piper come to town. The adults followed, too, their older, more mature eyes sparkling with amazement and childish delight.

"Where did you find him?" Jake whispered into Laurie's ear.

"I didn't. It must have been Meg."

"For my first feat of magic," Elfin the Magnificent announced, "I'll need a volunteer." He looked around the room, and pointed at Joseph. "You, young man, are perfect. Please, join me if you will." He swirled his cape, and bowed, beckoning Joseph toward him.

Joseph looked at his dad for permission, his eyes wide and a little frightened.

"Go ahead, son," Jake encouraged, gently pushing Joseph's back, ushering him before the odd little man who reminded him, strangely, of an elf he'd once seen in a drawing of Santa's workshop.

Elfin the Magnificent removed his top hat, holding it between himself and Joseph. A little bit shorter than the child, and maybe a few pounds heavier, the magician with a decidedly pronounced ski jump nose, and shiny green shoes that curled up at the toes, waved his hand quite dramatically over the top of the hat. "Do you believe in magic?"

Joseph nodded.

"Then let's see what I have inside." Elfin started to stick his hand inside, then stopped, grinning instead at his audience. Tilting his head back and forth, he circled his hand over Joseph's head, then tapped him lightly on the nose. "I'm a psychic too, you know. Let's see." He pressed a hand to Joseph's brow. "Your name's Joshua, right?"

Joseph rapidly shook his head. "No," his little voice creaked.

"Oh goodness. How could I have made such a mistake?" Elfin lightly touched the scar on the boy's chin, then threw his hand in the air. "Of course. You're Joseph, and Joshua's your twin brother."

Joseph nodded.

The partygoers oohed and aahed.

"Have you been naughty or nice this year, Joseph?"

"Nice—" He looked at his dad for confirmation, then back at Elfin. "Most of the time."

Elfin grinned at the group, particularly at Jake. "Ah, an honest child. You've raised him well, sir." He looked back at Joseph. "And what do you think I'm going to pull out of my hat?"

"A rabbit?" Joseph's eyes widened as he looked into the depths of the magician's eyes, and into the dark center of the hat.

"A rabbit?" Elfin the Magnificent grabbed his stomach as his infectious laughter captured his audience. "Did you hear that folks? He thinks I'm going to pull a rabbit out of my hat. But that's what ordinary magicians do, and," he added, lightly tapping Joseph on the nose with a stubby index finger, "I'm no ordinary magician." He pushed the hat closer to Joseph. "Why don't you put your hand inside, young man, and tell me what you find."

Tentatively, Joseph lowered his hand into the top hat, digging around inside, while the party-goers looked on in awe. With a puzzled frown on his face, Joseph pulled his hand from the hat. "There's nothing inside."

"Oh, my. That won't do at all." Again, Elfin waved his hand over the hat. "Try it once more."

Again, Joseph reached into the hat, searching deeper, and deeper, as if the hat was swallowing his arm, and when his entire arm was hidden, he smiled, eyes wide with delight, and pulled it from the hat. He opened the fist that clenched the magical object, and found—nothing.

The audience collectively sighed their disappointment.

Confused, childish eyes looked into sparkling, impish ones. "I feel something," Joseph said, looked at his hand, at the fingers that cupped an invisible ball of—nothing. His shoulders drew up in total disbelief. "But I don't see anything."

"It's magic. Remember? All you have to do is believe." Elfin tilted Joseph's chin toward him with the tip of his finger. "You do believe, don't you?"

Joseph, fresh-faced innocence radiating from his face, nodded over and over.

"Then hold out your hand, child." Elfin turned Joseph toward the audience, cupping his elbow. Joseph extended his arm. "Now, pretend you're holding a pretty little dandelion, frail and delicate, and blow."

Joseph looked at his dad for reassurance. Jake winked and nodded, amazed at what was going on before his eyes.

Joseph puckered his lips, and puffed at his open palm.

A glittering rainbow of confetti stars exploded from his hand and into the air, raining down on the partygoers, stunned at first, then filling the room with applause and laughter and cheers.

Elfin the Magnificent humbly bowed. Joseph bowed. The crowd moved closer, their hair and clothing sparkling like the nighttime sky, filled with glitter and light. Jake lifted Joshua onto his shoulders for a better view of Elfin's magic, and Jacob squeezed through bodies so he could be right up front.

Laurie stood in the background and watched in awe, wondering what it was about the little man that seemed so terribly familiar. He looked like no one she'd ever seen before, yet there was some-

thing about his rosy cheeks, his mirthful smile, and
the twinkle in his eye.

"My, my, my," she heard Elfin the Magnificent
say, and suddenly she knew. He reminded her of
Merry. Had she sent him? Was he a magician, or
was he part of Merry's magic?

"And now for my next feat, I need another assistant," she heard Elfin proclaim, loud and clear,
above the cheers. "Oh, my. Who should it be?"

A path seemed to clear through the people filling the Grange and Elfin the Magnificent strutted
toward her. "Ah, if it isn't little Miss Laurie Langtry." He took her hand, lightly bestowing a kiss on
the backs of her fingers. "I'd be honored to have
your assistance."

Laurie found herself curtsying, feeling like Cin-
derella at the ball. "I'd be delighted."

Elfin led her through the crowd and stopped in
front of his magic-making box. "Now, don't move
from this spot, child."

Laurie obeyed as she watched Elfin search the
crowd again. "You, young man." He pointed his
wand at Jake.

Jake looked around, wondering if the little man
was pointing to him, or to someone else standing
beside him.

"Yes, young man. Jake, I believe it is?"

Jake nodded.

"I'll need your assistance too."

Jake stepped forward hesitantly and stood at
Laurie's side, absently taking her hand, weaving
his fingers through hers.

"No, no, no, young man. You can't hold her
hand. Not yet, anyway." He crooked his finger,
beckoning Jake toward him.

He flung open the door of his star-painted box. "Please, step inside if you will."

Jake crouched low and squeezed his body through the opening. "What now?"

"Test the walls, the ceiling, the floor."

Jake pushed on the walls and the ceiling, and stomped his foot on the bottom. He knew the man planned to perform some kind of magic trick, possibly make something disappear, but he didn't see how that could be possible. There were no trap doors in the solid pine.

Jake stepped out, and Elfin smiled up at him. "It's very strong, this box of mine. And"—he winked at Laurie when Jake again took her hand, then turned to the crowd—"my box can make all your wishes come true."

"I have a wish," someone in the crowd called out, and others followed suit, caught up in the excitement, everyone wanting a chance to be part of the magic.

"And what would you wish for?" Elfin asked, standing in front of Laurie and Jake, looking from one to the other.

"I have everything I need," Laurie said. "I'd like to give my wish to Jake."

"And you, young man. What is it you wish for?"

Jake squeezed Laurie's hand. "May I give my wish to one of my sons?"

Elfin grinned, and spun around, his red and green cape swirling about him as his laughter filled the room. "A perfect choice." Elfin stopped, his cape settled at his sides. "But which son?"

Jake looked at his three impish towheads. They all deserved so much more than he could give. How could he decide? But the decision was made for him when the twins pushed their brother toward the magician.

"Ah, Jacob. The light of your father's eye."

Jacob scratched his head, and so did his father, and Jake wondered for at least the tenth time how the little man could possibly know their names.

Elfin took Jacob's hand and led him to the front of the box. "What do you wish for, child?"

Jacob looked at his dad. He looked at Laurie. Then he shrugged his shoulders and dug his hands into his pockets. "I don't think you could make my wish come true."

Jake's heart sunk. It was the mother thing again, and he prayed Jacob wouldn't ask Elfin for that. He couldn't stand to see his son's hurt when the wish could not be granted.

Digging into his pockets, Jacob finally pulled out a fist. "Maybe you could turn this into something really nice." He opened his fingers, and resting in his palm was a dirt-crusted stone, one he'd picked up on the path between his house and Laurie's. "It's not the best rock I ever found, but maybe you could make it a little nicer."

Elfin took the rock from Jacob's hand, inspecting it closely as he pinched it between his thumb and index finger. "My, my, my. Haven't seen a stone like this in a mighty long time. Did you know, young man," Elfin said as he gently cupped Jacob's chin, "that some of the finest castles in Europe were built on foundations made of stone just like this?"

Jacob shook his head, and his eyes widened at the mention of castles.

"It's true, child. Now, let's see if we can make it the foundation for something just as spectacular." Elfin set the dirty stone on the solid floor of the box, closed the door, and fastened its shiny brass latch.

"Step forward, Laurie. I need your help in performing this feat of magic."

Laurie moved away from Jake, ruffled Jacob's hair just like she'd seen his father do time and time again, and took the wand Elfin was holding out to her. "What do I do?" she asked.

"Watch closely, Jake. You never know when you might be called upon to do the same thing."

Magic? Jake didn't believe in it, but there was something compelling about Elfin the Magnificent, something mystical. The little man knew their names, after all. So he watched, but doubted he'd ever be called upon to perform anything more magical than turning fields of grass into bales of hay, or making downed fence posts stand straight once again.

"Close your eyes, child," Elfin said, "and repeat the words 'I believe' three times. Then open your eyes, tap the wand against the door, and stand back."

Laurie looked into Elfin's wise, wonderful eyes, and nodded. She believed in magic, and she so very much wanted Jacob's wish to come true.

She closed her eyes and stood quiet and still before the cabinet. She felt like Dorothy, wishing to go home. She hadn't been told to do it, but she clicked her heels three times, closed her eyes tighter, and thought of homes. The cabin. The farmhouse. And castles. "I believe," she said, her voice only a whisper. "I believe." Louder now, and she took a deep breath and smiled. "I believe wishes come true."

She opened her eyes, stepped forward, and gently touched the wand to the cabinet door, holding it there until the box began to shake and shimmer, and glittery stars exploded from the top just as they had from Joseph's hand. The wand slipped from her fingers, clattering to the floor, rolling across the planks to Elfin the Magnificent's feet.

The little man picked up the wand and touched it once again to the cabinet, and the shaking eased. He turned, swirled his cape, and grinned. "Step back, child," he said to Laurie, and she gladly obeyed, taking her place beside Jake, wrapping a loving arm around Jacob's chest and pulling the boy against her as they waited.

Elfin the Magnificent released the latch on the cabinet door.

The crowd grew silent.

Breathing ceased.

All eyes stared, transfixed on the spot where the rock had been.

Slowly, Elfin opened the door. "My, my, my," Elfin said. "I do believe my assistant has performed a very great feat of magic." He turned toward Laurie and Jake and Jacob, his hands open, and there in his palms rested a crystal castle of spires and turrets, magnificent in its splendor, setting high atop a mountain of shimmering glass.

"I believe this is yours, child." Elfin held the crystal castle out to Jacob, but the boy didn't move. "Take it, Jacob. It's what you wished for."

Jacob tentatively touched the glass, smoothing his fingers over the carving, then wrapped it into his hand. "Thank you."

"It's my pleasure, young man. Now"—he swirled around in his cape—"I believe my work is done for today."

"But we want more magic," Joseph and Joshua called out.

Elfin only smiled. "All the magic you need is right here," he exclaimed as he waved his wand at the festive room and guests, "at this wonderful celebration."

He twirled his cape one last time, basking in the glory of continuous applause. "Thank you, thank you, thank you," he called out, and spinning around on the heels of his curled-toed shoes, he moved like a mini-whirlwind through the crowd.

Silhouetted by the setting sun shining through the doorway, Elfin the Magnificent opened his arms to his captive audience. "Dance. Play. Eat. Drink. And celebrate. It's a joyous occasion," he proclaimed in a voice that reverberated through the room, "and a night of magic."

Elfin disappeared from the Grange, and music once again burst from the speakers and filled the room, young and old danced, and sang, and recounted the wondrous things they'd witnessed, some believing, some questioning, but all caught up in the fun and excitement of the night.

"Dance with me, Laurie," Jake asked, pulling her into his arms.

But she slipped away, her fingers sliding along his as she broke from his hold. "I didn't get to thank him. I'll be right back." She ran toward the door, but all she saw was an instant flash of light, a glitter of stars.

"He's gone," she said, when she felt Jake at her side, his hand resting on her shoulder, his fingers playing with the short hair at the nape of her neck. "I'm glad Jacob got his wish, but I wish I'd made my own." She looked up at Jake, her eyes tinted with a hint of sadness. "Does that sound selfish?"

His head shook, and his eyes smiled with tenderness. "What would you have wished for?"

"That the stalker would disappear. That I could be free again."

"I'd wish that too, Red." He looked out into the approaching darkness, and found the first and brightest star in the sky. "I'd wish for that, too."

13

Jake and Laurie slipped back into the ranks of the merrymakers. Taking Laurie easily into his arms, he twirled her around the floor, hoping she'd forget the fear that still awaited her, wondering if the stalker would hold true to his word, and show up before the night was over.

Somehow, they managed to laugh, to eat, and drink. Chubby Checker sang while Laurie taught the boys to twist. Jake thrilled the older women, dancing them skillfully around the room as if he were Fred and every woman was Ginger. Mrs. Adams and Bert Ramsey had chairs set on either side of the disc jockey and talked music till the party waned. And Meghan and Kurt forgot the music and just held each other tightly, swaying to a rhythm that was only their own.

Darkness came. They stood outside and swirled sparklers in circles and triangles, and watched roadside stand fireworks shoot ten feet into the sky, and fizzle on the ground.

And when the end arrived, Kurt, who wowed his congregation every Sunday as he stood behind the pulpit, took the DJ's place on the dais, and addressed his friends and neighbors.

"It's been a truly magnificent evening, a Fourth

of July we'll all remember for a very, very long time. I'd like to thank Mrs. Adams for her exceptional organizational skills, and for baking the best apple pie in the county. I'd also like to thank Meghan O'Reilly and Laurie Langtry for the great decorations, and entertainment I'm sure we'll never, ever forget.

"I know you're all tired and you'd like to gather your belongings and loved ones and head for home, but I'd like to announce one more thing." Kurt directed his gaze at Laurie, and she tried to hide behind Jake, but he refused to let her budge.

"I'm sure most of you have met Laurie Langtry, either tonight, in the last few weeks, or years ago when she lived here as a child. She was Annie Flynn back then, a name, I'm sure, many of you would like to forget. But she's proof of the power of faith, of believing that miracles can and do come true."

A tear slid down Laurie's face. She didn't want Kurt to say anything more, she just wanted to hide.

"A few weeks ago, Laurie asked me to build a castle."

Everyone laughed, and Laurie rolled her eyes, flashing Kurt a frown that said the Lord might forgive him, but she never would.

"Now, now"—he raised his voice and hands to hush the group—"there's no need to laugh. Let me tell you about this castle. It's a big play structure, with turrets, and towers, and drawbridges, a couple of slides, and ladders and swings, and Laurie asked that it be built in the park next to the church."

Laurie felt the tightening of Jake's hand on her arm, and looked into his eyes, wondering what he was thinking about her change in plans. What she saw was tenderness, and something that just might resemble love.

Kurt continued when the people in the Grange grew quiet, when their whispers ceased. "Laurie didn't want me to say anything, she didn't want anyone to know she'd donated the money. She was afraid the people in town might think she was trying to buy friendship, something she'd never known when she lived here as a child. She didn't tell me her reasons, but I'd like to venture a guess, and those of you who've gotten to know her since she returned to town, will know it's the truth. Laurie wanted to give to the children of this town something she never knew when she was growing up. She wanted to give them a place of their own, a place to play and have fun, a castle where make-believe can become very, very real.

"I won't embarrass you any further, Laurie. I just want to say thank you. And, to the rest of you, we're going to need a lot of help constructing the castle. We've had fun today, coming together as a community, and I know you'll all want to get together again. I'll let you know the work date so you can take time out of your busy schedules to make a dream come true."

"It looks so empty now," Laurie said to Jake as they took one last peek inside of the Grange. The balloons had gone home with children, the drapes had been taken down until the next Fourth of July, the DJ was gone, as was all the leftover food. The boys slept in the back of the Jeep, and the hall stood stark and still and dark, except for the magical box Elfin the Magnificent had left behind.

"It looked better today than it ever has before. You made it special, Laurie. Special for everyone."

"I don't know if I did it for everyone, or if I did it for me. I've lived so long with bad memories of this town and the people, I wanted to replace those memories with good ones."

"I have a memory for you, Laurie," a familiar, haunting voice said, as a yellow rose flashed in front of Laurie's eyes, and the hard steel of a gun pressed into her temple.

Jake jerked around to face the wild black eyes of the stalker, a madman no longer hiding behind a mask.

"Don't move again, Jake."

Jake stood there, powerless, and watched all color drain from Laurie's face as the stalker wrapped his arm around her struggling body and pulled her into his chest, the petals of the long-stemmed rose brushing over her lips. The crazed man's finger rested on the trigger. One move, and Laurie's life could come to an end. But he had to save her. He had to.

"Impressive magic show tonight." The stalker continued to smile. "I watched it all, and you didn't even know I was here. You've never seen my face, have you Laurie? You've never felt my lips against your skin, have you, Laurie?" He lowered his mouth to her forehead, lightly brushing her brow, her temple.

Jake raised his hand slightly, hoping to get it within range of the man's arm while he focused his interest on Laurie, hoping he'd slip just enough that Jake could knock the gun from his fingers.

"I see you, Jake."

Jake froze.

"I've seen everything." He buried his lips into Laurie's cheek while his eyes remained on Jake. "I can give you more than he can, Laurie. I've waited for the right moment to take you away. Tonight's the night."

Tears streaked down Laurie's cheeks. "Please. Let me go. I'll give you anything."

"Yes, Laurie. You'll give me anything—and everything."

Laurie struggled, and Jake saw the madman's finger loosen on the trigger as he fought to keep her from moving. It was his only chance. A mad, insane moment, but it was the only opportunity he might have.

Jake drew back his fist and drove it hard and fast through the air, smashing it against the madman's hand, and the gun crashed to the ground. In another swift move, he kicked the gun across the room, latched onto the man's slicked-back black hair, and dragged him away from Laurie as the man strained against Jake's grasp, his arms and legs battling to get hold of the situation, and Jake.

"Get the gun, Laurie," Jake yelled, as he worked an arm around the man's neck in a stranglehold, but she stood there, motionless, and stared at the man who'd taken away her peace for way too long.

"She doesn't want to hurt me." The stalker groaned when Jake hooked his ankle around the man's right leg, pulling it from under him, off-balance, and sending them both crashing to the floor.

"She wants you to disappear," Jake hissed into the man's ear as he moved his body on top, pressing his knee into the stalker's back, finally maneuvering into a position where he could grip his wrists.

Jake held him firm against the floor. He tried to control his heavy breathing enough to speak to Laurie. She hadn't moved. Her eyes had glazed

over. But he couldn't let go of the stalker and go
to her. All he could do was talk.

"Laurie. Listen to me, Laurie."

"Don't listen to him, Laurie. He's the crazy man,
not me." Jake wrapped the fingers of one hand
around both wrists so he'd have one free, grabbed
hold of a hunk of the man's hair, and jerked his
head back.

"Shut up! Do you hear me. Shut up!" He
slammed the man's head against the floor, stunning him, stunning himself at his actions.

"Look at me, Laurie!" Her head turned slightly,
but he saw no emotion, only emptiness. "Dammit,
Red!" he yelled. "Snap out of it! I need your help."

Slowly, she moved toward the gun, reached for
it, then hesitated, her fingers just a fraction of an
inch from the handle. She turned back to Jake. "I
can't."

"That's okay, Laurie," Jake said softly. "We
don't need the gun. I've got him. He's not going
anywhere."

"You're sure?" Her voice strained with fear.

Jake nodded. "There's a phone outside the door,
Laurie. Call the sheriff."

"I'm afraid, Jake."

He smiled, wishing he could take her into his
arms and comfort her, but that would have to wait.
"No one's going to hurt you. Go outside. Call the
sheriff, then come back inside. I'll be right here."

Like a zombie she walked out of the room and
into the night, and the stalker came out of his stu-
por, jerking back his head, trying to gain leverage
with his feet and legs to throw Jake off-balance,
and all thoughts of Laurie left Jake's mind.

Taking control again, Jake wrenched the man's
arms tighter behind him and shoved himself to a

standing position, pulling the stalker with him. He dragged him across the floor, the man's black and white alligator boot heels attempting to dig into the floor, trying to stop, or get away.

Jake stumbled toward the magician's box. The walls and floor and ceiling were sturdy. He'd tested them himself. There was no way the man could get out if he could just get him shoved inside. And then he could comfort Laurie until the sheriff arrived.

Tired of fighting, tired of struggling, Jake continued across the room, the box seeming a million miles away instead of just a few yards. Finally, he reached the open door, turned, and shoved the beast into the container, slamming the door onto the man's fingers as he tried to exit.

"You're not going anywhere." Jake's voice was low, menacing, and hateful as he slammed the door again, opening it just a crack as the fingers disappeared, and he closed it one more time, securing the latch. With a heavy sigh, he leaned his back against the door and stared at the gun laying just across the floor. He wanted this man out of Laurie's life. It would be so easy to put the gun to the stalker's head. But then, he realized, he'd be no better than the evil man he'd trapped inside.

It seemed like hours, but it had probably been just a minute or two since Laurie had left the room. He wanted to hold her. He wanted to comfort her, just as much as he wanted her to comfort him. His arms and legs ached from the struggle. His mind swirled with thoughts of waiting for a trial, sitting day after day in a courthouse while the man inside pleaded not guilty by reason of insanity. He envisioned the man spending six months in an institution somewhere, then being set free. He pictured him finding his way back to Laurie's house with another yellow rose.

The thoughts seized him. His breathing labored again. He couldn't let the man go free. For Laurie. He had to end it now.

One foot after the other he moved across the floor, his fingers wrapping around the handle of the gun, one finger resting on the trigger. Again, he stood in front of the box and listened to the pounding inside. It would be so easy. So very, very easy.

He closed his eyes and prayed. "Forgive me, Lord."

He opened his eyes again and reached for the latch. His fingers trembled.

He raised the gun, pointing it at the door. "Oh, God. What am I doing?"

Distraught, he dropped his arm to his side, and pressed his forehead to a painted star on the door. He took one deep breath, then another. "Disappear. Please. Just disappear."

Jake set the gun on the floor next to the box and stood back. Again he closed his eyes, and clicked his heels three times, willing himself to believe. He had to believe. He had to.

"Jake?"

Don't open your eyes, he told himself. Don't look at Laurie now. Finish what you were about to begin.

All thoughts left his mind. He didn't know if Laurie spoke. He didn't know if the stalker still struggled inside. All he knew was he had to believe. He filled his chest with air and a lightness came over him, a feeling of joy, as though all would soon be right and good.

"I believe," he whispered.

"I believe."

A smile formed on his lips, and his mustache twitched.

"I believe."

He opened his eyes, and at his feet lay Elfin's long red wand. He hadn't seen it there before. He didn't question it now.

Leaning over, he picked up the wand and tapped it against the box the stalker was trying so hard to free himself from.

And just like before, it began to shimmy. It shook fiercely, stronger than before, as if all the power in the universe had wrapped itself around the box. Suddenly, a glittering of lights and stars burst from the top.

Jake threw his shoulders back and stood straight, tall, his muscles no longer aching from stress or strain. He touched the box again with the wand, and the fireworks display disappeared, and all was quiet, except the woman standing at his side.

"Jake?" She touched his arm, and it was the most comforting feeling he'd felt in his entire life.

He lifted her to him, swinging her around and around and around. "He's gone, Laurie. He's gone."

"What are you talking about?"

"The magic, Laurie. Didn't you see the magic? I've made him disappear."

She put her hands on his cheeks as he held her, and they met eye to eye. "I want to believe, Jake." A tear slid down her cheek and he kissed it away.

"Did you get the sheriff?"

She shook her head. "I couldn't get the phone to work."

"Good. Then we don't have to explain any of this."

"Explain any of what?"

Jake looked into her eyes, at her tears, and realized maybe his jubilation was too quick a reaction. He didn't know if anything had worked. He didn't know if the stalker had disappeared. All he knew was that the box had shook. But that could have been the stalker. Fireworks had exploded from the top, but, again, that could have been just some crazy magician's theatrical device.

But he wanted to believe. He really and truly wanted to believe.

He put his hand on the latch, but Laurie quickly covered it with hers, horror written on her face again. "No, Jake. He's still inside. You can't open it. It's a trick."

Gently, he put his callused fingers on her face and kissed her lips. "Believe, Laurie. Just believe."

With doubt still wrapped around her, she moved her hand and let Jake release the latch. Slowly, deliberately, he opened the door just a crack. There was no noise. No movement.

He opened it a little further, a little further, then jumped when he heard the first clanking noise.

Laurie gripped his arm, as the clanking became a steady rhythm.

Jake opened the door wide, and they both peered into the darkness.

There, in the center of the cabinet floor, stood a wind-up toy.

Jake laughed.

Laurie cried.

And the mechanical man in black and white prison stripes, ball and chain clamped tightly around his ankle, took another methodical, continuous swing with his pick at the rocks strewn around his feet.

Jake stepped onto the porch, a blanket and towels thrown over his shoulder, and closed the screen door behind him. "You feel like walking down to the stream with me?"

Laurie had curled up in the swinging chair on the porch, while Jake tucked the boys in bed, and let her fear drain away into the star-filled night. He'd held her for the longest time as they stood in the middle of the Grange hall, the toy clanking away in the background. When they headed for home, they left the toy behind, locked away in the box, something to think about at some other time. But not tonight.

And now he wanted to go for a walk, and he probably wanted to talk, when all she wanted to do was crawl back into his arms and stay there forever. But she smiled, and held her hand out to his, loving the rough skin that touched her pampered flesh.

Quietly, they walked along the path that led to the boys' favorite swimming hole, a place lit by the stars and the moon, hidden from prying eyes, but not so far away that they couldn't see the cabin, or hear a child's voice if one should call out.

Laurie climbed on top of a rock and sat on the cold, moss-covered surface, pulling her knees close with her arms wrapped tightly around them.

Jake stood before her, casually pulling off his boots and socks as if it was something he did in her presence all the time. He unsnapped the pearlized buttons of the red, white, and blue plaid cowboy shirt he'd worn to the party, pulled it from his jeans, and dropped it to the ground.

"I'm going for a swim," he said. "Will you join me?"

She shook her head, and continued to watch as he slipped out of his jeans and walked, naked and splendid, into the cold pool of water. He looked lonely and confused, and it took only moments for her to strip out of red linen and sequins and thousand-dollar boots to join him.

He came back to the rocky bank as she walked toward him, and picked her up into his arms, like a babe, and cuddled her close as he headed into the waist-deep water.

"Thought it might be a good idea to wash away the memories," he whispered, lowering himself, and Laurie, inch by inch, into the calm, cold water. She slid her arms around his neck, her fingers threading through the curling hair that cascaded over his shoulders, and tucked her head into the hollow of his shoulder.

"It's over, Jake," she said, as the water splashed her breasts, but the comfort of his arms kept her warm. "I can go back to New York now."

She could feel his muscles flinch, feel his hands tighten around her leg, around her arm, as if to tighten his hold so she wouldn't slip out of his grasp.

"Yeah, I guess you can, Red." She felt his kiss, the way his lips settled in the curls on top of her head, and hesitated, lingering a moment or two, as if he didn't want to take them away. She felt his heart beating harder, felt him take a long, deep breath. "Hold on tight, Laurie. I'm going under."

She did just as he'd told her, digging her head deeper into his chest, grasping even tighter to his neck, and she swallowed air less than a second before they dropped under the water. She was there just a moment, maybe a second or two, before he lifted her back to air, his head following shortly, tilted back, his hair dripping, and shimmering in the moonlight.

Her teeth clattered together. "Cold?" he asked as she looked into his eyes, at the face earlier beaded with sweat, now beaded with tiny drops of water that shined like diamonds in the starlight.

She nodded. "But I do feel better, like some of the shock washed away."

"Had the feeling it might help." He carried her out of the water, giving no thought at all to making love, wanting only to hold her, knowing it might be the last time.

He set her on the ground and draped a blanket around her shoulders, wrapping her tightly, then dried his body with one towel and fastened the other around his hips. Pulling her down with him, he leaned against the rock she'd sat on earlier, and cradled her in his lap. "Tell me what you like so much about New York."

Laurie rested her head against his chest. "The opera. Theater. The lights of Times Square." She lifted her head and looked into his eyes, and he forced himself not to kiss her. "There's not much I don't like. There's so much I left behind." She yawned, and closed her eyes. "So much I have to do when I get back."

Weaving his fingers through her curls, he pulled her head closer to his warmth, and listened as her breathing steadied, and watched her eyelids relax over her beautiful emerald eyes. She slept, probably the first truly relaxing and peaceful sleep she'd experienced in years.

Jake watched the moon move westward in the sky, sitting for nearly an hour as he wound his finger around curl upon curl in her hair. Why had he even hoped she would stay? he wondered. Why had he thought there might be a chance?

Tonight, he'd given her back her life, her freedom, and destroyed all hope he'd ever thought of having her with him forever.

Attempting not to disturb his sleeping beauty, he leaned over and grabbed her clothing, her boots, digging her key out of the pocket where he'd seen her put it earlier.

Slowly, he stood, lifting her gently in his arms, paying little attention when the towel slipped from his waist, paying no attention at all to the rocks that cut into his feet as he walked the path toward the house he'd hoped for a fleeting moment they might share someday.

Slipping the key into the door, he quietly closed it behind him and headed for her bedroom. Laurie's eyes never opened, not even when he pulled his arms from under her so she could snuggle into the comfort of her own bed, not even when he pulled the blanket from around her, and wrapped it around himself. He looked at her body, naked and beautiful, but his loins didn't ache for her. Not tonight. Only his heart ached. He pulled the covers tightly around her neck, and lightly kissed her forehead.

He went to the window and stared out at the stars, looking for one in particular, but knew he'd already exhausted a lifetime worth of wishes when the stalker disappeared. Instead, he went back to the bed and looked down at Laurie one more time.

"I wish you wouldn't leave," he said, no longer believing wishes come true, and leaned over to gently kiss her Betty Boop lips, so sweet and innocent in sleep. "Good night, Red," he whispered, and walked out of her life.

14

Laurie woke when the first light of day beamed through her window. She smiled, and breathed deeply, loving her first morning of freedom.

And then she peeked under the covers. *Oh, Lord!* she was naked. Had Jake carried her to her room? she wondered. Had he stayed? Had he wanted to make love when all she'd wanted to do was sleep?

Oh, Lord! What a way to start the first moments of her new life. She had to talk to him. Now.

Clambering out of bed, she saw the outfit she'd worn to the party draped over a chair, her boots sitting neatly at its side, just the way Jake's had sat next to his bed. She ran to her closet, ripped out a t-shirt and cutoffs, slipped into both without bothering with underwear. In the bathroom, she quickly picked out curls, wondering how it could be tangle free when it had gotten so wet the night before and hadn't been combed. She brushed her teeth, washed her face, and grabbed a pair of tennis shoes, struggling into them as she skipped out of her bedroom, finally running down the stairs, and zoomed past Merry.

"My, my, my, but you're in a hurry this morning."

"I have to go see Jake," Laurie said as she

breezed through the kitchen, letting the screen door slam behind her. She jumped over ground squirrel holes and cow patties, and climbed the fence rather than opening and closing the gate, which would take too much time.

She had to tell him she loved him. She had to tell him she couldn't wait to get everything taken care of in New York so she could come back to Bunch Gulch permanently.

Tramping up the porch steps, she took a few calming breaths, then knocked on the door.

No answer.

She knocked again.

Still no answer.

She tried the knob, but it was locked. She looked around. The Jeep was gone. He must have gone into town, she thought, and her shoulders slumped. All she'd wanted to do was throw her arms around his neck and kiss him. But she'd missed her chance.

Slowly, she walked back to the farmhouse, opening and closing the screen door with ease this time, and slumped into a kitchen chair as Merry bustled around the room making what smelled like sausage and bacon. She remembered that morning when they'd eaten in the middle of her big old bed, and made love afterward. She wanted Jake there with her again.

"If you'd given me half a moment, child," Merry muttered, halfway scolding Laurie with eyes that beamed over the tops of her glasses, "I would have given you this letter I found this morning."

Laurie took the white envelope from Merry's hand, ripped open the flap, and unfolded the lined notebook paper.

Laurie—

Hated to leave without saying goodbye, but thought the boys might enjoy a camping trip. We haven't been away from the ranch in months, and now that you're leaving, and I don't have to keep an eye on you any longer, figured we might as well get away. Hope all goes well for you in New York.

Jake

Laurie stared at the words, then she crumpled the note. "He's left, Merry." She shook her head, unable to believe what he'd written. No emotion. Not a word about caring, or missing her, or hating to see her go. Nothing. "I've been wasting my time. He doesn't want me. He doesn't care."

"Oh, pish posh! Of course he cares. He got rid of that stalker, didn't he?"

Laurie looked at Merry out of the corner of her eye. Her brow furrowed. "How did you know about that?"

"That? Oh, you know, child. I just have a way of knowing things. But that's not what's important now. What's important is you, and Jake."

"Forget it, Merry. He's run away from me, so I'm going to do the same. If he thinks I planned to go back to New York permanently, I might as well make his thoughts come true."

Merry looked toward the ceiling and shook her head. "Oh, Nicky, Nicky, Nicky. Whatever am I going to do?"

"You're going to help me pack."

Merry's hands shoved into her ample hips, and she stood her ground. "I have no intention of doing any such thing. Go to New York if you must. Clear up anything that's left to be cleared up. Then

you come back here immediately, young lady.
You've a love life to mend, and it can't be done
half a continent away."

Jake sat on the front porch step, carving a castle
into the face of a pine book shelf he planned to
mount on the boys' bedroom wall. He heard the
crunch of gravel and looked up to see the prettiest
redhead who'd ever caught his eye, stolen his
heart, and run away.

He looked back down at the wood, the fingers
holding his carving knife trembling, and he tried
to steady his hand just as much as he tried to
steady his voice. "Back from New York so soon?"
he asked, staring at the toes of her rich-lady blue
suede cowboy boots when they stopped in the
gravel just inches from his own scuffed and
muddy blacks.

"Yeah. Took almost three weeks to get everything taken care of back there, but at least now I
won't have to go back unless I want to."

His eyes raised to look at Laurie through his
pale blond lashes. "You get a dose of opera and
the theater while you were gone. Enough to last
you another month or so?"

Laurie dropped down on the step beside him,
running a petite, freckle-covered finger over the
rough edge of the castle. "Saw *Phantom* for the
ninth time. No opera, though. No symphony. Too
busy with real estate agents and movers. The rest
of the time I spent writing."

"Finish your book yet?" The small talk was killing him, but he couldn't think of anything else to
say.

"Not yet. Getting close, though."

They sat in silence while he carved, and he inhaled the scent of her perfume, something expensive from one of those highfalutin New York stores, he imagined. But, hell, it smelled good, although he preferred the smell of her in fresh mountain water and a blanket washed in Tide.

He jumped when she put her hand on his arm, the sun beating on that diamond bracelet of hers, nearly blinding him with its glare. "I missed you, Jake. I wanted to see you before you left, but you'd already headed out on your camping trip."

"Had fun, too." He dug his knife deeper into the wood. "Sorry I missed you, but I'd been ignoring the boys. Don't plan on doing that anymore."

"But you're going to ignore me, aren't you?"

He stopped cutting, set the wood and knife down beside him, crossed his arms over his knees, and leaned forward, staring out at the farmhouse in the distance. He'd lived through two weeks of hell after he found out she'd gone back to New York, and it had taken him a week to build a wall around his feelings again. He wasn't about to let it fall down now. "I'm not going to ignore you, Laurie. I'm just not going to let you get under my skin again. I told you before I was afraid you'd run away. But you did it anyway—"

"I didn't run away, Jake. I had to go back to New York. I had an apartment there I had to sell. I had a contract hanging over my head and people wanting to know if I ever planned to sign. I had a hell of a lot of decisions to make. And I made them. And now I'm back. For good."

Jake scratched his eyebrow and tilted his head to look at her. God, she was pretty, and those Betty Boop lips were coated in burgundy lipstick, just begging to be kissed. But he turned away. "I'm glad you've made your decision. I made mine, too." He dusted his hands off on his Levi's and stood. "I'm not getting involved with a woman again." And he walked away from Laurie toward the pasture where the boys had been mercilessly teasing Sue Ellen, heedless to what was going on between their dad and the woman they'd begged him to make their mom.

"Damn pigheaded crazy stubborn fool!"

"Oh, my!"

Laurie stormed into the living room and stood in front of Merry, her booted foot tapping faster than the click of Merry's knitting needles. "He's not getting involved with a woman—ever again. That's what he told me, Merry."

"Oh, my!"

"I need more than an *oh my*, Merry. I need help."

"I take it you're not going to run to your office all in a snit over this?" Merry asked, her eyes twinkling as her cranberry cheeks swelled with merriment.

"Not on your life. Jake McAllister's going to get married. To me—whether he wants to or not. So, do you have any suggestions?"

"What would one of your heroines do?"

"This isn't fiction, Merry. It's real life."

"Yes, I suppose it is. Such a pity, too. All the really good things seem to happen only in books."

Laurie grew wistful. "My heroes never made my toes turn up quite the way Jake does. And they never—"

"My, my, my, child. If my Nicky heard you talking that way he'd ban me from being your housekeeper."

"Okay, I'll stop daydreaming, if you'll help me

come up with an idea to make Jake mine, for good."

Merry appeared to give the dilemma a lot of thought. She squinted, her lips twitched from side to side, and then, she tapped her finger to her nose. "Writers write, child. So that's what I suggest. Get a pencil and paper, and dream something up."

Laurie dropped down on the couch. "You're a big help, Merry."

"Yes, dear, I know." Merry scooted out of the rocker and headed toward the kitchen. "No time to sit there pouting, young lady. You've work to do, and just remember—" A sudden clash of thunder rolled across the sky, shaking the house, and the crystal vase on the coffee table. "Oh dear, Nicky might not approve of what I'm about to say, but—" Lightning streaked through the treetops, and Merry shuddered. "Sometimes," Merry spat out the words, speaking as fast as she could, "drastic situations call for drastic solutions."

15

Laurie strolled along the well-worn path, snatching up a wild yellow daisy, plucking away petals. "Loves me. Loves me not. Loves me. Loves me not. Loves me."

Smiling, she tossed the naked stem over her back, looked toward the heavens and begged the powers that be for help with one more miracle, and for forgiveness. She needed the first just as badly as she knew she would need the second.

The sun chose that moment to peek out from behind the clouds that had rolled in that morning, and a bright ray of light shot down from the sky to illuminate the man of her dreams. She chose to look at it as an affirmative answer to all her prayers, and picked up her step as she neared the porch.

Jake's muscles stretched and pulled as he vigorously rubbed sandpaper over the porch railing. His eyes flickered away from his work when Laurie stepped into his line of vision. For one short moment he looked into her eyes, then immediately returned his focus to his work.

"Need some help?" she asked.

"You any better at woodwork than you are at cooking?"

"Never given it a try. Probably not, though."
She grabbed hold of a pillar and hugged it, gazing
around the wooden column at Jake's naked shoulders and arms and hands. She wanted him. Desperately.

"Haven't seen you out and about much lately,"
he said, wiping away the fine film of dust with an
old rag, his eyes averted. He might as well be talking to the rag for all the interest he seemed to show
in her.

"Finished my book." She heaved a sigh, raised
her eyes heavenward for guidance, then pulled an
envelope from the back pocket of her jeans. "Took
it into town this morning, and sent it on its way.
Hope you don't mind, but I picked up your mail
while I was there."

His eyebrows raised, and he tilted his head, fixing her with a skeptical frown. "Tom just handed
you my mail?"

"Not *just*. He was sorting the incoming stuff
when I showed up, and I mentioned I might as
well take yours since I live so close. He gave me
the usual hard time, you know how he is." She
sighed again, wondering if she should just scrap
her plan and head back home. But when she
looked into those Montana blue-sky eyes that were
staring at her, then at the letter, she knew she had
to continue. "You haven't been very neighborly
since I came back from New York, so I figured I'd
need an excuse to get halfway close to you. And,
well, I guess I was pretty insistent with Tom. I told
him you wouldn't mind." She tilted her head
down, staring at her hands wringing the wood she
clutched like a life preserver. Slowly, she raised her
eyes, gazing at Jake through her lashes. "You don't

mind, do you?" She'd never fought so hard in her life to be sweet and demure.

"Suppose not."

She held the envelope out to Jake.

He dropped the rag over the railing and took the envelope, examining the front, which Laurie had looked at over and over again. No return address, only Jake's name and address typed on the front, with a faint cancellation reading Los Angeles. He frowned as he slipped his finger under the flap and slit open the top. "Hope you don't mind me taking a quick look." He held the letter up to the light as if looking for a sign of something disastrous within.

"No, go ahead."

He pulled out the contents, unfolded the nondescript white paper, and halfheartedly smiled. "Well, I'll be. It's from Amy." He shook his head and a stray strand of hair flopped on his forehead. He looked almost happy to hear from her, and Laurie wished with all her heart she'd never given him the letter.

He leaned against the railing, and she watched his eyes scanning the words, watched his Adam's apple rise and fall heavily in his throat. Watched tears slide from his eyes. He slumped to the steps, the letter floating down to the ground as it slipped from his fingers, then he stared, blank and empty, at the ground.

"Jake?" Laurie sat beside him, resting a sympathetic, comforting hand on his thigh. "What's wrong?"

"She wants the boys." The words were a whisper of shock and disbelief. "She hasn't given a damn in four years, and suddenly—suddenly, she wants them back."

"But, you have legal custody, don't you?"

He raised his head, his reddened eyes looking into hers, then past her, to the boys clambering over the old downed tree. "She wanted a quick divorce. She never asked for anything. It didn't seem necessary to fight for custody when it was understood I'd have them." He slammed a tightened fist against the pillar. "How could I have been so stupid?"

"You trusted her. That's all." She put her hands to his cheeks, wishing there was something she could do, something she could say to comfort him. Softly, she caressed away a tear.

"Yeah, I trusted her, and now I'm getting screwed." He shoved off the porch, headed toward the boys, but stopped at a gate and crossed his arms over the top rail.

Laurie ignored the way he pushed away from her. She refused to leave him. Not now. He needed her, whether he knew it or not.

She stood behind him, hands in her pockets, wanting to touch him, but forcing herself to hold back.

"Are my reasons for mistrusting people a little clearer to you now, Laurie?" he asked, although he never looked her way.

"We've all been hurt, Jake. Sometimes, though, you just have to forget and move on."

"How do you propose I forget this? Huh?"

"That's not what I meant. You have to trust someone, Jake. Maybe me?"

He spun around in anger, but when Laurie saw his face, all she noticed was fear. "What am I going to do, Laurie? I can't let her have them. I can't."

"Get an attorney."

He shrugged his shoulders, standing there quietly, for a long time, staring at his kids, looking at the lush green pastures, at the pines, and the mountains surrounding his valley. And then he again folded his arms over the top of the gate. "I could try to get in touch with her, see if we could talk this out."

"Do you know where she is?" Laurie asked, although he'd told her many times they hadn't talked in years, that he hadn't a clue to her whereabouts.

"I didn't look at the letter close enough. I didn't see an address, or a phone number, but she's got to get in touch with me sometime if she really wants to do this."

He ran his fingers through his hair. He was more distressed than he'd been when the stalker held a gun to her head, and she wished, once again, she'd never given him that letter.

"Can I do anything, Jake?"

"Yeah, sure," he said sarcastically. "You could buy this place from me, give me enough money so I could run off someplace where she couldn't find us."

"What!" His fight might be gone, but hers wasn't. "You're not about to sell this place. Not to me, not to anyone. And you're not going to run away. That's your big hangup, remember? People don't run away. They fight. So, dammit, Jake! Fight!"

"Don't lecture me, Red."

"And don't give me orders," she snapped.

He spun around. He had anger in his eyes this time, and Laurie wanted to crack open a bottle of champagne and celebrate. "What do you propose I do?" he barked. "Get some high-priced lawyer to give me advice?"

"Sure. Why not?"

He threw up his hands. "And how the hell am I supposed to pay for that? Huh? You see money falling off the trees around here?"

"No, but as you stated before, I've got a heck of a lot just burning holes in my pockets. Let me help."

"No."

"Why don't you just swallow some of that ridiculous pride of yours and think straight?"

His chest heaved, hard and labored, and Laurie almost cried when his mustache twitched. "Not a chance." He stormed away, and once again left her standing all alone.

Jake called every phone number he'd ever had for Amy and placed call after call, even trying her parents but got no answer, just disconnect recordings everywhere.

He sat half the night staring at his checkbook, at his savings passbook, but there wasn't enough money to hire a lawyer—not a good one, not even a bad one.

At three in the morning he crept into the boys' room, adjusting blankets, brushing stray strands of hair from their brows, and kissed each gently on the forehead. He loved them more than life itself, and he didn't have a clue what he'd do without them.

The next morning, shaved and showered, and feeling like hell because he'd never closed his eyes during the night, he packed the boys into the back of the Jeep and headed into town. He went to Tom Harrington and asked for a job working in the store. But Tom had just hired a nephew to help him out. He wasn't qualified to sell real estate, or insurance, and neither office needed a janitor or clerk. It was summer and the teenagers had all the minimum-wage jobs. The only thing Jake knew how to do was ranch and carve. He already knew he couldn't make money at the first, and he needed money fast and couldn't rely on the second.

He stopped at the church, hoping to talk to Kurt, but the pastor had gone to Helena till Sunday, the note on the door said, and Meghan was mysteriously missing, too.

Hell!

He bought ice cream cones for each of the boys and headed for home, slamming on the brake when he drove past Laurie's drive. He shoved the Jeep into reverse, backed up a short ways, then shoved it into first and drove up to the front of the house.

"You boys wait here a minute," he instructed before hopping over the door, and running up the porch steps. He banged on the screen, and a moment later little Laurie Langtry appeared at the door, her emerald eyes looking like great big dollar signs. He tried to shake the vision away, but it was there, and it wasn't going to go away.

"Afternoon, Jake," Laurie said in that sweeter than honey voice.

"You know any good lawyers?" he growled, and knew he'd live to regret his question.

"My, my, my, don't you look all in a dither."

Laurie watched Merry shuffle into the living room with her ever-present tray of food. She wasn't the least bit hungry, and she wasn't in the mood for company, but she knew offering those excuses to Merry would get her nowhere.

She set the magazine she'd been staring at for an hour beside her on the sofa. "I'm not in a dither, Merry. I'm feeling a bit like Jezebel—and trust me, it's not a pleasant feeling."

"Well, child, I've the perfect thing to brighten your mood. Look, I've brought fresh gingerbread with whipped cream, just the way you like it."

"I suppose it won't do any good to tell you I'm not hungry."

"No, it wouldn't. So why don't you settle for telling me the truth. Aren't things working out with you and Jake?"

"Things are going just fine. Everything's according to plan. Perfect, as a matter of fact. So perfect, I think I can already hear wedding bells."

Merry set the gingerbread on the coffee table, and placed a pudgy hand over Laurie's. "Ah, Laurie child. Isn't this what you wanted?"

She wanted it more than a lifetime of gingerbread and whipped cream, more than a lifetime of being number one on the *New York Times* bestseller list. She leaned her head against the back of the couch and stared at the ceiling. "For the first time in my life, Merry," Laurie whispered, "I just don't know if the end justifies the means."

Jake clenched the phone between his ear and his shoulder, scribbling note after note, while he listened to words that must have been scripted in hell. His expressionless eyes stared at the paper. All feelings, all sense of caring, deserted him the moment he received Amy's letter. Now, talking to Laurie's attorney friend, he still had no feelings, not even fear, or dread, or anticipation.

"Yeah, I understand," he said, dropping the pen

and gripping the phone. "I'll do it as soon as possible."

Jake hung up the phone, stared at it, then picked up the receiver and stabbed out a series of well-remembered numbers. "Hello, Meg," he said, both simple words catching in his throat like glue, and he just barely heard her words of concern. "No, no. I'm fine. Look, can you watch the boys for awhile?"

He twisted the cord on the phone as she talked. "I'll be there soon. Thanks, Meg."

In less than ten minutes, he dropped the boys off at Meg's, hopped back in the Jeep, and strained every gear as he peeled out of town.

Laurie sat cross-legged in the grass and pulled thriving weeds from the base of her roses. Her bare knees were crusted with dirt, right along with the seat of her too short to be decent cut-off jeans, and pink cotton halter top. A trickle of perspiration ran down the hollow of her back. If she'd known Jake McAllister was going to slam his brakes in the middle of her dusty drive, she might have dressed for the occasion.

She pushed her sunglasses up on her nose with the tip of a dirty glove, and watched Jake hurdle the door of the Jeep and stomp across the yard, planting both feet firmly in place before her. If only he knew what those tight jeans and muscled thighs did to her insides as he stood smack in front of her eyes.

From where she sat, he looked like an angry giant, but when she looked into his eyes, all she saw was a cloak of indecision.

The time had come. It was what she wanted. She just wished she didn't feel so damn guilty.

"Can we talk?"

"Here, or in the bathroom? I'm a mess."

He didn't laugh, just put his hands under her sweaty arms and pulled her to her feet.

"Is this going to be another one of those talks I'm not going to want to hear?" she asked, but once again, he said nothing. Somehow, although he glared into her eyes as if looking into a crystal ball for all the answers, he wove his fingers through hers and stalked off, his stride so long Laurie had to run to keep up.

When they reached the old well, he dropped her hand and leaned against the rocks, folding his arms resolutely over his chest. "I talked to your lawyer this morning."

Laurie bit the inside of her cheek and looked away. She couldn't come up with any quips to throw his direction, her wit as dry as her throat. "Does he think he can help?"

"Not unless I get married," he spit out, his words followed by laughter full of unspoken sarcasm. "I need a wife, he said. And money in the bank. I need to show that I can provide them with proper clothing and shelter and food. Hell, Laurie, I always thought just being a good dad was all they needed."

"Well, you're the best dad I've ever encountered."

"The courts could care less. Money talks. You should know that by now."

Laurie's teeth moved from her cheek to her tongue. She was getting sick and tired of hearing that line of bull about money being the greatest thing since woman invented the wheel.

"Look, Jake." She swallowed deeply, working up the courage to withstand his next blast of hot air. "If you need money, I could—"

"I don't want your money," he fired back, just as she'd expected.

"Then what do you want?"

He pushed away from the well and walked to the wall of roses, snapping off a thorny, dark red bud. "You interested in getting married?"

She came within a hairsbreadth of choking on his pathetic proposal. "Don't know," she answered, trying to make light of her lie. "No one's asked."

"Don't make this difficult, Red. I'm asking."

"Pretty sorry proposal if you ask me."

"Oh, hell." He slammed a fist into an open palm and started to walk away. But he stopped, and she could see the muscles of his back expand and contract as he fought for breath, and maybe a little composure. "Look, Laurie. I don't want anything permanent. Just a temporary fix, something to make things look good till the lawyer can get me permanent custody."

"Well, that's got to rank right up there with getting a proposal from Bluebeard."

"You want me to get flowery?" He swept up a handful of daisies, roots and all, and shoved them into her hands. "You want me down on my knee?" He dropped down in front of her and tossed his hat toward the well. "Look, Red, right about now I'll do just about anything to get a wife."

"But you only want a temporary fix?"

"Yeah, just till I get papers saying the boys are mine."

"That means you rack up your second divorce."

"One. Two." He shrugged. "What's the difference."

"You're awfully cynical. I thought you were proposing."

He plowed his hands through his hair and got up from the ground. He stalked around the clearing like a caged animal, and finally halted, his chest to her face.

She looked up and smiled.

He looked down and frowned.

"Okay. Here's the proposal. Marry me. Name only; no consummation. We can have a prenuptial agreement drawn up saying I get nothing when we call it quits. No money, no nothing. I don't want anything from you but a marriage certificate I can show to the attorney. When I get sole custody of the kids, we can call it quits."

Laurie turned away, unable to face him. She hadn't expected this. It wasn't what she wanted. Didn't he know she loved him? Didn't he know how much she needed him? Absently, she plucked the petals from one of the wild yellow daisies, reciting to herself, once again, the age-old words. Could the daisy have lied the first time around? *Loves me, loves me not. Loves me, loves me not. Loves me.* She'd plucked the last petal, and wanted to believe that the words were true. He did love her; he just didn't know it.

Yet.

"You want me to marry you?" she asked, turning around to face him.

"Yes." His word was almost a whisper. "Yes, Laurie. I want you to marry me."

"Then here's my deal." She paced now, like a power-mad executive laying out the rules, while she clasped her trembling hands behind her back, the pathetic stem of the poor wilted daisy hanging from her fingers. "No prenuptial agreement. What I have is yours. What you have is mine, and that includes the boys."

"I don't know."

She jerked around and the blaze of her eyes defied him to speak another word. "*And*, no divorce. I won't ask you for anything you don't want to give me, but I don't believe in divorce, and I'll never give you one."

"I could take you for all you're worth if we split up."

"You won't."

"How do you know?"

"I've trusted very few people in my life, Jake. But you I trust. I wouldn't marry you if I didn't."

"I wasn't a great husband the first time around; I doubt things will improve. You're taking a pretty big risk, 'cause I just don't think I'm cut out for wedding bells."

"Maybe you weren't a great husband because you didn't have the greatest wife. Maybe you weren't cut out for each other. Maybe it had nothing at all to do with being cut out for marriage."

"Hell, Laurie. It doesn't matter if I'm good husband material or not. I need a wife. I need a mother for my boys. I can't give you anything in return. I have no money, no job, just me, the boys, the ranch."

"And a hell of a lot of pride."

"Yeah, well, I never claimed to be perfect." He pinched another rosebud from the twisted mass of vines and stuck it close to her face and smiled. "So, Red, are you going to marry me or not?"

Couldn't he just tell her he loved her? Couldn't he at least tell her he liked her, that they could have fun together, even if they did nothing but yell and fight? No, not Jake McAllister.

Crooking an index finger under a button on his shirt, she pulled him close, stood on tiptoes, and casually kissed his lips. "So, Jake. When should we tie the knot?"

16

Victory had been hers that day, yet Laurie felt more like the spoils of war than the conquering hero. She'd wanted Jake's proposal so desperately, anything was worth the price to capture him. Now, she felt only shame for what she had done, and sadness over the outcome. A lie seemed a lousy foundation for the beginnings of a lifelong commitment.

Merry bustled into Laurie's bedroom with cocoa and cookies and a dose of cheer, but even that couldn't pull Laurie from the depths of bleakness and doom. "My, my, my, child. You look as though you've got the weight of the world on your shoulders."

Laurie turned away from the window where she curled up with a pillow clutched to her stomach. "Well, Merry, I've managed to rack up one more success in my life," she moaned. "You'll be happy to know Jake and I are getting married."

"Ah, but the bride doesn't sound the least bit happy."

"If he ever finds out what I've done, he won't forgive me."

"Oh, pish posh!" Merry set the tray down on the edge of Laurie's desk and shoved her folded arms under her bosom. "I'm not going to stand here and tell you what you did is going to be smiled upon by the man up there." Merry's gaze turned toward the ceiling, then lowered again to stare at Laurie over the rims of her spectacles. "But I'm sure there's been a guardian angel or two who's done something a little on the wrong side of up and up to help her charge. Not to say it's right, mind you. But my goodness me, child, what's done is done. If I'm not mistaken, the time will come when you'll have to answer for your indiscretion."

Laurie groaned.

"Until then, young lady, just remember. He loves you. He'll forgive you."

"But that's the problem, Merry. He doesn't love me."

"Nonsense, child. The man's crazy in love, he's just too much of a fool to realize it. Now, I suggest you dwell on all that loves-me-loves-me-not stuff later, and think about wedding plans."

Laurie clutched the pillow even tighter to her chest. "There's no time for anything fancy, Merry. We're getting married this weekend."

"Oh, no, no, no. That won't do at all."

"It's what Jake wants."

Merry zapped Laurie with a scornful stare over the top of her glasses. "And when did you start doing what Jake wanted? What's happened to little Laurie Langtry, the woman who's always wanted the best and gotten it?"

"I've gotten what I want—I think. Maybe I shouldn't ask for more."

Merry shoved her hands tightly under her ample bosom and shook her head. "This isn't like you at all. Now, you get out of that window seat right this minute and write out a guest list."

Laurie rolled her eyes and tossed the pillow across the room. Slowly, she unfolded out of the window and wandered to her desk, pulled out her chair, and slumped.

"That pathetic, sulking attitude just won't do at all."

"I feel pathetic."

Merry raised her eyes. "Oh, Nicky. What did I ever do to deserve this?" She plopped her bottom down in the chair next to Laurie's desk, and put a pudgy hand on top of Laurie's slender one. "I've been thinking, Laurie child. Considering your pathetic nature, perhaps we should have black roses at your wedding and—" Merry put a crooked finger to her mouth. "Yes, that's it, devil's food cake."

"I prefer pink roses," Laurie mumbled.

"I see."

"And carrot cake with cream cheese frosting."

"My, my, my. There's ever so much to plan."

Laurie looked at Merry out of the corner of her eye and cracked a wicked grin. "Since when did you ever think there was too much to do?"

"Since I got the crazy notion that you needed my help. Of course, child, you've appeared to perform your own miracles, and need very few of mine."

"Well, I seriously doubt I could pull off the best wedding Bunch Gulch has seen in nigh on a century if you weren't at my side."

"Yes, that's very true. Now, child, there's much to do. So, I suggest you dream up the perfect wedding, and I'll make a special wish, and"—Merry winked—"if I know my wishes, all your dreams will come true."

* * *

Laurie haunted every bridal shop in Missoula and came up empty. She breezed through department stores and specialty shops and bought video games and movies for the boys, a box of chocolates for Merry that she wanted to devour herself, and a Remington bronze of a cowboy mending fences for Jake.

On a scale of one to ten, her shopping spree ranked a pretty high eight on gifts for everyone else, but a zero for herself. The wedding gown she'd dreamed of didn't exist, and in spite of the money she offered, the two dressmakers she contacted had their hands too full to take on anything new in such a short amount of time.

As the stores in the mall were starting to close, she dashed into a lingerie shop and grabbed everything that caught her eye. A black lace teddy, a sheer, white silk negligee, and, on a whim, black stockings, garter belt, and black and red panties and bras, the skimpiest she'd ever owned. If they'd had a whip, she might have bought it, too. It might come in handy for the day she had to smack a little sense into Jake McAllister.

Heading for home, tired and disappointed, she lost all sense of direction, and found herself near the university on a street lined with quaint, unobtrusive homes. A peculiar fog rolled in and surrounded her car, and she pulled to the edge of the street, fearful of driving any further.

The mist swirled about her, and finally cleared just enough to see a sign on the cottage just a few yards away. "Holly's, where dreams come true." How appropriate, she laughed to herself. The place was strung with Christmas lights, and hanging on the front door, over the "Open" sign, was a wreath of holly. She'd often browsed Christmas shops in the middle of July, but it was late, she was tired, and it seemed a crazy thing to do well past 9 P.M. But the cheery lights beckoned, and the fog still shrouded her view, so she hopped out of the car and treaded lightly up the pebbled walk.

Stepping into the shop felt like stepping back in time, to the early days of the Old West, an absolutely delectable researcher's feast. An intricately tooled leather gun belt hung from the wall, reminding Laurie of one she had described in her last novel, right down to her hero's initials etched into the silver buckle. A mint-condition sleigh she could easily picture being drawn by a dappled gray when the snow drifted high. The McAllisters had owned one, woven with holly at Christmastime, and Laurie had wished so often to share in their outings.

"There's another room in the back if you're interested in clothing," a deep, cheery voice commented before the white-bearded man appeared from behind the counter. In red flannel shirt and suspenders, he looked as though he'd been miraculously ripped from the heyday of the Old West and transported through time.

"Could you show me?" Laurie asked, trying not to let her hopes swell.

"Of course, child." He studied her, his red cheeks glistening almost as brightly as his eyes tucked away behind wire-rimmed spectacles. "You have a gleam in your eye, child, like a woman about to be married. If it's a dress you're looking for, you've come to the perfect place."

She smiled.

His belly shook.

"If you can find me the perfect dress, I'll be forever in your debt."

"Well, let's just see." He held open a swinging door and Laurie entered a room muted in the soft light of Tiffany lamps, the glass wreathed in sprigs of holly. A kettle hummed on top of an old black pot-bellied stove, spewing out scents that had become so familiar to Laurie in the past month—cinnamon and apples, peppermint and pine.

She strolled about the room, fingering a tall beaver hat, a red taffeta umbrella, looking brand new instead of a century old. But something even more wonderful caught her eye. A long-fringed rawhide coat, bleached nearly white, devoid of any beaded ornamentation, just the foot-long fringe that hung in a W formation across the chest and back. Buffalo Bill could have worn it in a parade, or for his wedding, and she wanted it for Jake—her own wild west hero. It would make a perfect wedding gift, she thought, as she smoothed her fingers over the soft, velvety fabric of the jacket, thinking of smoothing her fingers over Jake's chest on their wedding night.

A sudden squeaking sound made her turn. The old man was wheeling a mannequin toward her—a tiny mannequin with springy red curls—clothed in the dress of her dreams, a high-necked Victorian confection, prim and proper and perfect, with a train at least ten feet long swirled in a pool about the bottom.

Slowly, she inched toward the mannequin, awed by the gown. She touched the ivory satin, the delicate lace dotted with thousands of seed pearls, and a tear slid from her eye. "It's beautiful."

"A dream come true, if you ask me." The jolly old soul chuckled.

"May I try it on?"

"Oh, no, no, no, child. That won't be necessary at all. It's yours, made just for you."

Laurie shook her head. "But that's impossible."

"Nothing's impossible, if your beliefs are strong."

"My mother said something like that once."

The old man chuckled again. "Heard those same words myself from a pretty young thing. Must be nigh on twenty, twenty-five years ago. Had red curls, she did. Like yours. Not much bigger than you, either."

Laurie's heart thudded. Could this jolly old soul have known her mother? "Where did you meet her? Was it in this shop?"

"Oh, no, no, no. I move around a lot. As I recall, it was in New York. She was looking for a birthday present." He put a finger to his lips, his thumb twirling the curl of his fluffy white beard. "Bought a silver picture frame. No, come to think of it, we made a trade. She didn't have much, only a pretty smile, and an old necklace her father had given her. Wasn't worth much, and she sure hated parting with it. But she wanted that frame. Told her I'd keep the necklace till she could buy it back. She never came for it though."

"I suppose I'd be wishing for the impossible to hope you still have the necklace."

"Well, I don't know." He walked over to an antique bird's-eye maple bureau, his knee-high black boots clomping on the hardwood floor, and rummaged through the top drawer. "My, my, my," the man muttered.

Laurie half-expected to see Merry's face rather than the old bearded man's when he turned around, but she forgot his familiar words, his similarity to Merry, when he held up a delicate silver necklace, the star suspended from it just as tarnished as the chain. And she knew, she truly believed, it was the necklace in the old faded picture she'd found in her attic, the photo she believed to be of her mother and grandfather. "Not much to look at," he said.

But Laurie could see through the coating of black to the shine beneath. "It's beautiful," she said, a tear slowly running down one cheek. "It just needs a little polish, that's all." Laurie took it from the old man's hand, fingering it lovingly, finally holding a piece of her mother close. "I'd like to buy it, and the gown."

"Ah, then you do believe it will fit?"

"I believe."

The old man smiled, and his eyes twinkled. "It's getting late, child. I'll box these things up for you right away. Shall I wrap the veil, too?"

Laurie nodded, and before she knew it, she was standing at the street corner next to her car, a candy-cane–striped box tucked under her arm. She opened the door and shoved her boxes into the passenger seat, remembering, she hoped not too late, the rawhide jacket she'd wanted for Jake. She turned and rushed back to the shop, but the closed sign was hanging in the window, and her knocks and ringing of the bell went unanswered. She slowly walked back to her car, wishing she hadn't forgotten. She had the Remington, but no amount of gifts could ever repay Jake for what she had done to him.

The fog rolled away from the street, surrounded Holly's, and when the sparkling lights disappeared, and the cottage faded into the mist, Laurie wondered if she'd dreamed the entire scene.

She climbed into the driver's seat, and cracked

open the lid of the box. The tarnished silver star, pillowed in a bed of midnight-blue velvet, sat atop her pearl-spattered gown, and twinkled in the light of the moon, and she knew, once again, that someone, somewhere, had looked down upon her and granted her another wish, another miracle.

Laurie wanted to marry him. It's all Jake could think about. She wanted to marry him—forever—and it was all going to happen tomorrow.

Tomorrow.

Jake groaned. He hadn't bought her a gift. Or a ring. For nearly a week he'd thought the entire thing—this crazy marriage of convenience—would fall apart, that Laurie would change her mind and run, but she hadn't, and now he was at a loss.

Sadly, he looked in his savings account, in his checking account, and in his wallet. How could he purchase the band that would tie them together, when he could barely scrape together enough to keep a roof over his family's head, food in their bellies, and pay the infernal taxes. She deserved so very much more than he could ever hope to give her.

As he drove into Missoula the evening before his wedding, when most other men would have been celebrating with bachelor parties, Jake thought about the new life he'd be starting tomorrow. Things were changing. He'd have a wife, even if it might end up being in name only, and his sons would have a mom. They'd loved the idea. They'd hooted and hollered and told their dad they didn't care if Laurie couldn't bake cookies. They'd eat peanut butter for the rest of their lives just as long as she was always around to tell them stories, and hop over ground squirrel holes, and laugh when they tackled her to the ground during a game of football. She was, after all, just as lousy at sports as she was at cooking.

But Jake had never smelled anyone so sweet, like the dew-kissed roses she'd been picking just that morning when he'd stopped by for coffee and a neighborly chat about where they should live when they got married, his place, or the place that should have been his.

"Tomorrow afternoon it's yours again, Jake. My wedding gift to you," she'd told him, and he'd had too big a lump in his throat to even say thanks.

He didn't deserve the house, he told himself, and he'd never deserve Laurie, as long as he wasn't pulling his weight. He had to make money, and dammit, maybe Laurie was right. He needed to market his skills as a craftsman. Maybe people would buy his woodwork. He'd never be able to match Laurie's millions, but it was something, and maybe next year on their first anniversary, he wouldn't have to struggle to buy his wife a gift— not the way he knew he was going to struggle tonight.

Tonight. Somehow he'd buy a ring and tomorrow he'd place it on that dainty little freckle-covered finger. He'd kiss Laurie's Betty Boop lips that had done nothing but tease his days and haunt his nights. They'd be man and wife, he'd sell his crafts, and he'd send proof to Amy that he was married and could provide quite well for his sons. Never again could she claim to have grounds for custody.

He'd have his boys.

And if he was lucky, he'd have Laurie.

Forever.

Damn! The glass entrance door to the mall was locked when he arrived, but he refused to give up hope. He stood in the middle of the parking lot, as store lights flickered off around him, and turned his eyes to heaven. He made a wish—for help—on the brightest star he could find.

He drove up and down every street in the center of town, but not one jewelry store had lights on inside.

At a stoplight, he pounded his fist on the steering wheel and berated himself for his foolish fears, and when the light turned green, other lights flashed—he could see them out of the corner of his eye—and he made a hasty left turn the wrong way on a one-way street, but he didn't care. The lights beckoned, and he had to check them out.

They weren't shocking neon, they were nothing more than simple strings of multicolored Christmas lights just like the ones he strung on his cabin every year. He slowed, stopping at the curb to read the sign on the door. "Holly's, where dreams come true." He smiled and shook his head, grinding the Jeep to a halt, and hopped over the side of the door. Only in his dreams, Jake knew, could he ever afford something worthy of Laurie's hand.

A bell rang when he entered, and he carefully closed the door, trying to keep the noise from ringing out again. And then the scents enveloped him—cinnamon and nutmeg, apple cider and peppermint. The same things he had smelled in Laurie's house the first time he'd been in her kitchen, and a familiar tightness wrapped around his heart, just the way he remembered her arms enfolding him the first time they'd made love.

He prowled through a shop filled with old and new, and something familiar caught his eye. A child's saddle just like one he'd received on his sixth birthday. The memory hit him as if the scene had been captured on video and was being played back before his eyes. His father carried it from the old Dodge pickup to the redwood patio table, and his schoolmates paid no attention whatsoever, they were too busy eating chocolate cake and vanilla ice cream. But one person had been interested—a little girl peeking from behind the big pine at the edge of the property, her red hair a mass of unruly curls, her eyes wide as if she didn't believe the sights. Oh, Laurie, he sighed, realizing just how lonely she'd been as a child.

So many good memories he had, and in so many of those memories, there was a little girl in the background who didn't fit in.

Across the room, in a corner lit by Tiffany light, Jake found a white Angora kitten curled on a fluffy red pillow. He remembered another present, a kitten popping its head out of a birthday gift box and latching on tightly to his shirt. "Snowball," she'd been dubbed, and she'd go to no one but Jake, at least that's what he thought, until he'd seen her in Laurie's lap, both of them sitting comfortably on the branch of a tree. He'd felt so sorry for her that day, and he'd offered her his kitten, but she'd pushed it away. "My grandmother says cats smell up the house," she'd yelled, and once again ran away.

This time he'd offered her his name, and a place in his life. Would she run away again?

The kitten rolled on its side and stretched, righting itself slowly, moving cautiously toward Jake's long legs. He stood next to his boot, rubbing against his leg, and Jake leaned over and scratched the top of his fluffy white head.

"My, my, my. Never seen the little thing take to a stranger like that."

Jake spun around at the sudden sound of the jovial voice, and stared into the rounded face of a man to match. "I seem to have a way with animals."

"Yes, I can see that, son." The old man's rosy cheeks were just as round as his belly, and his thick hair and fluffy beard matched the snowy brightness of the kitten. He wore a red plaid shirt, wide black suspenders, and black pants tucked into knee-high boots. Jake came close to laughing when he realized just how appropriate the man looked in this shop. A sack full of toys flung over the man's shoulder would have completed the picture.

"Is there something I can help you with? A gift for a child, a loved one?" He tilted his head, eyebrows raised. "Your bride, perhaps?"

"Bride," Jake admitted, and smiled at the sound of the word. "I need a ring."

"I see," the proprietor said as he walked behind a glass display case filled with glittering jewels Jake knew he'd never be able to afford.

"I don't have much money," Jake stated, his voice soft, his eyes lowered to the cat still rubbing against his leg. He leaned over and picked up the kitten, cradling it in one arm while he scratched behind its ears and under its chin. The kitten stretched and nodded to make sure Jake hit all the right places.

The man looked at Jake over the tops of his spectacles. "You're in rather a hurry, I imagine."

"The wedding's tomorrow."

The old man nodded. "Afraid she might change her mind and run away?"

"Something like that."

The man leaned on the counter, shoving his glasses a notch higher on his nose. "Well, young man, you don't look like the kind of fellow a girl would run away from. The way I see it, you're the one who's scared."

"First marriage didn't work out. Guess I'm afraid this one won't either."

"Do you love her?"

Jake didn't have a clue why he was talking to this stranger about his life, about Laurie, about his feelings for his redheaded firebrand. But he knew exactly how to answer the man's question. "It's impossible not to."

"My, my, my. I felt the same way about my little lady all those years ago, haven't changed my feelings since. Scared half out of my wits I was back then, but she's given me an eternity of happiness, even if she does ignore my wishes much of the time."

"Sounds like your wife and my Laurie could be the best of friends."

The old man nodded, and his spectacles slipped just a fraction of an inch down his cherry red nose that looked as if he'd spent many a day and night in the cold.

"So, do you have any rings?" Jake asked.

"Well, let's see." The man pulled out a tray of silver bands, of emerald-cut diamonds mounted in platinum, teardrops in gold, an entire array of beautiful pieces far, far beyond Jake's means.

"They're beautiful, but—well—my finances are a bit strapped."

"Don't worry, son. When it comes to gifts, I've never failed to have just the right thing."

Reaching to the bottom of the counter, he withdrew a small purple velvet box, and set it on the glass in front of Jake. "Why don't you open this, and tell me what you think."

As if it knew Jake would need both hands, the kitten dug his claws into his shirt and climbed up his arm, resting on his shoulders, snuggling his head against Jake's neck.

Jake grasped the top of the ring box between his thumb and index finger, and lifted the tightly fitted top. The dim light above the counter glinted off the blood-red rubies, two hearts connected, side by side, fastened to an endless band of gold.

Jake looked from the ring, to the proprietor, his eyes red with sadness that he could never buy Laurie such a beautiful gift. "It's perfect, but I can't."

"Ah, but if you could, this is what you'd want?"

Jake nodded his head but recognized the folly of his wants. "If I could, yes. But it's impossible."

"Empty your pockets."

Jake's eyes narrowed. "Pardon?"

"Let me see what you've got in your pockets."

He'd known the moment he walked into Holly's that something wasn't quite right, and now the proprietor wanted to see the contents of his pockets. He thought it strange, especially when he'd already told the man he was close to broke.

But for some reason he obliged, digging first into his left pocket, pulling out a purple stone Josh had given him earlier that day, a Swiss army knife, and Joseph's rabbit's foot, which he'd purposely picked off the boy's dresser the day he asked Laurie to marry him.

"Not much here," Jake stated.

The old man tilted his head toward Jake's right side, and flashed a questioning stare over his spectacles. "There's still that pocket, son."

"Nothing there but a handful of change."

"Let's see."

Jake pulled out the coins, setting the nickels, dimes, and quarters on the counter. "Unimpressive, isn't it?"

The old man put an aged yet strong finger on one of the coins, slowly moving it aside, as he did over and over again, until only one remained. "It has no markings," the man stated, lifting his eyes to see Jake's face.

Jake took the coin, holding it in the palm of his hand. "My grandfather gave it to me when I was five. It used to be a silver dollar, but I've carried it a long time and I'm afraid it's worn pretty thin."

"Does this coin bring you good luck? Is that why you carry it?"

"No," Jake shrugged. "It's just special, something to remind me of someone I cared for."

"Ah, I see. Well, I believe we can make a fair exchange. Your coin for my ring."

Jake's jaw dropped, his brows knit together. "No, no." His head shook. "I couldn't part with it."

"But the ring." The old man lifted the box, holding it out before Jake's eyes. "It's what you want. It's the perfect gift for the woman you love."

Jake looked at the ring, at the old silver coin he held in his palm. "I'm sorry. I can't."

Jake turned away, ready to walk out of the store, but the old man's words stopped him.

"You have no money, and you'll find nothing like this anywhere else."

Jake sighed, and his shoulders dropped.

"Sometimes," the old man stated, "it takes more than money to purchase a true gift from the heart."

Jake faced the old man, his hands at his side,

one palm gripping the old silver coin. "It's worth nothing," he said, holding out his hand, unfolding his fingers, looking again at the dull piece of silver.

"Its worth is immeasurable, son."

Jake fought back a tear as he took the purple velvet box from the old man's outstretched hand, and replaced it with his priceless, faceless silver dollar.

"You'll not regret this, son," the proprietor said as he folded the coin into his hand.

A cuckoo clock on the wall behind the counter chimed ten times, and the proprietor yawned as Jake put his belongings back into his pockets.

"It's late, young man, and you have a very important day ahead of you tomorrow." The old man gripped Jake's arm and led him toward the door. "Don't worry. I'll take good care of your coin."

"Is there any way I can buy it back?"

The old man winked. "We shall see. We shall see."

Jake stepped into the doorway, and the kitten on his shoulder stretched. He shoved the velvet box into his pocket, and gently pulled the kitten from his shirt. He held the little face close to his. "You belong here, little one."

"No, no, no. Take him, son."

"But . . ."

"Run along, my boy." The old man began to close the door, gently shoving Jake and the kitten outside. "And tomorrow, two hearts shall bind two hearts," he said, his mirthful smile turning to a chuckle as he removed the welcome sign and closed the door.

Jake climbed into the Jeep, putting the kitten in the seat beside him, wrapped in an old blanket he always kept in the back. He pulled the box from his pocket, cracked open the lid, and looked in awe at the precious gem he'd purchased with an object worthless to others, but priceless to him. So many miracles had happened to him lately, but everything seemed too good to be true. Surely, he fretted, something horrible would come along and burst the magic bubble that surrounded him.

Turning the key in the ignition, he took one last look at Holly's. The engine roared. The lights dimmed on the quaint little cottage, then flickered off, and the magic glow disappeared. But in his hand, a wedding ring glistened in the moonlight, and he looked toward the heavens and thanked his lucky stars.

17

"My, my, my, aren't you just about the prettiest bride I ever saw."

Laurie spun around in a swirl of satin and lace, the luster of the pearls almost as radiant as the smile of delight on her face. "All brides are pretty, Merry." She twirled again in front of the floor-length oak-framed mirror. "But I feel beautiful to-day. I've wanted this all my life." And then her voice lowered, as if she were whispering a sacrilege. "I just hope I haven't made a mistake."

"Pish posh! How could marrying the man you love be a mistake?"

Laurie tilted her head, looking at Merry through a sheer veil of fine ivory tulle, thankful no one could see the swollen tissue around her eyes. "Marrying Jake isn't a mistake, Merry. I'm just afraid the means of getting him to marry me is going to backfire. And if it does, if he leaves me, I think I'll die."

"Now, now, now. I absolutely refuse to hear talk like that today." Merry busied herself with the gentle folds of the gown, making sure not a one was out of place. "You're marrying the man you love, and that other little matter will work itself out." She reached under the tulle and softly caressed Laurie's cheek. "You've brought a lot of happiness to that man and his family. Nothing else really matters. Do you understand?"

Laurie nodded. Gathering the satin at her hips in her cold, nervous hands, she lifted the whirlpool of gown just inches from the floor, and crossed to the window seat.

"My, goodness gracious, child. Couldn't you stand still for just one moment?"

"I just wanted to see all that you've done outside, Merry."

"Well go right ahead and look all you want, but please, don't move." Merry adjusted the crown of pale pink and white rosebuds, woven with baby's breath and a few sprigs of holly she insisted was for luck. "My, my, my, when that young man of yours gets a gander at you, he's going to think Christmas came early and Santa had been listening to all of his prayers."

Laurie laughed, capturing Merry's cheer and pulling it into her heart. She parted the curtains, looking at the clear blue Montana sky hovering serenely over the garden, the white gazebo Kurt had hastily erected in the last two days strewn with pink roses and ribbon, and row upon row of white folding chairs. "And then, again, Merry," she teased, "he might think someone sent a letter to Santa saying he'd been naughty and not the least bit nice."

"Why, whatever do you mean?" Merry asked, clutching her hands to her bosom.

"He wanted a quick wedding. No frills. Few guests. Getting married isn't exactly his idea of fun, and all this fuss could scare him off."

"Trust me, child. He won't run away."

Laurie fussed with the pointed tips of the pearl-trimmed sleeves edging over her wrists, and twisted the plain gold band she'd stuck on the middle finger of her right hand, waiting for the moment when she'd exchange rings with Jake. "I do love him, Merry."

"Why of course you do. So, I suggest you go downstairs right this minute and repeat those words in front of him—not me."

The satin and lace train trailed behind her as she glided toward the stairs. "Are you sure you won't change your mind and give me away?" Laurie asked.

"No, no, no," Merry said, shaking her head. "I'd rather look down from above on such a happy occasion. I can see all the smiles, and all the happiness. Besides," she busied herself around Laurie's bedroom, picking up haphazardly thrown jeans and tennis shoes, "as I told you before, Nicky's asked me to come home, so I'll be out of your hair for awhile, at least on your wedding night."

"But when will you be back?"

"When you need me, child. When you need me."

Laurie raised a hand from the banister and blew a kiss to the sweet old woman she feared she'd never see again. "Thank you, Merry."

Merry's eyes sparkled, and tears of joy slid down her rosy cheeks.

"Oh, hell! What's she gone and done now?" Jake halted at the footbridge crossing the trickle of a stream, and quickly calculated the number of people gathered outside the house, the men, women and children dressed in their Sunday best, and filling row upon row of chairs.

Kurt put a calming hand on Jake's shoulder.

"You didn't really think she'd buy your idea of a small wedding, did you?"

"She promised. It was supposed to be you, Meg, and the boys, not half the town."

"I've heard a few of Laurie's friends flew in from New York, too."

Jake sighed, digging a finger inside the neck of the white banded collar shirt. He'd ranted and raved for half a day about not getting all gussied up for a two-minute wedding, but Meg shoved the shirt under his nose and insisted. "You think Laurie will ever do what I ask?"

"She agreed to marry you, didn't she?" Kurt laughed, his lumberjack bellow filling the air.

"Yeah, but she's insisting on having everything her way in that, too."

"Sounds like the lady knows what she wants."

Jake snorted and shook his head, wondering how he'd gotten himself into such a fix. He stomped along the path, sticking his hand once again in the pocket of his best pair of Levi's, and touched the edges of the gold and ruby ring, the two hearts joined together—forever.

He thought of Laurie—her Betty Boop lips, her sweet curvy body, her firebrand temper—and he knew he was doing the right thing.

"For the first time in a long time, Kurt, I know what I want, too," Jake admitted out loud. "There's a feisty little redhead up ahead, who's gonna make me the happiest man alive." But he sure regretted the way he'd asked her to become his wife. *In name only.* Hell! He really regretted that.

Half the faces he and Kurt passed as they strolled down the aisle looked familiar, half he didn't have a clue. He'd be spending the biggest part of his wedding reception shaking hands and making small talk. Was Laurie doing this to get even?

He stood in front of the gazebo in full view of at least fifty gawkers, feeling like a lousy actor waiting for an assault with rotten tomatoes. He wanted it over with, and he wanted out of there. What he really wanted was to just be alone with Laurie. He'd missed her.

When, he wondered in growing impatience, would the pianist behind the obscenely big and shiny black grand start the music? And where on earth had Laurie found all the fancy trappings in such a short amount of time?

Hell! He sighed, uttering the word under his breath, but had the odd, uncomfortable feeling from Kurt's frown of reprimand that his thoughts had been heard, and Kurt wasn't the least amused.

So he tried to stand still, and wait, but just like any one of his boys, he fidgeted, balancing on one rawhide boot, and then the other. Finally, he clasped the edges of the fringed buckskin coat he'd found on the end of his bed early that morning. He swore he wouldn't wear it, swore he wouldn't accept something so expensive, which obviously had to be from Laurie. But it had lay there on that bed like a scarlet woman waiting for an innocent man to make up his mind, and he finally had to try it on for size. It fit like a kid glove and felt like one, too, smooth and soft, and the best gift he'd ever received—except for Laurie's promise to marry him.

He plunged his hands deeply into the pockets as he waited, surprised to find something cold and hard and round. He gripped it in his fingers and, slowly, withdrew the object from his pocket. Shaking now, Jake opened his hand, and there in his palm lay his coin—his old, faceless, priceless coin. How, he wondered, could it be there? How could Laurie have known? He searched the faces in the crowd, looking for the old gentleman from Holly's. But Jake saw only a sea of people, none with long white hair or beards.

He looked toward the house, to Laurie's bedroom, hoping to catch a glimpse of the beautiful woman who'd not only given him the jacket of his dreams, but had somehow, miraculously, recovered the precious gift he'd received long, long ago. But all he saw in the window was Merry's cherubic, smiling face, peeking through the curtains, and then a gentleman behind her—an old man with long white hair. A beam of light shot from the sun and glinted off the window, and in an instant, they were gone.

The music began, and Jake forgot about the coat, his coin, and the old man and woman who'd disappeared in a flash of light. All he thought about was the catch in his heart. All he heard was the light tinkling of piano keys.

The sweet melody of "When You Wish Upon A Star" filled the air. Another woman might have selected "We've Only Just Begun" or some such nonsense as the overture to her wedding, but not Laurie. Of course, one of the things he'd liked so much about Laurie Langtry was the way she never ceased to amaze him, the way she'd lie on the floor with his boys and build castles out of Legos, or dance around the room with an imaginary sword, or believe in wishes and dreams. She was magical, and somehow she'd enchanted his life.

And then he saw his boys. Joseph and Joshua followed Jacob down the steps of that big old farmhouse, dressed, like their dad, in their best jeans with the fewest holes. Laurie hadn't tried to change them, hadn't tried to change him, one more thing for which he was grateful.

The boys tripped and shoved and skipped their way down the aisle in perfect McAllister fashion, but obeyed when Kurt took hold of belt loops and ushered them into place. Jake winked at his towheads and had never felt so proud.

Meghan came out next, but rather than watch the pretty woman walk down the aisle, Jake glanced at the man in the gazebo, noting the beam of happiness radiating from Kurt's face. He might not have seen that if it hadn't been for Laurie—his Laurie.

Suddenly, the tinkling of piano keys became a rumble, deep and resonant like a drum roll, and all heads turned toward the door. But the traditional wedding march Jake expected never began. "When You Wish Upon A Star" continued, stronger now, more vibrant, and Laurie Langtry, resplendent in her gown of old, stepped into the doorway, tiny, petite, and to Jake, the most glorious creature he'd ever seen.

Laurie clutched the shiny silver necklace hanging around her neck, and thought of all the times she'd wished upon a star. Today, all her wishes were coming true. Slowly, she removed her hand from the chain, letting the star rest over her heart, and she sensed her mother was there beside her, that she wouldn't be walking that aisle all alone.

She looked toward the gazebo and waited until Meghan stood beside the boys, waited until Jake stepped into view at the end of the aisle. Oh, Lord. Her heart beat faster. He was wearing the buckskin jacket, the one she'd forgotten at Holly's. The one she'd wished she could see him in. She couldn't help but smile, knowing another one of her wishes had come true, hoping that the man upstairs had forgiven her major trespass. She smiled, too, because the man of her dreams stood only a walk down the aisle away, and he looked even more handsome and wonderful than the hero her vivid imagination had conjured.

She waited until her heart calmed before she floated down the stairs. At that moment, she saw no one but Jake, heard no music except the song of joy playing in her heart.

She stood beside him now, her hand in his, and Kurt's words, his prayers, flitted through her mind as nothing but a haze. They repeated vows, and she unconsciously slipped the band from her finger and clutched it tightly.

Kurt stepped forward and placed something into Jake's hands. It sparkled, but it could have been a brass washer for all she cared. All that mattered was that Jake was slipping it on her left hand, slowly, his fingers trembling, hers calm and steady and ready. His smile warmed her heart, his gaze heated her soul, and she saw not one ounce of displeasure, no sign of doubt.

When she slipped the simple band on his finger, he clasped her hands before she could draw them away, and squeezed, his smile reassuring, and, if she wasn't mistaken, full of love.

"I now pronounce you husband and wife. You may kiss your bride, Jake," their friend the minister announced, his laughter ringing through the air like old faithful church bells.

Slowly, Jake lifted the tulle, drawing it over the wreath of rosebuds, smoothing it away before touching her chin lightly with warm, trembling fingertips. Softly, gently, he kissed her lips, caressing away a tear as it cascaded down her cheek.

And then it was over. He stood straight and tall, and clasping her hand tightly, they turned toward the guests.

"Ladies and gentlemen," Pastor Elliott announced, "may I introduce Jake and Laurie McAllister."

Jake shoved the door closed on Kurt's Bronco, taking one more peek at the sleeping boys in the back. "You've kept those fellows way too much lately, Meg. Are you sure you don't mind?" he asked through the open passenger window.

"It's your wedding day, Jake. I think Laurie might appreciate spending tonight and a few others alone with you." Meg winked, and Kurt's infectious laughter rang out from the other side of the car.

"I've got a gift for you, Meg. A little something to thank you for your friendship and help over the years. Guess I won't be needing it quite so much now." He looked at Laurie and smiled.

"You didn't have to do that, Jake," Meg admonished.

"Yeah, I know, but I've seen that old plastic box you keep your paints and brushes in. Thought you might like something a little nicer. It's only pine, but I've got it polished till it shines brighter than those brown eyes of yours, and carved a honeysuckle vine around it."

"Oh, Jake. It sounds lovely. When did you find the time?"

"He doesn't sleep much at night," Laurie answered, tucking her arm through Jake's. "I hope that's going to change."

Jake slipped his arm from Laurie's grasp and

wrapped it around her waist, pulling her close, wishing she was even closer. "Can't deliver it for a few days, but I didn't want you to leave without knowing how much I—how much we care."

"There's something for you, too, Kurt," Laurie added.

"I haven't done a thing except read a few words."

"Well, you read every Sunday, and that lectern you keep your Bible and notes on is in as sorry a state as that broken stained-glass window. Got you a new one in my barn."

"It's beautiful, Kurt," Laurie said, remembering the intricacies of the cross Jake had carved on its face, the deep, smooth grooves cut away bit by bit by a craftsman who, in her mind and heart, knew no equal.

"Thanks, Jake. I'll look forward to leaning on it next Sunday. Got to say, I'm glad to see you putting that woodworking skill of yours to good use."

Laurie felt Jake's fingers tighten about her waist, and a gentle tug as he pulled her even closer. "Decided to try and make some money at it. Got an even bigger family now, and I can't let the little woman"—Laurie's head jerked up at his words and she shot him a fiery glare, but Jake only winked, and his mustache twitched—"be the only creative breadwinner in the house."

"Well, I'll put in a good word for your success."

"I'd appreciate that. The man upstairs has been awfully good to me lately. Hate to ask for anything else."

"He's always good to you, Jake. It's just that sometimes he performs his miracles in mysterious ways. But, now, I think Meg and I'd better get out of your way, leave the two of you alone."

Jake drew away from the vehicle, keeping Laurie fastened tightly at his side. "Guess we'll see you bright and early on Saturday for the castle raising," he announced. "If the boys need anything before then . . ."

"They won't, Jake," Kurt stressed, as he started the engine and shoved the Bronco into gear. "We'll see you in a few days." Kurt's words disappeared in the wind as the last of the wedding party drove away.

Alone. They were finally alone.

Jake wove his fingers through Laurie's, leading her toward the gazebo where they'd been united in marriage only a few hours before. Pulling her down beside him on one of the benches inside, he leaned against the latticework, stretched out his legs, and crossed his ankles. "Any regrets?" he asked.

"No." It had been the happiest few hours of her life, and she'd pressed the memories deeply into her mind and heart, trapping them there for all eternity. "I am glad it's over, though. I've never cared for crowds or being the center of attention."

"Then why all the people? Why such a big production? You knew how I felt."

"I've never been married before. I wanted a day to remember, not something hasty, something easy to forget."

"How could you forget a marriage to someone like me, Red, someone who asked you to marry him out of necessity, because he needed a wife so he could keep his sons?"

She twisted the wedding ring he'd slipped on her finger, looking down at it now, remembering how her heart beat uncontrollably when she'd seen his beautiful gift. She rubbed her finger over the rubies, like she would Aladdin's lamp, and wished her heart and Jake's would join together like those of the ring. "If necessity had been the only reason, Jake, you wouldn't be sitting here beside me now, and you wouldn't have given me something so beautiful."

"It didn't cost much."

She looked from the ring to his eyes, and sensed he'd come close to selling his soul for the ring. "If it had cost only five cents, Jake, I'd still promise never to take it off."

"So, you think you're here for the duration— good, bad, or indifferent?"

She smiled. "Good. Bad. I'm not so sure about indifferent. That's a bit hard to swallow, but I'll give it a try."

Drawing her hand to his lips, he softly kissed the backs of her fingers, holding them tightly, brushing them gently over the evening roughness of his cheek and jaw, until he found his heart, and held her there. "Getting tired?" he asked, gazing at her through dark, searching eyes.

"A little," she answered, wishing she could read his thoughts.

"It's been a long day." She felt him swallow, deep and hard. His mustache rested at ease over his lips. No twitch, no humor. "Maybe we should go to bed."

She heard no anticipation in his voice, only the sound of a man who'd fought hard to accomplish a goal, and now needed sleep, and time to recoup. Where were the lover's words, the groom's whispers of endearment, of longing, of passion—erotic and consuming?

Quietly, they strolled to the house, his hands clasped behind his back, hers holding the folds of the gown she still wore, and she fervently wished he'd sweep her into his arms, carry her over the threshold, and make her his lover, not just his bride. But it didn't happen. He stood in the doorway, a man afraid, and waited for her to walk inside.

Why wasn't her heart pounding, anxious and excited? Why wasn't she reveling in her first night of marriage, running to put on a silken negligee, to lie innocent yet seductive in the bed they'd share forever?

Convenience. Necessity. Did he really believe those were the reasons they'd become husband and wife? At one moment he acted the consummate lover, the next a distant friend, and the confusion haunted her. Yet, she'd said she'd accept anything just to be at his side. But *anything* was so much less than she wanted.

Once again they stood at a threshold, this time just outside Laurie's bedroom door, what could also be the threshold of the beginning of their life together. She opened the door but sensed Jake's reluctance, so much different from the last time they'd been in the room together. "You're not going to come in, are you?" she whispered, disappointed that he was pulling away.

"It doesn't seem right," he said, studying the toes of his boots, and she wished he'd look into her eyes and see how much she needed him. "You're a beautiful bride, Red, and I want you." He plowed his hands through his hair. "God knows I want you. But this marriage is all wrong. It shouldn't have been for the boys, it should have been for you and me."

Never had she seen a man's heart doing such heavy battle with his brain, and she knew she couldn't intercede. He had to work it out on his own. But why, oh why, she wondered, couldn't he have gone to war before their wedding night?

"Help me with my gown, Jake." She breathed the words out on a seductive sigh, and turned her back. "Please?"

She sensed his turmoil in his slow, hesitant reaction. And then she heard his boots shift on the floor, and felt the electrical sparks of his fingers gliding over her elbows, his calluses rough against the satin and lace, trailing casually over her shoulders to the high neck of the dress. Carefully he worked at the first pearl button, slipping it from its tight satin loop, the pads of his fingertips accidentally brushing against the soft short hairs at her neck.

She inhaled, her breasts rising high at his erotic touch, the dress tightening, pulling across her back. His warm breath caressed her skin as he came closer, trying to see the buttons in the dim light of the hall. *Kiss me, Jake. Please, kiss me*, she silently prayed. Did he have any idea what his touch was doing to her, how good it felt to have his fingers tracing the curve of her spine as he loosened the confines of her gown?

"Do you think you can manage the rest?"

His words hit like a shower of ice. She closed her eyes for only a moment, forcing her anger and frustration out in a deep, not quite defeated sigh. How could he possibly act so nonchalant when his very touch and nearness was killing her?

She turned, leaning against the doorjamb, hating to ask him to perform another exercise, doubting she could handle the merest brush of his skin against hers—but she had no choice. She stuck out her arm. "Could you undo the sleeves?"

He smiled. God, how she loved his smile, the

way his mustache twitched, and as he fumbled with more tiny buttons, as his fingers trembled, she let her gaze roam down his body to the spot where her attention had once been drawn, to a spot where denim had faded just south of his zipper.

Again, she looked at him and smiled. He was tormented, frustrated, most definitely horny, and in absolute misery—and she was loving every second of his wretched discomfort.

"Thank you, Jake." She breathed the words as he took a step back, his chest rising and falling so heavily even the fringe of his coat trembled. "You looked very handsome today."

A tinge of embarrassment crept up his neck. "It's the buckskin jacket. Thanks, Red. I always wanted one."

"It's not from me, Jake."

He laughed. "I suppose Santa Claus dropped it off in the middle of the night?"

Laurie only smiled, caressing her hand over the soft, velvetlike leather covering his chest. "Maybe he did," she said, and believed it.

She floated over the threshold, her billowing gown of ivory trailing like a slow parade of clouds. She swirled the skirts in behind her, and gripped the edge of the door, putting her cheek to the cold hard wood, as she slowly inched it closed. "Good night, Jake," she whispered, praying he would put his hand to the door and stop her from shutting him out.

He didn't move, just stood there looking at her with reddened eyes. "Good night, Laurie." He turned in an instant and stalked down the hall.

And Laurie closed the door. She couldn't bear watching him walk away.

* * *

Jake plopped down on the couch, stretching out, willing his body to relax, praying the tightness in his heart, his chest and his groin would ease. God, how he had wanted to follow her into that room.

Dammit! Why hadn't he? He'd admitted over and over to himself that he was stupid, that he knew she loved him, that, heaven forbid, he couldn't think of spending even one moment of his lifetime without her. So why did he persist in this obscene and ridiculous charade?

He tried to analyze his insanity, but he couldn't pinpoint one thing. *Pride?* Possibly. He hated the fact that she could support them and he couldn't, that she could be his children's savior, and he couldn't, not yet anyway. *Stubborn?* Most definitely. If he wasn't so stubborn, he would have said to hell with his pride. *Fear?* Yeah, his fear was overwhelming, but the thing he feared the most— that Laurie would run away from him once he fell in love with her, once he allowed himself to love her—was the one thing his pride and stubbornness would drive her to.

Hell!

He sat up, tore off his jacket, and threw it over the back of the couch, then yanked his shirt from inside his pants, coming close to ripping the buttons off Meghan's gift before he relegated it to the back of the couch along with his coat. He couldn't remember living through such a warm summer, but from the very moment Laurie Langtry nearly ran him down in the middle of Main, he'd been hotter than hell. Laurie was his warmth. Laurie stirred his blood.

Heaven forbid—he wanted her.

* * *

Laurie pulled the silky white negligee over her head, capturing a thin strap before it slipped over her shoulder. Without thinking, she closed her eyes and slowly, easily, twisted the strap around her fingers and dragged it across her shoulder, over the top of her arm, feathering her skin with her touch, wishing, pretending, that her husband was standing behind her, easing the gown from her body. But her fingers didn't zap her with a bolt of electricity the way Jake's did, and the arms she wrapped around her chest didn't lessen her loneliness.

For that, she needed Jake.

The charade was ridiculous, but no more ridiculous than spending her wedding night alone in her bedroom while her husband slept on the couch. They hadn't even argued, that was the damnable thing about the whole predicament.

She jumped at the rattling slam of the screen door downstairs, ran to the window, and crawled on to the window seat, drawing back the curtains to watch her husband running along the path in the dark, toward his old home.

All her hopes drained from her heart, and she buried her face in her hands and wept. All she'd wanted was a home, and love. Now, it appeared she had neither.

When she looked up, Jake had gone, and lights burned brightly throughout the tiny cabin. Dropping the curtains to hide the moon that shone inside, she went to her closet and pulled down her favorite, comforting old chenille robe, slipped into it and her bunny slippers, and silently left the lonely confines of her room.

Upstairs at her computer, she sat in the green glow of light from the screen, tears cascading down her cheeks, and poured her soul out in the story she'd neglected for far too long.

Page after page, her fingers clicked over the keyboard, one word blurring into another as she wrote, the story taking on a new life, far beyond what she'd originally envisioned, all of her frustration over the wedding night she should have been sharing with Jake being transferred to paper in a soulful, mesmerizing love scene like none she'd ever created.

Lost in her words, she missed the pad of feet across the wood plank floor, missed the thump of the heavily beating heart behind her, but the light touch on her shoulder sent her fingers smashing against the keys, and crazed letters skittering across the screen.

"You shouldn't be spending your wedding night this way." His voice was soft and sincere, his touch the tenderest of caresses, even through chenille.

She slipped the mouse up to "save," and swiveled around in her chair, her tearful, blurry gaze meeting the taut, muscle-bound spans of his stomach, and somehow she knew she could touch him, that he'd allow her that joy.

His skin felt so good and right under her fingers, cool from the night air. "I thought you'd gone home."

He tilted her chin, his thumb softly brushing over her lips and the hollow below. "I am home, Laurie."

"Do you mean that?"

He nodded, then smiled, pulling her up from the chair and into his arms, holding her tight against his chest. She felt the calm, steady breathing of a man who knew he belonged at her side, and she knew, without words, without further action, that he loved her.

"I almost forgot your wedding present," he said, moving inches away from her, and sweeping a basket up from the floor, holding it between them.

Meow.

A slight smile tilted her lips as she drew away the soft cotton towel, revealing the small ball of fluffy white fur. Black eyes stared up at her, a tiny mouth widened in a yawn. It closed its eyes, accepting her, feeling comfortable with her, and once again slept.

"Why a kitten?" she asked.

"You don't remember?"

She shook her head.

"Try."

She caressed the fur, gently running her fingers over the long, soft hair. The kitten purred, its motor running loud and strong, and that day so long ago came back to her. "You had a cat like this once."

He nodded. "She wouldn't go near anyone but me, yet I found you playing with her out in the pasture one day."

"You offered to give her to me."

"And you told me cats were foul and stinky and did nothing but scratch furniture and tear drapes."

"I was horrible, and you were trying to be nice."

"I knew it was your grandmother talking, not you. I think I always knew what you were going through, but I couldn't do anything about it."

"You tried. You invited me to parties."

"I didn't try hard enough, Laurie. None of us did, not anyone in the whole blasted town. You didn't deserve the life she made you live."

"It doesn't matter. Not anymore."

"She wasn't the only one who used you, though. She wasn't the only one who berated you. I did the same thing that night when I threw up on your dress. Everyone laughed, even me, but I saw the hurt in your eyes and I did nothing about it."

Laurie touched her finger to his lips. She didn't want to hear anymore. "It's in the past, Jake. It's over. I started again, a new life, and it was the best thing I ever did. I want to start another new life now, with you, and the boys. Let's never dredge up the past. Please."

"Can we forget my lousy proposal, too?"

She nodded, and he grabbed her hand, and tugged her from the room, down three flights of stairs.

"What on earth are you doing?" she laughed, as her bunny slippers scuffed along the floor.

"Starting over." He kept on pulling until they crossed the living room. He threw open the front door and stopped just outside on the porch. Sweeping Laurie up in his arms, he planted a hard, firm, and fast kiss on her lips. "I promise to make you happy, Red. I promise to wipe out every bad memory you ever had."

"You already have."

"Then I promise to give you new memories. Many new memories, beginning right now."

Her hands slipped into his hair, thick and tousled, and long overdue for a haircut, just the way she'd grown to love it. This is where she had begun when she'd crept upstairs to write, her hero and heroine standing on the porch on their wedding night, her heroine's first taste of lovemaking only moments away. Somehow, maybe it was a miracle, but her words were being transported to real life, and she thanked the heavens she hadn't finished the chapter. This was her story now, her reality, and she wanted so very much to be surprised when she and her true-life hero reached the bedroom.

"Mrs. McAllister?" Jake studied her face, his look questioning. "Is something wrong?"

"I was just wishing you'd hurry up."

18

"Welcome home, Mrs. McAllister." Jake carried Laurie across the threshold, kicking the door closed as he kissed the beautiful bride captured in his arms. He raced up the stairs, two at a time, his Laurie light as a babe in his arms.

She slipped from his loosening embrace and stood next to the bed, reveling in the wonderful, magical touch of his masterful fingers trailing upwards from her shoulders to her cheeks, his hands, rough from years of manual labor, softly circling her skin, the sensitive area below her ears. A soft cry involuntarily escaped from her lips, and she reached upward, standing on tiptoes, wanting a kiss, needing it desperately.

He took her mouth, slow, easy, nipping her lips, parting them, exploring the warmth inside, and she followed his lead, tasting, touching, wanting so much more but patiently waiting while she studied and learned all the intricacies of her husband's kisses.

Suddenly he pushed away, a grin where passion once had been. "What's this?" he asked, his fingers grasping the chenille of her robe. "Y'know, Red, you look cute as hell in that old robe and those bunny slippers. But it's our wedding night, Mrs.

McAllister. Couldn't you find something—well—a little more appropriate?"

She took a step back, her fingernails scraping the bare skin of his arms as she pulled out of his grasp. She kept her eyes on his face, watching him travel the lengths of her arms, to her fingers, as they worked the knot tying the robe together. Loosened now, she parted the robe, and watched the heaving of his chest when the first traces of silk appeared. She pulled the robe from her shoulders and let it drop heavily to the floor in a heap about her feet.

She stood before him in the white silk gown, one strap slipped from her shoulders, dangling near the bend of her elbow. Lightly, he touched the warm skin next to the fallen strap, the nearly invisible hairs of her arms bristling at his touch as an uncontrollable chill raced through her body, making her tingle in the deepest, most intimate parts of her soul.

He sat on the bed, taking her fingers and drawing her close between his Levi's-clad legs. Standing before him, she rested her hands on his shoulders as he leaned forward, kissing one breast where the silk had fallen away, revealing just the slightest touch of darkened pink flesh. His mouth, warm and moist, kissed the hardened nipple through the clinging sheer fabric, and she knew she'd gone to heaven. Her head fell back, rolling from side to side, her breathing heavy and labored, as each hot kiss caressed her like thunderbolts shooting through her veins.

Digging her fingers into his hair, she pulled him closer, wanting to be part of him. Capturing another strap, he brushed it over her shoulder and she felt the soft flutter as the gown slipped between them and puddled against his thighs. He buried his face between the roundness of her breasts. She heard him breathing in her scent, her very being, as his warm, sweet mouth kissed her skin.

His hands clasped her bottom and pulled her tight. She could feel the hard length of him against her legs, wishing there were no barriers between them, wanting to touch him, to share with him the same glorious delight he was offering her. Reaching down, smoothing her hands over his chest, she found and released the buckle of his belt, snapped open the waistband, and slid her fingers over the zipper.

He captured her hands, helping her remove the final barriers between them, then stood before her, naked and magnificent, his Olympian god body nearly as powerful as the love she felt for him inside her heart.

"You're staring again, Red."

"I plan to do it for the rest of my life. Hope you don't mind."

"Only if you let me do it, too."

"Be my guest."

And he did, from the tips of her crimson-polished toenails, to the red springy curls on the top of her head, slow, and lingering, his seductive scrutiny turning her limbs to putty, and finally, he molded her in his hands.

"I love you, Red."

She smiled. "I love you, too."

He captured her then, pulling her toward him, lifting her on to the bed, imprisoning her in the grasp of his arms as she gladly imprisoned him between her legs. There was no time, no need for tenderness or touching or exploring, now there was only time for passion. He was at the very threshold of her being, warm and hot and driving, and then he was inside, filling her with the love she so desperately wanted, the love she'd never known before, not in all of her thirty-two years.

She clasped her hands around his neck, digging deep, reaching out for his lips, capturing them, tasting his passion, trying to concentrate on his mouth while she reveled in wave upon wave of erotic joy. They belonged together. She'd known it forever, and now they were one, and she'd never let him go.

And then she thought no more of what had been or what was yet to be, she thought only of what was happening at the moment, of the millions of sensations coursing through her body, all good, all divine, all powerful. Her muscles clenched, contracted. Her nails dug into the skin of his back, needing something strong to hold onto as every nerve ending in her body erupted in overwhelming, excruciating pleasure.

One last time he drove into her, his breath held, his body, balanced above hers, quivering now, just the slightest bit. She could feel it, feel his release, his joy, transferring through her, making a memory to last forever.

He collapsed against her, burying his head against her neck, while he tried to restore calm to his body, suddenly rolling over, pulling her on top. She rested her head on the dampness of his chest, listening to the strong, quickened beat of his heart, feeling the expansion and contraction of his lungs. His fingers played with the curls of her hair, hers traced the cord of muscle in his arm.

"There's so much you don't know about me, Red," he finally said. "There's so much I don't know about you."

"We have forever to learn. But for now, I know I love you, and it doesn't seem like anything else is important."

"You might think it's important someday. I rise early. I work hard all day. I'm exhausted at night when I come in the house and I'm dirty and sweaty, and . . ."

She sat up, straddling his waist, a finger covering his lips. "I know all those things. I've watched you for weeks. I've seen you early in the morning milking Sue Ellen outside the barn. I've watched you feeding carrots and apples to Reb. I've seen you sweaty and dirty, and I've watched you pace outside on the porch, smoking your pipe."

"How could you see some of those things?"

She shrugged her shoulders. "I'm not a proud woman when it comes to you, Jake McAllister. I've used binoculars. I've sat in that window over there and watched you, and wanted you."

Gently, he cupped her breasts, circling her nipples with the pads of his thumbs till they hardened, begging for his kiss. "You're a shameless woman, Mrs. McAllister, but I promise, I won't pace any more. I'll be right here, every night, and no matter how exhausted I am, I'll never be too tired to want you."

"Then want me now, Jake." She kissed him, moving away just a fraction of an inch to look into Montana blue-sky eyes filled with passion. "Want me now."

Jake lazed in bed, fascinated by the way Laurie stepped into her tight, tight jeans, the ones that thoroughly hugged her thighs and hips and stomach, parts of her he'd grown to know so well in just two days. He'd explored every nook and cranny, even between the toes she now stood up on as she struggled to zip up her pants and fasten the snap. "Need some help?"

"You're much better at undoing clothes."

"That's the kind of help I was thinking of," he said, fluffing the pillow behind his head, and crossing his hands behind his neck, watching in awe the way her soft, succulent breasts bobbed as she moved, remembering, quite fondly, the way they felt in his hands, against his lips, and tasted on his tongue.

"I thought you wanted breakfast?"

"It could always wait."

"It waited yesterday, and so did dinner. I'm starving, even if you aren't."

She adjusted her bra, fastening the hook between her breasts, as if dressing before him came naturally, and was something she'd done her entire life. It was one of those things about marriage he'd missed, the openness, the ability to walk around naked or disheveled, with morning mouth and sleep in your eyes, and still be loved.

"I take it the honeymoon's over?"

"We've barely left this room for three days and, if you'll recall, we promised the boys they could come home tonight, and we're working on the playground today."

He hadn't really forgotten, he just wanted to ignore it, he wanted to spend another three days in bed, with Laurie in his arms. He wanted her in them now. He moved Snowball from his chest and settled the ball of fur on top of Laurie's pillow, then threw back the covers. Slowly, he climbed out of bed, stretching the kinks out of a back that had been in bed nearly seventy-two hours, and strolled toward her, his bare feet padding softly on the hardwood floor as he came up behind her, wrapping his arms about her waist as she picked out the curls in her hair.

She turned, the softness of her breasts rubbing against his belly, her warm lips trailing across his chest, to the base of his neck. He felt her bare toes touching his as she stepped on his feet for height, felt the cold metal button of her jeans biting into flesh that was stirring, growing, once more aroused, and needing her. He tore at the button, ripping it from its hold, freed her from the zipper, from the jeans, from the satin bra and bikini panties, and carried her once again to the bed, and loved her.

Breakfast could wait.

"So, the newlyweds have come out of hiding," Kurt teased as Jake and Laurie rounded the front of the Jeep and walked across the playground. Her hand was tucked safely, lovingly, in his, and he absently caressed the skin at the back of her hand with his thumb. Would she ever tire of his touch? she wondered, and knew the answer would have to be no.

"Against my wishes," Jake grumbled. "Hope those kids of mine . . ." He looked down at Laurie and winked. "Excuse me. I hope *our* kids haven't been any trouble."

"Set them in front of the TV with a good movie, a tray of cookies, and they're quiet for hours. Gives a man ideas about having a few of his own."

Jake's mustache twitched as he slapped Kurt on the back. "Tell you what. I'll pack them off to you next time they're holy terrors. Give you a taste of the flip side of fatherhood."

"Daddy!" Jake's head snapped around to the far

side of the park when he heard three boyish voices call out.

They scrambled over stacks of logs, and tools, and bags of cement, rushing toward their father's arms.

Jake grabbed the twins into open arms, swinging them up to his chest, kissing their foreheads, their cheeks, their noses, so outwardly happy to finally have them close. But Jacob distanced himself, standing at Kurt's side, looking from Laurie, to his dad, then back to Laurie again.

Laurie knelt, extending her arms, hoping he'd come to her. Jake had told her so many times how much his oldest son wanted a mom, had told her how happy he'd been when Jake told the boys Laurie was going to be his wife. Yet, why was he holding back?

Slowly, Jacob advanced, and Laurie reached up to brush away a lock of unruly hair from his brow. He didn't draw away, even when Laurie cupped his cheek and kissed his nose.

"Is it okay if I call you Mom?" he asked, the words precious and endearing, and straight from his heart.

She smiled, fighting desperately to hold back a tear. "I can't think of anything I'd like better. But maybe you should ask your dad, too."

"Dad?"

Jake bent down, a twin clasped in each arm. "What is it son?"

"Can I call Laurie Mom?"

Jake glanced at Laurie's bright and blissful face, at his son's questioning frown, and nodded. "You all can, if you want," Jake stated, ruffling his oldest child's messy mop of hair.

And Laurie couldn't hold back any longer, she

just let the tears flow from her eyes as Jacob grabbed her around the neck in a hold that would have made a defensive tackle proud.

A pair of worn black work boots stepped into the midst of the happy group, a throat cleared, and Laurie looked up and saw Tom Harrington, hammer in hand, a carpenter's tool belt around his waist. He was one sight Laurie hadn't expected to see.

"Morning, Tom," Jake greeted, extending his hand.

"Morning." Tom shook Jake's hand, then turned to Laurie. She studied his eyes, the faint trace of a smile she didn't recall ever having seen before. "Morning, Laurie."

Surprised at his greeting, Laurie wiped her face with the back of her hand and offered him a hesitant smile. "Hello."

"I owe you an apology," Tom admitted, his eyes downcast as he adjusted the heavy-hanging belt of tools. It didn't appear to need adjusting, but it appeared pious and pure Tom Harrington needed something to do with his hands. He cleared his throat again. "I haven't been fair to you since you returned to town, and I suppose I wasn't fair to you when you were a kid, either."

"It doesn't matter, Tom."

"No, no, hear me out." He put up a hand to stop her words. "I knew your grandmother. I had a run in with her a time or two. She treated you poorly, and I should have done something about it. But, like a lot of other people in this town, I guess it was just easier to ignore, and figure you were cut from the same mold."

Laurie smiled, the blasted tears once again falling. "Thank you, Tom. I always hoped the people of this town would accept me. I guess it's a good thing I married Jake, or I might have gotten run out again."

"Marrying Jake had nothing to do with it," he interrupted. "We heard about the hymnals and the new stained-glass window."

Laurie looked at Jake, wondering how he'd react at this newest revelation, but all she saw was a smile, and he wrapped his arm around her waist and pulled her close.

"Kurt's brimstone hasn't been quite so fiery since you fixed him up with Meg." Tom laughed, instantly repenting his comment and dropping his stare once again to his belt when Kurt's lumberjack hand clamped down on his shoulder. "Of course, there's the castle, and, well, just the way you made people feel good on the Fourth. It's not your money, Laurie, it's you, just you. We talked about it after the party, and I sort of elected myself spokesman to apologize to you on behalf of the entire town."

Laurie felt Jake's arm tighten around her, thankful to have him standing at her side. "Apology gladly accepted, Tom."

"Is there anything I can do to make up for the past?"

Laurie bit the inside of her lip as she thought about his offer. And then she knew. "Maybe you could let Kurt know if you run into any kids who look like they aren't getting a fair shake at home, give him a chance to check it out and see if there's anything we could do to help."

"It's a promise."

Laurie never imagined herself kissing Tom Harrington, but she clutched his arms and, standing on tiptoe, kissed his cheek.

"You planning on doing any work today?" Kurt asked, slipping an arm around Tom's shoulders.

"Suppose so," Tom answered, pulling the hammer from his belt. "Lead the way, Pastor."

"You okay?" Jake asked, cupping Laurie's face in his hands when Kurt led Tom and the boys toward the building site.

"In spite of the tears, I've never been better." She stood on tiptoes and kissed his lips. "Come on, Mr. McAllister. We've a castle to build."

The uprights had been cemented in concrete two days before, Kurt advised them as he rolled the plans out on an old redwood tabletop, and Laurie saw her dream from every angle, and in color, from Meghan's sketches to Kurt's detailed plans.

"The slide won't be here for another week or two," Kurt said, "but I've managed to get everything else we'll need from materials I had on hand and from the lumber supply in Hamilton. Seems to me we should be able to christen this baby before the end of the day if the weather holds out and more help shows up."

"So," Laurie said, "where do we begin?"

Kurt handed out tools and directions like a pro. Meg worked at Kurt's side, having him alter the plans here and there when something didn't appear to be working quite right. Jake hammered and sawed and sweated right next to Tom and two local ranchers with young children who couldn't wait to storm the walls.

Laurie knew her skills when it came to carpentry were slightly less than nil, so she kept the kids occupied with stories of knights and dragons and damsels in distress. She played follow the leader and did somersaults in the grass, making numerous treks to the Jolly Kone for ice cream, sodas, and hot dogs, for hungry laborers and impatient conquering heroes-to-be.

As evening fell, Jacob proudly crossed the lowered drawbridge, mounted the stairs, circled the turret, and placed a bright red pennant on top of the highest spire.

A multitude of kids clambered over and around the castle, while the adults dreamed of being young once again. Slowly, one by one, people trickled away, and only the McAllister clan occupied the park.

"Pretty impressive," Jake said, as he and Laurie rested in the grass and watched their kids scrambling inside and outside the castle walls.

"I'd still like to have one at our place," Laurie said.

"The kids'll outgrow it."

"Someday," Laurie admitted. "Maybe we could have some more?" It was more of a question than a statement.

Jake nuzzled her neck, and she tilted her head to allow him easier access. She covered his hand with her own when he circled her waist, caressing her belly. "You want a baby?" he asked.

"We've never done anything to prevent it, before or after our wedding," she laughed. "I haven't thought about it much. I figured you already had three and wouldn't want any more."

Jake fell back on the ground, pulling Laurie with him. "Guess you don't know me all that well, Laurie, dear. I'd have a dozen if I could."

"That might be overdoing it a bit. Maybe one or two. Three max."

"Hell, Red, as far as I'm concerned we could have none and I'd be happy. Just you and me. But,

God, I sure do like having those little creatures around."

Laurie sat up, straddling Jake's hips, picking at his buckle. "I've never even changed a diaper, Jake."

"Trust me, I'm a pro. You learn quickly when you've got three in them at the same time."

"Well, if it's all the same to you, one at a time's fine. But I'd like to think about it later." She jumped up. "Right now, I'm going to try out the castle. Have to be a few benefits in being less than five feet tall."

"Have fun while you can, Red." Jake laughed. "When I get you home, we'll get down to some serious thinking. I might even give you a lesson or two on making tow-headed babies."

Laurie ran to the castle and scrambled up a ladder, chasing the boys from one parapet to another. When she was winded and tired, she stood near the tallest spire, and looked down on her husband. He was stretching out the kinks in his Olympian god body, lifting his sweat-stained Stetson to run a casual hand through his hair.

"Pretty impressive," she called down from above.

"Nah, those aren't my impressive moves. You just wait." He shoved the Stetson back on his head, lowering it toward his eyes. "I'm going to get the mail, then maybe we should head for home."

She couldn't think of anything better she'd like to do. But, until he returned . . .

"Hey, Mom," Jacob yelled, and her head spun around to the blond child holding a slick brass pole. "Try this out."

Laurie grabbed hold and, following Jacob's lead, slid down the pole, a much easier feat than the downspout she'd conquered months before.

They swung on monkey bars, scaled rope ladders, and scooted on hands and knees through a maze of secret pipe passages.

"Laurie! Boys! Get down here. Now!"

Anger rang in Jake's voice, in his stiff, straight-as-a-board stance, as he stood below the castle and yelled to his wife and kids.

"Come on you guys," Laurie urged. "Guess we'd better go."

"Could we go through the maze just one more time?" Joseph asked.

"Did you guys hear me?" Jake bellowed. "Let's go!"

"Don't yell, Jake," Laurie called down. "We're on our way." She couldn't see him, and couldn't even imagine the look on his face. She'd seen him hurt, happy, sad, angry, and passionate, but she'd never seen him mad—really, really mad.

Laurie gripped the slick brass pole, wrapped her legs around the cold metal, and slid, her fingers squeaking as she shimmied down.

"That's fun," she said, wiping her hands on the rear of her jeans as she and the boys walked toward Jake. "If you weren't so tall, I'd tell you to give it a try."

"I don't have time for stuff like that. Come on, let's go."

She grabbed his arm, wanting to know what was bothering him, but he jerked away. "What's going on, Jake? What's happened?" Suddenly, she found herself overcome with fear. Had he found out? Had he somehow learned what she'd done?

"We'll talk later." He stormed toward the Jeep, helping the boys into the back, jumped into the driver's seat, and started the engine.

Laurie climbed into the passenger seat, feeling hurt and dejected, fighting off another rush of tears. She wanted to reach out to him but realized now wasn't the time. She sat in silence on the short drive home, and even more silently helped Jake bathe the boys and put them in the queen-size sofa bed in the living room.

"Sleep tight," she whispered, kissing three foreheads when their father neglected his duty.

"What's wrong with Daddy?" Joshua asked as Laurie tucked the blanket under his chin.

"I'm not sure. But don't you fret about it." She lightly tapped his nose. "Roll over and go to sleep."

She watched silently as eyes closed and heads nodded off. Finally, she crept to the kitchen.

Jake was filling a juice glass with Jim Beam when she walked in, and when he saw her, he turned away quickly, downing a swig in one deep swallow. Her heart cried when he slid a chair out from under the table, slumped down, and buried his head in his hands.

She put a hand on his shoulder and he flinched, his muscles tightening under her fingers. There seemed to be nothing she could do, not now, maybe never again. "It's been a long day, Jake. Why don't you come to bed?"

He didn't move, didn't answer.

She stared at his back, his drooping shoulders, and sensing his defeat, and her inability to make things better, she turned to walk away. But she stopped at the kitchen door, knowing she couldn't leave without giving it another try.

He was swirling the amber liquid around in the glass, and she watched him put it to his lips once again and down the rest of the drink. He clutched the glass in his fist and she thought for a moment that he was going to heave it across the room. Instead, he slammed it down on the oak table.

As if sensing she was still standing there, still staring at him, he pivoted in the chair, anger and deep, deep loss, radiating from his eyes. "Go to bed, Laurie."

"I love you, Jake," she whispered through her tears.

"Yeah. I'm sure you do," he said, turning away once again.

Jake had no clue how long he sat at the kitchen table, or how much whiskey he'd poured down his throat. Time hadn't deadened his pain, and the whiskey hadn't burned away his anguish. He forced himself up from the chair, and, knowing he had to confront her, quietly mounted the stairs, stopping for only a moment to look at the boys. "I'm sorry," he whispered, wishing he hadn't allowed Laurie to get under his skin, wishing he hadn't allowed her into their lives. He'd vowed to never let another woman hurt them, but he'd broken his promise, and this hurt was far worse than any they'd ever known.

He listened at the door, but heard nothing, wondering if Laurie had fallen asleep, wishing he could, wishing he could wake up tomorrow and find out it had only been a dream, the worst nightmare of his life.

He turned the knob and met darkness, except for the blasted moon that poured through the window, lighting the bed, and the woman who lay curled in a tight ball, a pillow clutched to her stomach as if it could give her solace.

He closed the door and sat in the antique rocker not far from the bed.

She sat up, her eyes rimmed in red, her face blotchy from too many hours of crying. How easy she seemed to cry, to demonstrate her frustration and sorrow and anger through tears. He wished he could do the same. Oh, Lord, he wished right now he could blot everything out with tears.

But he had no tears—only emptiness. He pulled an envelope from his shirt pocket and pulled out a piece of paper. "I got a letter from Amy today."

Laurie looked down at her hands, clutching and wringing the pillow, holding onto it as if it were a life buoy that would pull her through the storm.

"Funny thing, Laurie. She told me she'd gotten married about a month ago. For the life of me, I can't understand why she didn't tell me that in the last letter." He opened the paper and began to read. *"He's older, with two grown children, both successful and living on their own."*

He stopped his reading, looking across at Laurie, at her trembling lips, at the tears that fell from her eyes and blotted the blue satin of the pillow.

"I know you've never forgiven me for leaving," he continued to read, *"but I know in my heart it was the right thing. I was never cut out to be a mother. You know it, and I know it. Now, I have what I've always wanted, a man who can afford to travel, who loves theater, who shares all my dreams."*

Jake wadded the paper in his fist, allowing it to slip from his open palm to the floor. "She never once mentioned the boys in her letter. Not one word."

He heard her sniff, watched her wipe her nose with the back of her hand, and attempt to rub away her tears with her fingers.

"Dammit, Laurie," he yelled. "Are you listening to me? Have you heard anything I've said?"

Her face was filled with emptiness, and the greatest sorrow he'd ever seen. But it didn't matter. He wouldn't go to her, wouldn't give her even one moment of comfort.

"Did you write the other letter, Laurie?"

She just stared at him.

"Answer me!"

She nodded.

"And the attorney? Who the hell was that?"

"A friend," she sobbed. "An actor."

"What did you think you were doing? Writing another one of your goddamned romance novels, twisting the plot to make everything work out just the way you wanted?"

"I told you I loved you but you tried to push me away. You told me to go back to New York. I didn't want to go, but I didn't want to stay if I couldn't have you." She took a deep, trembling, grief-stricken breath. "I would have done anything to make you mine."

He paced to the window and stuck a booted foot on the window seat, crossing his arms over his knee. His head slumped. "And what did you do, Laurie? You scared the hell out of me, made me think I might lose my kids. You knew where I was most vulnerable and you launched your rockets right into my heart. Maybe if you'd just waited . . ."

"Waited? For what? An occasional night spent in your bed? That's not what I wanted. I want a lifetime with you."

"Well now you've got nothing, Laurie. No more nights in bed, no more kids to spoil, no more me. The lifetime's over."

She looked so frail and hurt when she crawled from the bed, her shoulders slumped as she came toward him, putting her hands over his. "Please, Jake. I'm sorry."

"Sorry? Did you ever think about the boys?"

"I did think about them. They wanted a mother, and I wanted to be the one."

"Yeah, well now all they're gonna have are broken hearts. They're gonna be motherless again. Did you ever think about that?"

"I didn't think you'd leave me, Jake. I thought if you learned the truth you'd want to work things out."

"You thought wrong. Everything you've done is wrong."

"But I wanted you, Jake. I needed you. Please. Try to understand."

"Understand what?" He jerked away and stalked to the door. "If you're planning again to tell me you love me—don't bother."

"Were you lying when you said you loved me?" she asked.

"It doesn't matter, Laurie."

"It matters to me. If you love me, we can work things out."

"There's nothing to work out." He hesitated only a moment before opening the bedroom door, looking once more at the woman who'd slumped to the floor. "I'll get the boys early in the morning. Maybe you could stay up here till they're gone."

She looked up, all the fight drained away. "If that's what you want."

He nodded, and closed the door, leaning against it for a moment, wanting so much to go back in and comfort her. Instead, the tears fell from his eyes, and he walked away from the life and love he thought would last forever.

19

"My, my, my. Aren't you a sight to behold."

Laurie opened swollen eyes and stared across the darkened room at the figure who stood in the doorway, the first person, she was positive, she'd seen in weeks. She closed her eyes again, not wanting to deal with Merry or anyone else, and pulled the pillow over her head.

Merry bustled into the bedroom, parted the curtains, and snapped open the shade. "Hotter than Hades in here," she muttered, and pushed up the window. "There. Nothing like a little fresh air to brighten up the day."

"I like it just the way it is, if you don't mind," Laurie groaned as she lifted the pillow an inch to follow Merry's moves.

"I don't mind at all." Merry shuffled to the bed and planted her fists into her hips. "Goodness, young lady, you look as if you've been locked away in this room for weeks. Such a sight."

"I thought you were gone, Merry. Of course, everyone seems to be leaving me these days."

"Oh, dear. Feeling sorry for yourself, I see. Well, none of that now. Besides, I said if you needed me, I'd be back. Well, I am, and I have no intention of leaving until your life's back in order."

"Go away, Merry."

"No, no, no. Not on your life." Merry ripped the comforter off the bed. "Oh, dear me," she exclaimed, leaping back a foot or two. "If I didn't know better, I'd swear you hadn't bathed in a week."

"Probably longer," Laurie mumbled, clutching the sheet to her chenille robe. If Merry had asked, Laurie would have told her, flat out, that she'd had no reason to bathe, and not much reason to eat, either. The only comfort she'd found in weeks was sleep. And tears.

"Well, that won't do at all." Merry grabbed hold of the sheet and tugged. "Up! Right now, young lady."

Laurie gritted her teeth, the most exercise she'd had since she'd hiked up the ladder in the playhouse and slid down the pole. "I'd rather stay here."

"Absolutely not. I won't hear of it, and if I have to get help to get you out of there and into the shower, I will."

Merry stood there like a drill sergeant, staring down at Laurie, her arm extended, straight and strong, her index finger pointing toward the bathroom.

Slowly, Laurie slid across the bed, her body weak, her head spinning from lack of food. Somehow, she managed to stand, stumbling across the hardwood floor to the bathroom. She slammed the door behind her, but could hear Merry's loud, disgruntled "humpf" over the noise.

She leaned on the bathroom sink and stared at herself in the mirror, her greasy hair plastered to her head, curls matted in spots, and looking totally despicable. She'd seen derelicts lying in doorways on the streets of New York who looked better than she did right now. Under her eyes her skin had turned purple, her cheeks hollow, the once-profuse freckles blending now with the blotchy red of her face.

"Oh, God," she cried, slumping down to the floor, burying her face in her hands and sobbing once again. "Please, Lord," she finally prayed. "Help me get through this."

"Daddy?"

Jake looked up from the design he'd sketched on a sheet of graph paper, the hutch he was designing for Mrs. Adams nothing but a blur as his thoughts drifted to the farmhouse just a well-worn path away. "What is it, son?" he asked as Jacob climbed on to the couch next to him.

"Are we ever going back to Laurie's?"

"No."

"Why?"

What could he say to his son that he hadn't already said, over and over again, every day since they'd walked away? "Things just didn't work out," he said, knowing Jacob didn't understand, and refusing to say anything more. Even in his anger, he wouldn't say anything bad about the woman.

Jake dropped the pad of paper on the coffee table and pulled Jacob onto his lap, running his fingers through the boy's fine blond hair, and tried to forget bouncy red curls. But as much as he tried, everything about Laurie, including her lie, haunted his every waking and sleeping thought.

"It's always dark in her house, Daddy. We never see her outside."

How well Jake knew. He'd watched at night as

he paced the porch. Not once had he seen lights on in her office, in her bedroom, or anywhere else in the house. Before, she'd gone outside during the day, trimming roses, sitting in the sun to write, walking down to the stream to watch the boys' attempts to catch minnows in shallow pools. But for three long weeks, he hadn't seen her once.

"Do you think she's okay? Do you think she might be sick?"

"She's fine, Jacob. Don't worry about her."

"I thought you loved her," Jacob said, tilting his head up to look at his dad.

"Yeah, I thought so too." He ruffled Jacob's hair. "It's past your bedtime, son. Come on, I'll tuck you in."

Jacob crawled down from Jake's lap. "I can go by myself. I liked it when Laurie tucked me in. She used to sing lullabies."

"I could sing."

Jacob shook his head. "It's not the same, Dad." The boy disappeared down the hall and into his room, and Jake leaned his head back on the couch and wondered why everything had gone so wrong.

"I'm not sick, Merry, but I am sick of chicken noodle soup."

"Nonsense." Merry shoved another steaming bowl under Laurie's nose and held out a spoon. "Dig in."

Laurie rolled her eyes, shoved the spoon into the bowl, and stirred. She'd eaten enough chicken noodle soup in the last two days to fill Yankee Stadium and it looked as though there was no end in sight to Merry's fuss and calculated ministrations.

"Do you think he'll ever come back?" Laurie

asked, watching Merry fidget with a bouquet of roses she'd just brought in from outside.

"Do you want him back?"

"Of course I do." Laurie's words were indignant, her scowl heartfelt and lively. How could Merry possibly think she didn't want Jake back?

"My, my, my, but it's good to see a little life back in you, child." Merry put the vase of multicolored, sweetly scented roses in the middle of the oak table. She pulled a chair out next to Laurie and plopped her girth down on the padded cushion. "What you need, young lady, is a plan."

Laurie groaned. "That's what you told me before and look at the mess I'm in now."

"But that plan worked. You *did* get married."

"Yeah, and it lasted all of three days. Your thoughts and my plans are nothing but disaster."

"Well, child, I don't see that man of yours coming back of his own accord. I believe if you want him, you'll have to do some major editing on that last ending you wrote."

"You sound like my editor."

"You told me yourself your stories wouldn't be nearly as good if she didn't step in once in awhile and make you fix the mistakes you failed to see the first time around."

"Yeah, she's a miracle worker. Is that what you are, too?"

"Oh, I've been called many things in my lifetime. I suppose miracle worker fits in there someplace."

Laurie rested her elbows on the table and spooned some soup into her mouth, trying to think of a plan while her stomach turned somersaults. "Do you have any crackers to go with this?"

"Why of course, child." Merry went into the

pantry and came out with a box of saltines.

Laurie slid a cracker out of the box and munched on the edge. "So, Merry, where do we begin?"

"Hey, Dad!" Jake heard one of the boys call him as he stepped out of the shower. "There's some guy here who needs to see you."

Opening the door just a crack, he answered back. "Tell him I'll be there in just a second."

Jake hastily dried his body and slipped into his jeans, remembering all too vividly the way Laurie had done it that last morning they were together, her sweet, lush breasts shimmying as she struggled with the zipper. He shook the memory away, quickly running a comb through his hair, and headed for the front door.

"Can I help you?" he asked the man in dust-covered Wrangler's and a blue baseball cap with Angels imprinted across the front, the familiar halo circling the golden A.

"I've got a delivery outside for you."

Jake peered around the door and sighted the long horse trailer hitched to the back of a Chevy pickup with dual wheels on the back. "I didn't order anything."

"Your wife did," the man said, tapping his pen on the paper-filled clipboard.

"Well, if she ordered it, you're delivering it to the wrong place. She lives in the white house over there," Jake said, pointing to Laurie's house in the distance.

"No mistake, son. I got explicit orders to deliver this stuff to Jake McAllister. She told me you might put up a stink, but gave me specific orders not to leave until you accepted the delivery."

"I suppose she paid you pretty well, too."

The man shrugged. "Look, I haven't got all day. You going to come outside and help me?"

"Well, come in and get some coffee while I slip on some boots."

"If it's just the same to you, I'll wait outside. Nice morning. Won't be too many more before winter sets in."

Jake joined the man a few minutes later at the back of the trailer and peered inside. "Did she pick these out herself?" Jake asked, catching his first glimpse of horseflesh.

"Yeah. Seemed to know what she was doing, and what she wanted. Picked the best out of my herd, and didn't flinch a bit at the price."

"She wouldn't."

The man lowered the ramp and squeezed past the bay, guiding the mare backward down the ramp.

Jake took hold of the lead rein, scratching the white blaze on the horse's brow. "Pretty thing. She have a name?"

"They all do. This one's Magic. Your wife took quite a liking to her."

"She would." Jake led Magic to the pasture he'd recently fenced, removed the rein, and swatted her rump, sending the horse on a run, her head tossing as she enjoyed her freedom, her mane of red flying in the air, reminding Jake again of . . . Damn! Did everything have to remind him of his wife?

When the truck and driver drove away, Jake braced his arms against the fence, his sons standing beside him, looking at the handsome animals filling the small pasture. He'd long hoped the place would one day be home to one or two old nags. Never in his wildest dreams did he expect to see prime horseflesh. Besides Magic, Laurie had picked a quarter horse mare named Phoenix, a buckskin that Jacob immediately claimed as his, and calico ponies for the twins, Topper with the long black mane, and Trigger with white. And, of course, there was no doubt in Jake's mind which horse she'd selected for him. A black gelding, nearly two hands taller than the bay, sleek and shiny, stubborn and full of pride, appropriately named Beelzebub.

"Are they really ours, Daddy?" Jacob asked.

"For now."

He took one more look at the animals Laurie had tried to buy back his love with, and tried to control the unmerciful twitch of his mustache. "I've got some work to do inside," he muttered as he started to stomp away. "You guys can stay out here, but don't go into that pasture unless I'm with you, at least till we get to know them better. Okay?"

"Sure, Dad."

The boys climbed up the wooden cross-hatched gate and watched the horses and ponies inspecting their new home, while Jake stormed into the house, slammed his hat down on the back of the couch, grabbed the phone, and stabbed out Laurie's phone number.

"Hello." Sultry. Sweet. God, he'd almost forgotten how wonderful her voice sounded. Maybe it was another trick, another way to lure him back to her heart.

"What the hell's going on?"

"Is that you, Jake?"

His shoulders drew up in frustration. His jaw tightened. "Yeah, it's me. What do you think you're doing?"

"I don't know what you're talking about." Sweetness again. He could easily strangle her.

"The horses, Laurie. I'm talking about the horses. What are you trying to do?"

"Oh, that. Look, Jake, you might not mind living on a ranch with no animals but a lame-brain cow, a lop-eared mule, and a fussy old goose, but I do. I'm part owner now, in case you've forgotten, and since that's the state of our affairs, I plan to populate this place with animals of my choosing."

"And who's going to take care of them?"

"You are, of course. It's only right that you do your fair share."

"Fair share?" His voice raised loud enough she could have heard him without benefit of the phone. "Look, Red. I've got too much other work to keep me busy."

"Yes, Jake. I know. You've got more post holes to dig. You do that a lot."

"The hell with the post holes. I've got five orders waiting for headboards and hope chests, and I'm working day and night on a hutch for Mrs. Adams. I don't need you burdening me with anything else, especially five horses that need almost as much attention as three boys."

"I'm sorry, Jake, but I really am trying to build our ranch, and since you don't want me, *or* my help, you'll just have to do all the work. Besides, Jake, I don't know the first thing about animals."

"Bull! You picked out the horses."

"They looked good. I especially liked Beelzebub. Has a personality like a man I used to know."

His hands shook.

His mustache twitched.

And he slammed the phone down, refusing to listen to any more nonsense.

* * *

Laurie rubbed her ear, the sudden slamming of the phone reverberating inside. She smiled, sweet, secretive, and full of cunning. Jake McAllister was falling apart—and she loved it.

"So?" Merry rocked peacefully in her old maple chair, her knitting needles clicking madly as another afghan spilled to the floor.

"I think it just might work, Merry."

"That's wonderful, dear. Now, are you feeling at least a little bit better this afternoon?"

"I'm fine. Actually, hearing his voice made all the queasiness disappear."

"Good. Now, what's next?"

"Daddy!" Joseph ran into his father's room and bounced in the middle of the bed, straddling Jake's stomach. With a loud, oppressive groan, Jake clapped the pillow to his ears and tried to pretend he was asleep, since it seemed like months since he'd gotten any. He had three boys who cried half the night, something they'd rarely done before he'd had the misfortune of marrying Laurie Langtry. And he'd had multiple versions of the same recurring dream: Laurie astride Magic; Laurie astride Beelzebub; Laurie, naked and beautiful, astride—his hips. He groaned again. Hell, if he didn't know better, he'd swear some witch was filling his head with those crazy dreams, forcing him to stay awake, miserable and horny, just like he'd been every night since he'd walked out of their home.

"Wake up, Daddy." Joseph bounced on his stomach, grabbing hold of Jake's mustache as if the hair were reins.

"Whoa! Stop your jumping."

"But there's a big"—Joseph's voice raised an octave as he threw his arms wide apart—"big truck outside, lots bigger than the one that came last week."

"Oh, hell!"

Joseph clamped a hand over his dad's mouth. "That's not nice."

"Sorry." Jake sat up, lifting Joseph to the floor, grabbing his pants from the heaping pile of dirty clothes he'd allowed to collect next to his bed. After pulling on the jeans, he shoved his feet into socks, then mud-crusted boots, and headed outside into the early light of morning.

"You Jake McAllister?" the burly man walking toward him asked.

"Yeah." Jake strained his sleep-crusted eyes around the man to get a gander of the size of the semi. "My wife send you here?"

"Pretty little thing with curly red hair?"

"Yeah. That's the one."

"Sure did. Has a great eye for livestock. Must have been raised in the cattle business."

Jake didn't have the strength or the energy to refute the statement. "What did she buy this time?"

"Hundred head and two of my best bulls."

Jake eyed the single semi and trailer. "I suppose this is just the first truckful we've got to unload."

"I'll do another load this afternoon, and bring the bulls last."

"I suppose it wouldn't do me much good to refuse the shipment."

"No. She paid me real good, told me to stick around. Said you—"

"Might refuse," Jake interrupted. "Yeah, I know. She's been saying that a lot lately."

"S'pose we should get this load into your pasture. Days aren't quite as long as they used to be. Have the sneaking feeling it's going to be an early winter."

"I think the frost set in several weeks ago," Jake grumbled in a sarcastic whine.

Hours later, hungry and dirty and tired, Jake paced the porch, puffing furiously on a pipe that refused to stay lit, and waited for the boys to drop off to sleep. He fully intended to wait until midnight, then call, hopefully waking the woman who claimed to be his wife from the deepest of sleep.

When the moon was high in the sky, when he'd had his fill of waiting, he dragged the phone outside, its cord just barely reaching through the door. He slumped against the wall and slid to the porch, punching the numbers in the dark.

"Hello." He'd almost forgotten the sound of her sleepy voice, a voice that had whispered his name in the middle of the night when her fingers brushed over his stomach, arousing him, making him want her even more than sleep or food or drink.

"Hello?" She was awake now, and revenge was so, so sweet.

"So, Red. Have you had enough fun yet?"

"Hello? Who is this?" She was feigning ignorance, and he knew it.

"Is that you, Jake?"

What other man would call her in the middle of the night? he wondered. *Hell!*

"You know damn good and well who it is. What's going on, Laurie?"

"Hello, Jake."

He tried counting to ten but made it only to three. "How do you expect me to take care of all these things you keep buying, and take care of the boys, and my woodwork, too?"

"I'm tired, Jake. Couldn't we discuss this tomorrow?"

"No. We're talking about it now. I have three kids to take care of, five horses, a hundred head of cattle, and two bulls that are horny as hell."

"Are you horny, Jake?"

"Yes! No! It's the bulls. There's no way I can take care of everything, Laurie."

"It's what you always wanted."

"Quit giving me things, Red. I don't need your money anymore, so you can stop trying to buy your way back into my heart."

"Or what, Jake?" She was asking for an ultimatum. What could he say now?

"Or I'll go to Albuquerque with the boys," he bit out. "My mom keeps telling me they appreciate a talented craftsman there."

"I see. You're going to run away again. Is that what you plan to do?"

"I've never run away from anything in my life."

"No?"

"No."

"Like I said, Jake. It's late. Good night."

She hung up.

He heard the click. He wanted to dial her back, but had the feeling she wouldn't answer. And why should he call her back? What the hell was she talking about? He hadn't run. She'd lied to him. She'd done the worst thing imaginable. But he hadn't run. He'd walked away from her. It wasn't the same thing.

Laurie climbed out of bed, headed straight for the bathroom, and in a ritual that had become as common as brushing her teeth or hair, she lifted the toilet seat and threw up. She rested her head on the cold porcelain and wondered how much longer the morning sickness would last.

When her stomach calmed, she took a deep breath, and the other constant took over. Hunger.

She rinsed her mouth with water and splashed even more over her face, scrubbed her teeth with a healthy dose of toothpaste, secured her old che-nille robe around her still-slender stomach, and headed down the stairs, anxious to fill her belly with one of Merry's wonderful breakfasts.

But the kitchen was empty. Laurie frowned, heading to the living room, hoping to find her friend. The old familiar rocker and candy-cane-striped carpetbags were gone. No ball of yarn lay in a chair with knitting needles sticking out. The dozens of picture frames that had lined the mantel were missing. The doilies. The snowy white af-ghans. All memories of Merry had disappeared, except the ones in her heart.

Laurie slumped to the couch, tears, which flowed so easily now, beading up in the corners of her eyes. "You can't leave me now, Merry. Please. I need you."

Even though she begged, no one answered. The little old woman who'd brought magic into her life had disappeared. But then Laurie remembered her words. She would never leave without saying goodbye. That meant she had to be returning. Maybe this afternoon, maybe tomorrow. But she would return.

Faith restored, Laurie headed for the kitchen, poured a bowl of milk for Snowball, routed around in the refrigerator for juice and muffins, butter, and slices of the ham Merry had prepared a few nights before. She filled a plate, a glass, and carried everything to the table, anxious to sit down to eat. Lifting her glass, she started to drink, and saw the red envelope sticking out from under the ball of white fur sleeping in the middle of the table.

With trembling hands, Laurie pulled the envelope from under Snowball, opened the flap and took out a letter.

Laurie, dear —

I will miss you greatly, but I must say farewell. Summer is over, and it's my Nicky who needs me now. Complete happiness is just around the corner — so believe, child, always believe, for only then will love come true.

Merry

"I want to believe, Merry," Laurie whispered. "But please, don't leave me now."

"Are you talking to yourself?"

Laurie spun around in the chair.

Jake's silhouette filled the kitchen doorway as the morning sun beat down behind him. "I've talked to myself a lot lately. No one else to talk to." She wrung the ties of her old chenille robe. "The man I married deserted me, now my housekeeper's left."

Jake stepped into the kitchen, his hands filled with late summer wildflowers, orange and gold and purple, and Laurie wasn't sure which she smelled, the sweet scent of flowers, or Jake's aftershave, but both filled her senses with hope. "Could we talk?" he asked.

"There's ham and muffins in the fridge. Care to

join me?" She realized she was trying overly hard to sound normal and nonchalant, but she was deathly afraid of letting him know how dreadfully much she needed him.

"Thanks," he said, sitting down across from her, laying the flowers next to her plate, "but I ate at Meg's. She's taking the boys for a few days."

"I see." She picked at the ham. "Is she going to help you out while you figure out how to take care of the animals and do your woodwork?"

"No." Jake's hand slipped across the table, his fingers threading through hers as they rested next to her plate. "While I figure out how to take care of us."

"Is that more of a priority?"

His chest heaved with a sigh. "The cows, the horses, the property, and everything but you and the boys can go to hell for all I care."

"I'm sorry." She began to cry. "I thought you'd enjoy the cattle and horses."

"Dammit, Laurie." He thumped his fist on the table. "I do enjoy the horses, and the cattle, and the horny bulls, but I enjoy you a whole hell of a lot more." He reached across the table and caressed away a tear. "I don't forgive easily, and what you did's still eating away at my insides. But we're good together, Red, and we're not going to work things out if we stay apart." He plowed his fingers through his hair, and an incessant lock with a mind of its own fell again over his forehead. His gaze captured hers, his Montana blue-sky eyes almost melting her firm resolve. "Come back to me, please."

"But I never left, Jake. It's you who ran away. Remember?"

"Okay, okay, I said it wrong. I haven't slept for

five minutes since you—hell!—since *I* left. The boys do nothing but ask when they're going to see you again."

"You want me back because of the boys?" she interrupted, her eyes sad and disappointed.

"*I* want you back. *I* want to come back, because—because I love you."

"I see."

"What the hell is that supposed to mean?"

"I don't know, Jake." But she knew very well. It was all part of the edited version of the end of her story. "You woke me up in the middle of the night, now you're here interrupting my breakfast."

His jaw slackened and his mouth fell open. He looked at her in total and abject disbelief. "Do you want me to leave?"

"Do whatever you want, Jake," she murmured, low and soft, as if she didn't care. "I'm not keeping you here."

He slammed his fist on the table, pushed out of the chair, sending it clattering to the floor, and stomped to the door. Then he stopped. His shoulders slumped.

Laurie didn't hear the door, and she didn't turn around to see what was happening, to see what he would do, she only prayed that he wouldn't walk out the door—again.

His shoulders raised again, stiff and proud, and he turned around. "I'm not leaving you, Laurie. I was wrong to run away, but I refuse to do it again, even if you push me."

Kneeling behind her, he wrapped his arms around her chest and rested his cheek against hers. She hadn't felt anything so good or wonderful in weeks, and she wanted to apologize, wanted forgiveness for the wicked thing she'd done.

"I'm sorry Jake. I know I can never make it up to you. But I am sorry for what I did."

"Which time?" He caressed a tear away from the corner of her eye, and she felt the slight, teasing twitch of his mustache.

"What do you mean?"

"Are you sorry for pretending just a moment ago that you didn't care? Or for the crazy, misguided antic you pulled to get me to marry you?"

"Both, I suppose. But I promise, Jake. I won't do anything like that again."

He swept her out of the chair, cradling her in his Olympian godlike arms. "Don't make promises you can't keep, Laurie." He stalked from the kitchen, up the stairs, and into their bedroom, to the unmade bed where she'd slept so many nights alone, wishing he were at her side.

He lay beside her and stripped away the old chenille robe. "Did you know I'd be coming back this morning?" he whispered, fingering the silk gown she wore, his gentle caress the fulfillment of a million wishes.

"I prayed you would."

"Ah, Red. I've been praying awfully hard myself."

"What have you prayed for?"

"A new beginning for us. No secrets. No lies. A chance to forget what happened and start all over. I shouldn't have left you, not after all the harping I did about running away. I don't know why you didn't give up on me, or call it quits."

"I'm not a quitter, Jake. This place is my home. I'll never leave it, and I'll never leave you. And . . ." She didn't know how to tell him, didn't know how he'd react.

"And what?" Jake asked, his fingers gently caressing her silk-covered belly.

She put her hand on his, holding it tightly against her. "And this baby needs you just as much as I do."

Silence. All was silent as Jake gazed into her eyes, and she wished so much she could read his thoughts. When he finally spoke, his words were only whispered. "You should have told me. What if I hadn't come back?"

"I would have spent the rest of my life with a broken heart, but with a child I'd love forever. I wouldn't have given the baby away, Jake, or left it with someone else. I already lived through that, I wouldn't let my child live through it, too."

Jake pulled her tighter in his arms, saying nothing, just listening, and giving her warmth and comfort and love, things she'd lived without as a child, things she'd never have to live without again.

"I didn't grow up in a happy family, and I never got to know what it was like to have a mother around to love me. But I've watched you with the boys, and I hope I've learned a thing or two. If I'd had to raise this baby on my own, I'd just pray that I could follow in your footsteps."

Tears streaked Jake's cheeks, and he did nothing at all to hide them. "You don't need to follow me, Red. I've seen you with my boys and, trust me, God didn't scrimp on you when it came to mothering skills." He leaned over and kissed her lips, letting his tears mingle with hers. "You're the best thing that ever happened to me, Laurie, and out of all the gifts you've thrown my direction the last few weeks, this little one's the best. Well, actually, it comes a close second to having you back in my arms."

Laurie wove her fingers into his hair and looked deeply and passionately into his Montana blue-sky eyes. "That's where I've always wished to be, Jake."

"Ah, Red." He pulled her close, his mustache beginning a wicked path from head to toe. "Your every wish is my command."

Laurie crept out of the house long after the children had gone to sleep, long after her husband's embrace had eased and he'd drifted deep into dreams. She clutched the picture frame tightly in her hands and ran down the well-worn path with only the moon and stars to light her way.

She pushed open the door to the old red barn and went inside, flicking on the light, trying not to disturb the chickens roosting inside. Scooting around the sleigh they'd bought last Christmas, and two or three dozen bales of hay, she found what she wanted.

A midnight-blue box, painted with gold and silver suns and moons and stars, was hidden away in the darkness. It had to work, she told herself. It just had to.

"This is for you, Merry," she said. "You've done so much for me. Now I want to give you something in return, something I know you'll love."

Putting the picture frame inside the box and wishing it would find its way to Merry seemed such an odd thing to do, but stranger things had happened while Merry was part of her life. She'd waited for months for Merry to return, wanting so much to deliver her gift, but Merry hadn't come back. And tonight, when the Grange was lit with red, white, and blue lights, when fireworks exploded in the sky, she remembered the last Fourth of July, and a magical box.

And she believed.

She took another look at the family portrait. Her three towheads sat at her feet, and her husband, dressed in buckskin, stood behind her, cradling their babies, one in each arm. *"For Merry, who made all our wishes come true,"* she'd inscribed on the back. *"With all our love, the McAllisters—Jake, Laurie, Jacob, Joshua, Joseph, and our newest twins, Nicky and Merry."* She placed the frame in the cabinet and shut the door, closed her eyes, and clicked the heels of her bunny slippers three times. "I believe," she said. "I believe. I really and truly believe."

Opening her eyes, she tapped the closet with a candy cane left over from Christmas, and the box began to shake, and shimmy, and a burst of stars and glitter spewed from the top.

Laurie smiled. Her heart swelled, and she tapped the box one more time. The shaking ceased, and she opened the door.

The picture frame was gone, and in its place rested a red envelope, with Laurie's name clearly written across the front. She wasted no time slicing open the top with her fingernail, and pulled out a white, lace-edged card.

Laurie, dear—

I've missed you, child, and your gift to me is one I promise to treasure. I will keep it with me always, just as I keep you and your loved ones in my heart.

Magic is powerful, believing is too, but it's love that will make your dreams come true. So believe child, believe in the magic of love, and your wishes will be fulfilled—again and again and again.

                                        Merry

Laurie clutched the card to her breast and ran out of the barn to stand under a trillion stars. "Thank you, Merry," she whispered. "You were the best grandmother I ever could have wished for."

And Laurie's wishing star twinkled in the night-time sky, shining brighter than all the rest.

Epilogue

"Look Grandma. Look."

Laurie McAllister swiveled around in her desk chair, opened her arms, and captured the red-headed moppet, pulling her granddaughter to the comfort of her lap. "And just what is it you'd like to show me, Katie?"

"It's magic, Grandma." The child's emerald eyes were alight with joy as she pushed the picture frame away from her chest for Laurie to see.

"Why, wherever did you find that?"

"I was playing in the attic." The child's lower lip jutted out, and she looked down at her hands. "Mommy told me I shouldn't. She said you and Grandpa keep special things up there. But, gosh, Grandma, I figure if you have special things, you should share them with me."

"I suppose you're right."

"So you're not mad?"

"Not at all, Katie." Laurie touched the polished silver picture frame her granddaughter held in her pudgy little hands. "Why don't you tell me why you think this is magic."

"Look at it, Grandma. Real close," Katie cooed softly. "You can hardly see the picture anymore, but right there"—she poked her finger on the glass—"you can see a lady's eye. And you know what, Grandma?" Wonder and awe filled the child's face. "She winked at me. I didn't imagine it, either." Katie shook her head over and over and over again.

"No, Katie, you didn't imagine it."

The child nestled her head into the comfort of her grandmother's bosom and yawned. "Do you think she'll ever wink again, Grandma?"

"When you need a wish to come true, honey. Until then, why don't I keep her someplace safe, just for you."

"Okay, Grandma." The picture frame slipped from the child's fingers as she yawned again and closed her eyes.

Laurie set the picture frame on her desk, and made a mental note to tuck it safely away in the memory box she'd made especially for Katie. The child didn't need any special magic now. She had a home, and all the love and happiness a world of family could offer. But someday, maybe, she just might need a miracle or two.

"Am I intruding?" Laurie tilted her head up at the drawl of her husband's laughter-filled tenor. From head to toe he was coated in grass clippings, and the latest in a series of sweat-stained Stetsons was pulled low over his brow.

"Shhh. She's sleeping."

Jake crept across the room, his boots leaving puddles of dust and dirt across the hardwood floor. He scooped the child up in his arms and cradled her against his chest. "Caught this one climbing a tree earlier today. Hell if I know where they get so much energy."

"Suppose they inherited that from you." Laurie pushed out of her chair, pressed her hands to her back, and stretched the kinks out of her spine.

"You look like you've been wrestling bulls again, Mr. McAllister," she teased, attempting to brush an ounce of grass from the t-shirt that still stretched quite nicely over his somewhat aged Olympian god body.

"It's that damned castle. Whose idea was it to have thirteen grandkids over here at the same time, and who, by the way, told them I like being the dragon?"

"Not me. Must have been one of your kids, you've got seven of them as I recall, and you played that game with every one." Laurie brushed a quick kiss across his cheek. "How could they possibly pick anyone else, Jake. You spout fire so well, it's easy to see you're the perfect choice for the part."

"Ah, hell, Red. I'm getting too old."

"We're the same age. Does that mean I'm too old, too?" she teased, circling her husband, fluttering her fingers over his back, around his waist, and teasingly over the well-worn and faded spot just south of his zipper.

"I don't pay much attention to age where you're concerned." Carefully, he tucked his thirteenth grandchild into a corner of the couch and pulled an ancient red and white afghan over her tiny body, then grabbed his wife up in his arms, cuddling her close.

"Put me down, Jake. I have work to do. Heaven knows those books don't write themselves."

"You still modeling the heroes in your stories after me?"

"Right down to the most minute detail."

"What about the love scenes? Those modeled after us, too?"

"Some of my best research has been done lying next to you."

"Good." He nuzzled her neck with the sweetest and tenderest of kisses. "When we get those kids all tucked into bed tonight, what do you say we get down to some serious research?"

"I'm always willing to learn, Mr. McAllister. Always willing to learn."

His mustache twitched.

And her Betty Boop lips puckered in anticipation.

Discover Contemporary Romances at Their Sizzling Hot Best from Avon Books

THE LOVES OF RUBY DEE   *by Curtiss Ann Matlock*
78106-9/$5.99 US/$7.99 Can

JONATHAN'S WIFE   *by Dee Holmes*
78368-1/$5.99 US/$7.99 Can

DANIEL'S GIFT   *by Barbara Freethy*
78189-1/$5.99 US/$7.99 Can

FAIRYTALE   *by Maggie Shayne*
78300-2/$5.99 US/$7.99 Can

Coming Soon

WISHES COME TRUE   *by Patti Berg*
78338-X/$5.99 US/$7.99 Can

Avon Romantic Treasures

*Unforgettable, enthralling love stories,
sparkling with passion and adventure
from Romance's bestselling authors*

LADY OF SUMMER *by Emma Merritt*
77984-6/$5.50 US/$7.50 Can

HEARTS RUN WILD *by Shelly Thacker*
78119-0/$5.99 US/$7.99 Can

JUST ONE KISS *by Samantha James*
77549-2/$5.99 US/$7.99 Can

SUNDANCER'S WOMAN *by Judith E. French*
77706-1/$5.99 US/$7.99 Can

RED SKY WARRIOR *by Genell Dellin*
77526-3/ $5.50 US/ $7.50 Can

KISSED *by Tanya Anne Crosby*
77681-2/$5.50 US/$7.50 Can

MY RUNAWAY HEART *by Miriam Minger*
78301-0/ $5.50 US/ $7.50 Can

RUNAWAY TIME *by Deborah Gordon*
77759-2/ $5.50 US/ $7.50 Can